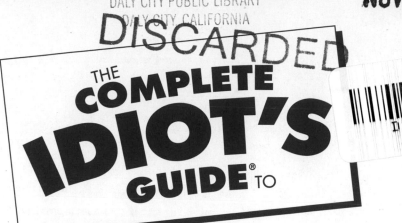

THE
COMPLETE IDIOT'S GUIDE® TO

Success as a Chef

by Leslie Bilderback, CMB

ALPHA

A member of Penguin Group (USA) Inc.

J

This book is dedicated to Bill, Emma, and Claire, to whom I owe all my success as a chef and a person.

ALPHA BOOKS

Published by the Penguin Group

Penguin Group (USA) Inc., 375 Hudson Street, New York, New York 10014, U.S.A.

Penguin Group (Canada), 10 Alcorn Avenue, Toronto, Ontario, Canada M4V 3B2 (a division of Pearson Penguin Canada Inc.)

Penguin Books Ltd, 80 Strand, London WC2R 0RL, England

Penguin Ireland, 25 St Stephen's Green, Dublin 2, Ireland (a division of Penguin Books Ltd)

Penguin Group (Australia), 250 Camberwell Road, Camberwell, Victoria 3124, Australia (a division of Pearson Australia Group Pty Ltd)

Penguin Books India Pvt Ltd, 11 Community Centre, Panchsheel Park, New Delhi—110 017, India

Penguin Group (NZ), cnr Airborne and Rosedale Roads, Albany, Auckland 1310, New Zealand (a division of Pearson New Zealand Ltd)

Penguin Books (South Africa) (Pty) Ltd, 24 Sturdee Avenue, Rosebank, Johannesburg 2196, South Africa

Penguin Books Ltd, Registered Offices: 80 Strand, London WC2R 0RL, England

Copyright © 2007 by Leslie Bilderback

International Standard Book Number: 978-1-59257-562-6
Library of Congress Catalog Card Number: 2006932986

09 08 07   8 7 6 5 4 3 2 1

Interpretation of the printing code: The rightmost number of the first series of numbers is the year of the book's printing; the rightmost number of the second series of numbers is the number of the book's printing. For example, a printing code of 07-1 shows that the first printing occurred in 2007.

Printed in the United States of America

Note: This publication contains the opinions and ideas of its author. It is intended to provide helpful and informative material on the subject matter covered. It is sold with the understanding that the author and publisher are not engaged in rendering professional services in the book. If the reader requires personal assistance or advice, a competent professional should be consulted.

The author and publisher specifically disclaim any responsibility for any liability, loss, or risk, personal or otherwise, which is incurred as a consequence, directly or indirectly, of the use and application of any of the contents of this book.

Most Alpha books are available at special quantity discounts for bulk purchases for sales promotions, premiums, fundraising, or educational use. Special books, or book excerpts, can also be created to fit specific needs.

For details, write: Special Markets, Alpha Books, 375 Hudson Street, New York, NY 10014.

Publisher: *Marie Butler-Knight*
Editorial Director: *Mike Sanders*
Managing Editor: *Billy Fields*
Senior Acquisitions Editor: *Paul Dinas*
Development Editor: *Jennifer Moore*
Production Editor: *Megan Douglass*
Copy Editor: *Nancy Wagner*

Cartoonist: *Shannon Wheeler*
Cover Designer: *Bill Thomas*
Book Designers: *Trina Wurst/Kurt Owens*
Indexer: *Brad Herriman*
Layout: *Ayanna Lacey*
Proofreader: *John Etchison*

Contents at a Glance

Part 1:   **You Have a Dream**   1

    1   Is a Culinary Career Right for You?   3
        As you pursue your dream, you need to understand the pros and cons of a culinary career.

    2   Culinary School vs. Learning on the Job   11
        Which path should you choose on your road to becoming a chef? School or work? The options are pretty straightforward, and each has its good and bad points.

    3   Getting Ready for the Next Step   21
        If you think your skills are up to snuff, and you're ready to enter the workforce, read this chapter first. Learn a few things the other books don't tell you.

Part 2:   **Getting a Formal Culinary Education**   29

    4   Getting Into Culinary School   31
        When looking at schools, recognize that while they generally cover the same material, their methods of instruction and degree programs can vary tremendously.

    5   Succeeding in Culinary School   45
        Just showing up is not enough to succeed. You must do well with homework, projects, finals, and grades. Prepare yourself to succeed.

    6   Enriching Your Culinary School Experience   53
        Since you paid all that money to go to culinary school, you ought to take advantage of everything it has to offer.

Part 3:   **Learning the Trade on Your Own**   63

    7   Learning to Cook at Home   65
        Before you step out into a working environment, learn to be comfortable cooking for friends and family in the comfort of your own home.

    8   Getting Book Smart   75
        Cookbooks have much to teach; you can learn more, in fact, than you could ever get in a culinary school.

9   Learning on the Job   87
     There is no better way to learn than on the job. Here are
     some easy ways to get the experience you need.

Part 4:   **The Job Search**   **95**

10   Entering the Field   97
     Learn everything you need to know about entry-level posi-
     tions. There are many to choose from, so pick the one that
     matches your long-term goals.

11   Looking for a Job   113
     Once you figure out what kind of job you want, you need to
     apply for it. Here is how to successfully navigate the job search
     process.

12   Making the Most of Your Shot   125
     You've got the interview. Don't blow it now!

13   Tricks of the Trade   133
     Now that you have your foot in the door, don't trip over it.
     Here are a few tricks to make you look like a seasoned profes-
     sional.

Part 5:   **Being a Successful Professional**   **147**

14   Building Restaurant Relationships   149
     Being a good cook is not enough. You need to know how to
     be a good employee, too.

15   Finding a Mentor   157
     Everyone needs a little help along the way. Keep your eyes
     open for someone willing to share his experiences with you.

16   Staying Healthy   165
     This is a grueling business. Staying in shape and eating right
     makes it a whole lot easier.

17   Honing Your Skills   177
     You're going to get bored, and any skills that you're not using
     are going to get rusty. Find a way to stay on top of your game.

18   Keeping Up with the Joneses   185
     Watch what's going on around you, and pay attention to the
     direction the industry is taking. Whatever happens in the res-
     taurant business will have an impact on your own success.

19 Culinary Careers 191
*There are lots of places to enter the field, including some you
probably haven't considered. See the big picture, and choose the
jobs that will round you out as a chef.*

Part 6: **Taking Charge** **201**

20 Moving Up the Ladder 203
*If you do your job well, people are going to notice. If you do a
really good job, you may find yourself in charge of something.
Here's how to get from here to there.*

21 Becoming the Boss 213
*There's a lot more to being the boss than making sure the
lettuce gets washed. People's livelihoods—including your
own—are at stake.*

22 Sanitation and Safety 223
*A restaurateur has the awesome responsibility of looking out
for the health and safety of the employees and customers.
Make it your business to know proper food-handling guidelines.*

Part 7: **Your Own Place** **231**

23 Owning Your Own Restaurant 233
*Everyone wants to open her own restaurant. And why not?
It seems easy, right? Well, not if you want to make money.*

24 Opening Up 241
*You need to take into consideration a few thousand things
when opening your own place. Here are just a few of them.*

25 Things You Don't Want to Think About 251
*These unpleasant aspects of business ownership may very
well determine the life or death of your business.*

Appendixes

A Additional Resources 259
B Culinary School Directory 265
C Glossary 293
Index 301

Contents

Part 1:   You Have a Dream   **1**

1   Is a Culinary Career Right for You?   **3**

Should You Be a Chef?...4

The Pros 4

You Are a Star..4

You Get to Do What You Love—and Get Paid for It!.....................5

The Cons 6

You Have to Work … Hard..6

You Have to Work in Unpleasant Conditions...............................6

You Won't Make Much Money...7

You'll Have to Work Nights, Weekends, and Holidays...................8

You Gotta Love It 8

2   Culinary School vs. Learning on the Job   **11**

The Advantages of Going Straight to Work...............................12

The Disadvantages of Going Straight to Work..........................13

The Advantages of Going to Culinary School...........................14

The Disadvantages of Culinary School 15

The Best of Both Worlds: Working and Going to School.........18

3   Getting Ready for the Next Step   **21**

Stamina 22

Speed...23

Patience..24

Teamwork 25

Cheerleader 26

Part 2:   Getting a Formal Culinary Education   **29**

4   Getting Into Culinary School   **31**

How to Find a School 32

How to Pick a Good Culinary School.......................................32

Find Out About the School's Reputation 32

Talk to Alumni 33

Study the Curriculum 34

Ask About Class Format and Size 37

Interview Instructors...37
Answers to the question, "Why did you become a teacher?"...........38
Ask About Accreditation...39
Get Job Placement Data..40
How to Avoid Getting Crushed by the Chef Mill.....................40
Do Your Culinary School Credentials Matter?.........................41
Certificates 42
Associate's and Bachelor's Degrees..42
How to Pay for School...43

5 Succeeding in Culinary School   45

Mise en Place Your Brain 45
Follow the Rules..46
Study..47
Teacher's Pet...49
Making the Grade 50
Recommendations...50
Networking 51
Mentors...51

6 Enriching Your Culinary School Experience   53

Working During School..54
You Get to See Another Side 54
You Can Apply What You Learn...54
You Expand Your Network 55
You Can Find a Mentor 56
Professional Organizations and Clubs................................56
The American Culinary Federation (ACF)...........................56
The International Association of Culinary Professionals (IACP)...57
The Retail Bakers of America (RBA) 58
The National Restaurant Association (NRA) 58
The James Beard Foundation...59
The American Institute of Wine and Food (AIWF)..................59
Women's Organizations 59
Campus Clubs...59
Bad Influences 60

Part 3:   Learning the Trade on Your Own   63

7   Learning to Cook at Home   65

Get Cooking 66
Go Shopping 67
   Experiment with New Ingredients.................................67
   Get Some Good Cookware 67
Try Everything 68
Read Books Cover to Cover 70
Find Some Guinea Pigs 72
Learn to Love Cleaning 73

8   Getting Book Smart   75

Classics 76
Reference 78
American Cooking..79
International Cooking 81
Special Disciplines...82
   Baking and Pastry 83
   Healthy Food 84
   Fish 84
   Wine 85
Just a Good Read..85

9   Learning on the Job   87

A Job by Any Other Name … 87
   Internships...88
   Externships...88
   Apprenticeship...89
   Volunteering Yourself 89
Baby Steps..91
   Catering..91
   Bakeries..92
   Delicatessens 94

Part 4:   The Job Search   95

10   Entering the Field   97

Where to Begin? 97
Entry Levels...101
   Personal Chef 101
   The Military 102

Hotels 104
Cruise Ships 105
Chain Restaurants 107
Independent Restaurants 108
The Front of the House 109
Make Your Choice 110

11 Looking for a Job **113**

Get Your Resumé Ready 114
Heading 114
Objective 114
Education 114
Work Experience 115
Additional Information 116
References 116
Cover Letter 118
A Few Words of Caution 119
Finding a Job 119
Call Upon Your Network 120
Read the Classified Ads 120
Do an Internet Job Search 121
Check Out the Placement Services 121
Waiting for Something to Happen 122

12 Making the Most of Your Shot **125**

Prepare 125
What to Wear 126
What to Bring 127
First Contact 128
Nailing the Interview 128
Tryouts 129
Your First Weeks 131

13 Tricks of the Trade **133**

Tricks for Comfort and Happiness 133
Drink Plenty of Water 133
Protect Your Hands 134
Clothing 135
Comfy Feet 136
First Aid 136

Tricks for Expediency...137
   Measuring..*137*
   Equipment...*138*
Handling..138
   Defrosting...*139*
   Cooling...*139*
Save Everything..140
Food Tricks...141
Organizational Tricks...143
Cleanup Tricks..143
Purchasing..144
Storage..145

Part 5: Being a Successful Professional   **147**

14 Building Restaurant Relationships   **149**
Communication Skills...150
Negativity..151
You're Not a Chef Yet...151
Common Courtesy...153
Common Sense..154
Burning Bridges..155
The Blacklist..156

15 Finding a Mentor   **157**
What Is a Mentor?...157
Skills Mentor...158
Taste Mentor...159
Attitude Mentor..160
Business Mentor..161
Lifestyle Mentor..161
What Do You Do with a Mentor?..........................162
   What if You Can't Find a Mentor?....................*162*
   What Happens When They Let You Down?.............*163*
Are You a Mentor?..163

16 Staying Healthy   **165**
All You Can Eat...165
Nutrition..167
   The Pyramid...*167*
   The Food Groups..*168*

Calories 170
Just Say No to Drugs and Alcohol 172
Smoking 174
Take a Lap 174
Avoid Injury 175

17 Honing Your Skills   177

Get a Second Job..178
    Where to Look *178*
    Why Bother? *179*
Entertaining 180
Catering 180
Volunteering 182

18 Keeping Up with the Joneses   185

The Latest Trend 186
Enjoy Life, Eat Out More Often..187
Reading 187
Professional Organizations 188
Competitions 188
Trade Shows 190

19 Culinary Careers   191

Job Descriptions 192
    Corporate Executive Chef, Regional Executive Chef,
      Executive Chef, Chef de Cuisine, Chef *192*
    Executive Sous Chef, Senior Sous Chef, Sous Chef, Kitchen
      Manager *192*
    Chef de Partie, Line Cook, Culinary Supervisor, Line
      Manager, Shift Manager, Cook 1 ....*192*
    General Manager (GM), Food and Beverage (F&B)
      Director, Food and Beverage Manager *193*
    Restaurant Manager, Dining Room Manager, Hospitality
      Supervisor, Maitre d'hotel *193*
    Executive Pastry Chef, Pastry Chef, Pâtissier, Baker,
      Pastry Cook, Dessert Chef *193*
Specialty Jobs...194
    Banquet Chef, Catering Chef..*194*
    Garde Manger..*194*
    Butcher..*194*
    Sushi Chef...*195*

Education 195
Research and Development 196
Manufacturing 196
Food Stylist 197
Food Purveyor 197
Specialty Merchandiser 198
Nutritionist 198

Part 6:   Taking Charge   201

20   Moving Up the Ladder   203

Is Management Right for You? 203
A Manager's Job Description 205
   Planning 206
   Organizing 206
   Leading 206
   Coordinating 207
Management Styles 207
   Scary Boss 208
   Touchy-Feely Boss 208
   Micromanaging Boss 209
   The M.I.A. Boss 210
Motivational Supervision 210
Friends vs. the Business 212

21   Becoming the Boss   213

The Beauty of Being the Big Boss 214
Hiring 214
   Plan 215
   Recruit 215
   Select 216
   Interview 217
   Check References 218
Easing New Employees Into the Job 219
   Orientation 219
   Training 220
   Employee Upkeep 220
Firing 221

22   Sanitation and Safety   **223**

   Sanitation 224
      Training and Certification 224
      Food-Borne Illness 225
      Viral Contamination 226
      HACCP 227
   Safety 227
      First Aid 228
   Training 228
      Disasters 230

Part 7:   Your Own Place   **231**

23   Owning Your Own Restaurant   **233**

   Understanding the Risks Involved in Opening a Restaurant ...234
   Creating a Business Plan 234
      What Goes Into the Plan 235
   Identify Funding Sources 237
   Ownership Types 237
      Partnerships 238
      Limited Partnerships 238
      Corporations 238

24   Opening Up   **241**

   The Concept 241
   The Market 243
   The Location 245
   The Menu 246
   The Layout 246
   Ambiance 247
   The Staff 248
   When It's Time to Expand 249
      Franchise 250
      Other Ways to Grow 250

25   Things You Don't Want to Think About   **251**

   Stumbling Blocks 252
      Fire 252
      Pests 254

Insurance...254
    Required Coverage...255
    Recommended Coverage 255
Theft 256

Appendixes

A Additional Resources   **259**

B Culinary School Directory   **265**

C Glossary   **293**

   Index   **301**

Introduction

I know you love food. So do I. In fact, I love some foods with an obsessive passion. Take bread, for instance. I love it so much that I trap my own yeast in starters built from special water and grains. I love it so much that I taught my kids how to knead dough before they entered kindergarten. I love it so much that I received my Master Certification in Baking. I love it so much that I have a wreath of wheat tattooed around my ankle.

If your goal is to enter the world of culinary arts, you need a similar level of affection for food and cooking. A love of popular new recipes or fad diets or celebrity chefs will not make you successful. Those interests can get you started, but they will not sustain you for the long haul. A deep passion for food and a willingness to work hard is what will propel you to the top. You've got to be willing to exert yourself—both mentally and physically—day after day. You must be eager to take on tasks that, to most people, seem like drudgery. And you must do it knowing that, in all likelihood, you will never get rich, will never be on television, and will never have the hottest restaurant in town. You'll have to do it for the love of the craft.

You need to love the history of cuisine, the art of culinary traditions, and the pleasure of serving good food to others.

I am not alone in my culinary romance. It is a common dream these days. Good thing, too, because the food industry is booming. People are busier. Many families are too tired at the end of the day to cook. And even if they had the time, many of today's young professionals wouldn't know their way around a kitchen beyond popping a frozen entrée in the microwave.

The food industry is also moving in new directions. People want to see fresher, healthier foods on menus. They want organic and locally grown produce, ready-made meals that can be served quickly and easily, and a nice dining experience with healthy options at a reasonable cost. Luckily for us culinary professionals, we can make money bringing healthier food options to the masses through restaurants, personal chefs, specialty-diet meal delivery, specialty food purveyors, and healthy-cooking courses.

All this hubbub over food is filling up culinary schools nationwide, and new schools are popping up all over the place. Culinary education is growing just as fast as (if not faster than) the industry itself is. There are more than 12 million food service workers in the United States, according to the U.S. Bureau of Labor Statistics, and the demand for trained workers is rising, with well over 700,000 food service managerial jobs nationwide.

Who is filling these schools? Some of these students are kids straight out of high school. But the largest group of new culinary students is comprised of middle-aged career changers. The good news is that you can enter the culinary field no matter what your age, ethnicity, or gender.

But before you send off your application to the Culinary Institute of America, you need to do a reality check. The world of the professional chef is hot, dirty, smelly, and crude. It's hard on marriages and children. It's definitely not for everyone. But for the right person, it can be wonderfully exciting, creative, passionate, and fulfilling. If you are that type of person, you probably already know it. If you are not, don't give up just yet. There is still plenty of room for you in the world of culinary arts. This book is going to help you get there, wherever *there* is for you.

The Complete Idiot's Guide to Success as a Chef has something to offer everyone, whether you already have a plan or you're just toying with the idea of becoming a chef.

Part 1, "You Have a Dream," lays it on the line and tells you exactly what you're getting yourself into. Be prepared for the cold, hard truth, because I don't hold back in describing what it's like to work in a busy kitchen.

Part 2, "Getting a Formal Culinary Education," is for those of you thinking about attending culinary school. It will help you find a school that's right for you and tell you what you need to do to succeed. If you're already in culinary school, this section will help you make the most of the experience.

If culinary school isn't for you, **Part 3, "Learning the Trade on Your Own,"** will show you how to become a chef on your own. It helps you build a good library, cook from it, and get the practical, real-life experience you need to get your foot in the door of the restaurant business.

Part 4, "The Job Search," explains the ins and outs of finding work as a trained professional, from writing a resumé to nailing the interview.

Fine-tuning your skills as a professional is handled in **Part 5, "Being a Successful Professional."** Playing nicely with others, taking care of yourself, and keeping your skills up are all a part of being successful.

Part 6, "Taking Charge," and **Part 7, "Your Own Place,"** assume you've enjoyed the ride so far. In fact, you've enjoyed it so much you're ready to take control. These final sections discuss everything from mid-level management to opening your own shop.

If you follow my advice and heed my warnings, there is every reason in the world to believe you can make this career your own. The country is becoming more and more sophisticated about food, and you can absolutely help shape the trends of the future. If you've got stamina and passion, you can get yourself trained and get busy cooking. Let me show you how to get started.

Extras

You'll find the following sidebars scattered throughout the chapters.

def•i•ni•tion

The kitchen has its own unique language, and these sidebars will help you decipher it.

Kitchen Tales

Here you'll find practical advice from industry professionals.

Behind You!

This is a warning used throughout the food industry to help prevent accidents and injury. Here, it is meant to show you what not to do.

Classic Cuisine

These sidebars contain tidbits of culinary history—the important people, places, and things of the past that have shaped what we do in the kitchens of today.

Acknowledgments

Thanks to Bill for proofreading, for letting me work when I needed to, for providing the new office, and for helping me bring the funny. Thanks to Emma for helping out when needed, for being totally random, and for making me laugh. Thanks to Claire, for helping too, and keeping me entertained with your beautiful music. Rock on! Thanks Mom, for showing me what's good. Thanks Dad, for the constant support.

To Paul and everyone at Alpha. To Andrea for being in the right place at the right time. To the crew of the *USS Salvor ARS-52* for bringing me on board and helping me hone my skills. To Dave Grohl and his Fighters of Foo and the Fabulous Green Day Trio for helping me work off the stress. To Dina Altieri, Dave Danhi, Ciril Hitz, Sherry Yerd (I mean *Yard*) and Tina Wilson for their thoughtful insight. Thank *U* very much.

Trademarks

All terms mentioned in this book that are known to be or are suspected of being trademarks or service marks have been appropriately capitalized. Alpha Books and Penguin Group (USA) Inc. cannot attest to the accuracy of this information. Use of a term in this book should not be regarded as affecting the validity of any trademark or service mark.

Part 1

You Have a Dream

I've spent half my career teaching culinary students. And I have spent almost as much of this time talking people out of culinary school as talking them into culinary school. This is because along with all the great students I have had the pleasure of teaching, I have had the misery of trying to teach the worst students in the world. More than a few of them had no business being in this business. The high turnover rate from this type of employee is damaging to this industry, and it is disheartening. But it is not as sad as the hundreds of hours, and thousands of dollars, I see wasted every year.

So if I don't think you will be able to hack it, I'll try to talk you out of it. More than creating fabulous menus or schmoozing glamorous guests, remember the long hours, low pay, intense heat, lack of benefits, lack of vacation pay, and lack of sick leave. Sometimes this news scares people off. Sometimes my warnings don't faze prospective chefs at all. People who are considering a career change for the right reasons don't worry about the money, security, hours, or stress. They crave it. This is the student I want, and this is the employee and co-worker I want. This is who I hope you are.

Chapter 1

Is a Culinary Career Right for You?

In This Chapter

- ◆ Understanding that loving food is not enough
- ◆ Reaping the rewards of kitchen work
- ◆ Overcoming the challenges of kitchen work

As you read this chapter, you might wonder if I am trying to discourage you from becoming a chef. Understand that I absolutely am not trying to do that. But I do think you should know what you're getting into. Too often potential cooks don't have a realistic sense of what cooking for a living is all about. For your sake, and for the sake of the culinary industry that I love, I promise to tell it like it is. I'm going to pull back the curtain and show you what it's really like to work as a chef, so you will have all the facts in hand when you decide if a culinary career is right for you.

I have met many people with their hearts set on becoming a chef, who have had their hopes dashed by a harsh and unexpected reality. I have also seen many fully informed people enter the industry and go on to become successful, happy chefs. The choice is yours.

Should You Be a Chef?

You love to cook. Your friends rave about your creations. Everyone says you should become a chef. Your favorite room is your kitchen. Your favorite TV station is the Food Network. You head straight for the cookbook section of every bookstore. You recreate menus you've seen at restaurants.

Everyone has a different reason for starting a new career. I bet you already have your own list of reasons. You probably think the job would be fun, fulfilling, creative, and interesting, right? Well, it certainly can be all those things. But before you submit your application for sous chef or shell out thousands of dollars to attend culinary school, you need to make sure you know what a career in the kitchen is really like. The cooking life isn't always as romantic as some people think.

Restaurant life is like a swimsuit. It often looks better in the display window than it does when you try it on. I've witnessed this harsh reality again and again as students drop out of the culinary schools I've worked in. These schools are as guilty of glamorizing the profession as the Food Network is. I have known and loved many admissions representatives, and I begrudge them nothing. They have a job to do, and that job happens to involve quotas. So it's no surprise that they leave out some of the more unsavory aspects of kitchen life. Luckily, you have me to lay it all out for you.

The Pros

So you want to be a chef, huh? I know exactly how you feel. It happened to me slowly, over a period of many years. I always liked cooking. I certainly always liked eating. From the age of 15 I worked in food service. But I never thought I would make it my career. I went to college and studied music and art. I planned on being a teacher. But something turned my head when I was done with all that. Maybe it was because I grew up watching Julia Child on television. Maybe it was because my mom knew what good food was and exposed me to it at an early age. Maybe it was because I lived in San Francisco, a city with more restaurants per capita than any other metropolis in America. Maybe it was because I discovered the California Culinary Academy and watched from across the street as the students walked to the BART station in their bright white coats, carrying tool boxes filled with knives.

You Are a Star

I think all of these circumstances contributed. But the thing that really made me decide to change directions was a job I had at a gourmet food shop. I took the job simply as a means of paying the bills while attending San Francisco State University. My duties included putting together platters of cheeses, meats, and terrines for our catering business. Surprisingly, customers, the staff, and the boss all loved my trays. They thought I really knew what I was doing. Apparently, mine were the best deli trays the store had ever created. This kind of approval is why I became a chef. It was the first time I had really pleased people on that scale. It was an incredible feeling. If I could please customers with a cold-cut platter, imagine the possibilities when I got my hands on real food!

Nothing in the world compares to the feeling of pleasing people with the things you create. When the chef tells you that the special you have created has sold out and asks you to make more, you are a triumph. When a waiter walks back to your station and tells you a diner thought your chocolate cake was the best thing to ever cross his fork, you are a star. When an article appears in the weekend restaurant reviews highlighting your unique use of flavor combinations, you are a success. When a celebrity sits in the dining room deciding which of your creations he wants to put into his million-dollar mouth, you are the champion. When you are asked to work the toughest shift because you are the best and most reliable cook on the line, you have arrived.

When you're a chef, everyone wants to know what you think—where to eat, what to order, how best to cook this and that. You are the expert. So much of America relies on frozen dinners and take-out for their meals that cooking has become mysterious. Consequently, the chef has become the magician. The chef is someone to be in awe of.

You Get to Do What You Love—and Get Paid for It!

But beyond the warm fuzzy feelings you get from the adoration of others, there is the actual work, which I love more than any of the praise and glory. I love to work all day and then come home and plan a big party menu. I love when I am asked to make a birthday cake for someone. I love when it's my turn to provide the buffet for coffee hour at church. I love when the Girl Scouts have a bake sale. I love when it's my turn to host the family for the holidays. Why? Because I simply love to cook!

I can work in the kitchen for hours, rolling out dough for mini tart shells, assembling tamales, or dipping chocolate truffles. I can tackle a recipe that requires the fine dice of 20 different vegetables because I truly enjoy chopping. I never buy a cake mix or pre-made pie dough or canned tomato sauce. I'd much rather spend an hour or two in the kitchen making my own. These idiosyncrasies of mine confuse the occasional onlooker, who will invariably exclaim, "It's so much work!" But they couldn't be more wrong, because for me it is so much fun.

Yeah, I know why you want to become a chef.

The Cons

My favorite part about the food business is the instant gratification I get from a job well done. It's not like writing a book and then waiting a year or more to see if people like it. With cooking, you know whether you have succeeded the minute your customers take a bite. You can see it on their faces. And you can see it in the dish station when the plates come back empty. Of course, sometimes the plate comes back after the first bite because it was not to someone's liking. And that's part of the food business, too.

If you truly love cooking, it is fun. But few people truly love cooking. Many people *mostly* love it. Remember, chopping 20 pounds of onions is cooking, too. You've got to love it, or at least be willing to get through it, to achieve your end result, whether your end result is onion soup, the end of your shift, or owning your own place. When you're repeating the same recipes day after day, pride in your craft becomes a critical element to achieving happiness. If you don't have pride in your craft, the entire experience can become extremely tedious and unpleasant.

You Have to Work ... Hard

Being a cook is hard work. You are on your feet for eight, ten, twelve hours a day—even more if you become successful. There is no sitting in a kitchen—if you do, your colleagues will mock you. Your back will ache from lifting heavy bags of flour, sacks of potatoes, and cases of veal bones. You'll develop foot problems. You'll ache everywhere.

You Have to Work in Unpleasant Conditions

And kitchens are hot. Cooks stand over open flames and reach into 500-degree ovens. Kitchens are so hot that you will sweat like a pig and smell like one, too.

Kitchens are also dirty. There's food all over the floor and garbage everywhere. There is so much grease that most restaurants have special traps for it. There is so much grease that it is collected in special bins in the back alley, and hauled away in the night by fleets of grease removal tankers. (And where there is food and garbage, there are pests. Bugs, rodents, dogs (it's nothing like *Lady and the Tramp*), cats, and even birds are common pests that cooks must routinely deal with.

Kitchens can be dirty in other ways, too. Sexual harassment is all too common, as are cursing and violent temper tantrums. Let's not forget the racial, ethnic, religious, moral, and political offenses. You'll need a thick skin or earplugs.

And there's no question, kitchens are dangerous. You'll be burned many, many times from open flames, hot oven doors, hot sauté pan handles, hot sheet pans, and hot tongs. You'll mistakenly use a wet *side towel* as an oven mitt. You will be burned by boiling liquids, molten sugar, and sizzling oil. Oh, and you'll be cut, too. You'll be cut by knives, electric slicing machines, saran wrap teeth, food processor blades, blender blades, broken glass, and sharp fish fins.

"Beautiful cook" is an oxymoron. Our hair is crammed into hats, the brims of which are stained with sweat. Our crisp white uniforms are smeared with remnants of the food we just sent out to the dining room. Our faces are aglow from the steam rolling off boiling cauldrons of chicken guts. We can't wear fragrance because it interferes with our ability to taste. Our fingernails aren't long because food will linger underneath and spread germs. We can't use fingernail polish because it flakes off into the food. Makeup is impossible to maintain in the heat and sweat. Excessive jewelry is a hindrance and a safety hazard.

def•i•ni•tion

A **side towel** is a small, kitchen-size towel, made of terrycloth or cotton, provided by a restaurant for use by its cooks.

I remember my first week out of culinary school, free of the rules and restrictions. I arrived at work wearing makeup and big hoop earrings. The first time I opened the convection oven my mascara melted, fusing my eyelashes together, and my earrings heated up so fast I got large circle-shaped burns on my neck.

Kitchen Tales

A chef's uniform looks snazzy on TV, but real cooks' uniforms are usually stained and mismatched. Sometimes the restaurant will provide the uniforms, which is a pretty good deal if you don't care what you look like. I had this perk once. If I didn't get to work early, my size would be gone, and I ended up looking like a sausage in pants that were *way* too tight. If the pants were too big, I used long strips of plastic wrap as a belt. I can't understand why that style never caught on.

You Won't Make Much Money

As a cook, you'll likely never get rich. Cooks don't typically arrive at work in a Porsche. They usually come on the bus. Cooks don't eat at work simply because food is all around. They eat at work so they can spend their measly paycheck on rent instead of groceries. And speaking of measly paychecks, they will be. You'll be making $7 to $9 an hour to start. Even an executive chef's salary is comparatively small.

Fifty thousand dollars a year is considered fantastic. Think carefully about how you live now and whether or not you like it. Quality of life, in terms of career gratification, might be your motivation for entering this line of work, but being a cook may actually decrease your quality of life in terms of material comfort.

You'll Have to Work Nights, Weekends, and Holidays

The best cooks work when everyone else is done for the day. You'll be working weekend nights, holidays, your birthday, and your anniversary (if your marriage survives your career). I worked the night of my high school reunion, the day before my wedding, the morning my daughter was born, every Thanksgiving, Christmas Eve, and Mother's Day. Life as you now know it now will cease to exist. You'll need strong support from family and friends who understand your responsibilities at work and can live with it. If they don't, you'll end up like all the other lonely, divorced, childless cooks I know.

Behind You!

Maybe you think that being a chef is your ticket to fame and stardom. It could be. But it probably won't be. Chefs who make it to television or open successful world-renowned restaurants are few and far between. If this is your reason for joining our industry, think again. We need people who will work hard to perpetuate the craft, not those who will bail out when the going gets tough. And if you haven't figured it out by now, the going is going to get tough.

You Gotta Love It

Perhaps you've found that my cons list is a bit harsh. Well, boo hoo. I told you I wasn't going to hold back.

If, after reading this, you still want to launch into this career, then bravo! Perhaps you and I are kindred spirits. I love being a chef. I love the heat. I love the stress. I love the challenge. I love comparing scars and horror stories. I love working with people I respect. I love talking dirt about the people I don't. But most of all, I love the culture of the kitchen. We all speak the same language because we have all lived the same life. I've had an instant connection with every cook I've ever met, no matter what country I was in, what language they spoke, or what food they served. It's one, big, happy, dirty, smelly, international family.

The Least You Need to Know

- ◆ Being a chef can be infinitely rewarding.

- ◆ Being a chef is physically challenging.

- ◆ Cooking is rarely glamorous.

- ◆ If you can survive the "cons" of cooking, you'll make a great chef.

Culinary School vs. Learning on the Job

In This Chapter

- ◆ The pros and cons of culinary school
- ◆ The pros and cons of learning on the job
- ◆ Getting the best of both worlds

So you refuse to be scared off by hard work, uncomfortable working conditions, and low pay? Good for you! So now what?

You need to learn the fundamentals, that's what.

You may already know how you intend to proceed, but hear me out. You have two basic options: go straight to work or go to school. Both offer many variations, which I discuss later in the book. (See my discussion of picking a school in Chapter 4 and a commentary on entering the field in Chapter 10.) And, as you might expect, both options have pros and cons.

I know plenty of excellent chefs who graduated from culinary school and just as many who learned the trade on the job. Their success rate seems to have little to do with the path they chose and everything to do with how they traveled along that path: where they stopped, who they met, and what they took with them. You will have to find your own direction. But whichever path you choose, be smart about it.

The Advantages of Going Straight to Work

The traditional path to becoming a chef is not schooling but working. For centuries, a chef became a chef by working his or her way up from the bottom.

Learning from the ground up teaches you the physical, hands-on business, not the textbook business. And this kind of experience is by far the most respected. The general consensus is that a working cook is a cook who can hack it. It's survival of the fittest. No self-respecting boss is going to keep a crummy employee on payroll. It's hard enough to own a restaurant with a crew that gets it, let alone with one that doesn't.

There are a couple big reasons to choose work over school and a few smaller ones. The main reason is money. When you work, you make money. And as much as you may insist that you're cooking for the love of food, it all boils down to earning a living. Sooner or later, you're going to wonder what's in it for you. That's when getting a paycheck can really boost your morale.

The second reason to choose going to work over culinary school is the experience. Experience counts more than a degree. On the job you will become an expert at everything you do within a couple weeks, at which point you'll probably be asked to train someone else. You'll memorize recipes for life. You'll become speedy at every task, simply because you want to get them finished. You'll learn good shortcuts and bad ones. You'll pick up useful tips from everyone you work with.

When you learn on the job, your lesson plan consists of creating actual food for actual people. Your management class will be figuring out how to get along with the jerk working the grill, the oblivious hostess, and the egomaniacal owner. You'll learn supervision when you see the backpacks and knife rolls leaving work larger than when they arrived. You'll learn nutrition by watching the tubby busboy steal chocolate cake when the pastry chef isn't looking. You'll learn purchasing at the end of each month when the chef asks you to stay late to take inventory. You'll learn the business aspects of running a restaurant by observing the success or failure of your workplace.

To be a part of the success of a business is an exciting thing. There is no better feeling than to work hard and actually see it pay off. You can only get this feeling on the job. On the other hand, to come to work and find a padlock and chain on the door is a terrible thing. And there is no worse feeling than learning your paycheck has bounced.

But both experiences are part of the business, and both will be a part of your education as an up-and-coming chef.

Classic Cuisine

Practically every European chef working today learned on the job rather than in school, including Wolfgang Puck (Spago), Daniel Boulud (Daniel, Café Boulud), and Ferran Adria (El Bulli). Many American chefs did it on their own, too. There's James Beard, Alice Waters (Chez Panisse), Lee Hefter (Spago), Nancy Oaks (Boulevard), Mario Batali (okay, he went to school, but dropped out), Traci Des Jardins (Jardiniere), and Thomas Keller (The French Laundry), to name just a few. These chefs all have different stories, but they all worked their way from the bottom up. Somewhere along the way they displayed a certain understanding of the culture of the kitchen, a love for food, and a desire to work hard and do their best. And somebody noticed.

The Disadvantages of Going Straight to Work

A chef who doesn't attend culinary school must somehow seek out broader culinary knowledge on his own. The best of them actively hunt for it. Knowing how to cook is one thing, but if you are exposed to the how and why of a recipe, you can apply that information to other recipes, troubleshoot, and eventually create something entirely your own. That type of learning, the exploration of the nuances of a recipe or technique, is not generally available to you on the job, unless someone is willing to take you under his or her wing. (See Chapter 15, where I talk about the importance of finding a mentor.)

The training you get on the job consists of a 30-second description of what it is you need to do or (more likely) a list of the 15 things you need to do. Then you have maybe a couple hours to get everything ready, so that you can pump out plates continuously from 5 to 11:30 P.M. There's no history lesson or note-taking; there is only doing.

At work, you will learn how the chef likes his or her stock prepared. It may very well be completely wrong, but you'll have to do it the chef's way. If you decide to challenge that procedure, you will likely face one of two outcomes. The chef may take the time to explain to you the thought process behind the stock recipe. He'll tell you why he chooses to roast the bones the way does, why he embellishes his *mirepoix* with kitchen scraps, and why he starts with boiling water. Perhaps you'll get to hear about his early years as a cook, and how his mentor taught him this method, and nurtured him into the chef he is today. Then you will be thanked for taking an interest in the minutia of his restaurant and maybe even be given a raise. Or, more likely, the chef will tell you to shove off. At work, it behooves you to remember which side of the bread your paycheck is buttered on.

def•i•ni•tion

> **Mirepoix** is a basic ingredient of most French sauces, stocks, soups, and stews. It's the combination of three aromatic vegetables—carrots, onions, and celery. The basic ratio is usually 1 part carrot to 2 parts onion and 2 parts celery, although we do whatever our chef tells us. Sometimes herbs are included as well. The mirepoix is usually sautéed in fat at the beginning of a recipe.

The Advantages of Going to Culinary School

For the right individual, culinary school can be a good fit. If you have realistic expectations and are not swept up in the allure of the tall hats (and tall egos), you can absolutely benefit. If you apply yourself, a culinary school can teach you not only the basic skills but also important lessons about yourself and what you are capable of. And if you are willing to keep an open mind, you will be exposed to more people and ideas than you'll know what to do with.

For the most part, the work you do in culinary school is theoretical. You make food, but in a much different way than in a restaurant. Culinary school cooking begins with a lecture about The Dish. You'll take notes on the history of The Dish and the culture it comes from, the way to purchase and store the food for The Dish, the variations on The Dish, and all the classic terminology associated with The Dish. You may even get to watch someone make The Dish. Then, for the next four hours, you and your team of three or four classmates will work on creating The Dish. This Dish Dance is not without value. While it is likely you will never actually make The Dish again, you will certainly use the techniques.

Large schools offer a broad education with specialized curriculum in topics such as pastry, butchery, nutrition, business, management, and a variety of international cuisines. These behemoth chef factories expose you to multiple cultures, varied points of view, and placement assistance for jobs you may never have considered. You'll also have access to professional culinary organizations that sponsor competitions, scholarships, and internships.

Smaller schools may offer only the basic skills, but they'll probably give you more attention. If the class size is smaller, the instructor is more likely to notice what you're doing. Smaller schools typically cost less as well. Culinary programs in places like community colleges are typically staffed by seasoned professionals who have been trained to teach.

I'm sure you can see the benefits of schooling. But besides the breadth of information, there is the time factor. You learn a great deal in a relatively short period of time. You can be out in the real world working within a year if you're good. You'll also make tons of contacts, expanding your network substantially. Fellow students, instructors, visiting chefs, and even administrators will all help you over time. I still bump into my instructors occasionally, at conventions or competitions, and through them, I have met many other important contacts who have helped me along the way.

The bottom line is that a culinary school can get you in the door.

The Disadvantages of Culinary School

Simply entering a culinary school doesn't mean that you will be presented all you need to know to be a successful chef on a silver *giradon*. You will need to apply yourself as you would in any school. You will have homework assignments, projects, pop quiz-zes, and final exams. You'll need to study, and you'll need to pay attention. If you are not willing to do these things, then the entire experience will be a waste of money. (See Chapter 5 for tips on how to succeed in culinary school.) The benefits are only available to those who take advantage of them. If you slide through, as many do, you'll miss a golden opportunity.

def•i•ni•tion

A **giradon** is a cart on wheels, used for classic table-side service. On it, dishes of many kinds are prepared right before the diners' eyes.

And although culinary school prepares you to make The Dish, which will no doubt look and taste wonderful, it's not a good preparation for the rigors of a production kitchen. The curriculum of a culinary school doesn't always address the kind of real-world issues you'll face once you get a real-world job. With its theoretical focus, a culinary school doesn't offer its students the one thing they really need to excel: repetition. The best way to learn anything, from piano to multiplication table to chopping onions, is to practice. At a culinary school, there simply isn't time. These programs are short as it is, and beyond the cooking classes, instructors have to cram in nutrition and purchasing and management and whatever else they decide is crucial to a good culinary education. They leave it up to you to find the time to practice your skills.

Kitchen Tales

When I first became a pastry chef, the customers at the restaurant who were celebrating a special event always got a message written in chocolate on the rim of their dessert plate. Unfortunately, my chocolate penmanship left much to be desired. But after my first Saturday night, I was an accomplished cocoa calligraphist.

That lack of real-life experience in culinary school can be a problem when the time comes to look for work. You cannot submit a resumé with a list of your classes—you must have a list of actual jobs. And the jobs should relate to the one you're applying for, not the job you had the summer after college selling puppets on Fisherman's Wharf.

By far the biggest downside to the culinary schools is their reputation. A common opinion in the food industry is that culinary schools produce snotty, arrogant graduates who are unable to handle the pressure of production. Of course, this is a stereotype. But it's a common enough stereotype that you'll need to prove yourself to overcome it.

Where does this stereotype come from? It comes from experience. After 18 months of schooling, many students graduate with the feeling that they've paid their dues. The culinary schools are booming now, thanks to the Food Network, and the emergence of chefs as celebrities. Whether or not that is good for the industry is debatable. Too many students enter with the Food Network as their goal, which is unrealistic. Many of these Emeril wanna-bes graduate thinking that they are ready to hit the big time and collect their six-figure salaries. The reality is that they'll be *lucky* to start out as a line cook, making $9 an hour.

Of course, to graduate anything is quite an accomplishment. But a diploma or certificate does not a career make. Like any other vocation, you need to work your way up. Funny, but you never hear of business school graduates expecting to be Chairman of the Board at World Wide Wickets immediately after graduation. Culinary graduates, on the other hand, expect to become chefs right away. Is this because the culinary field is looked upon as an easy discipline—similar to wood shop in high school, an easy A? Those of us in the business know better. Food service is still service. Despite our loosey-goosey class structure in America, the American dream is still to have servants. So becoming one shouldn't be that hard, right?

Wrong! It's darn hard! To get anywhere in this business, you have to prove yourself every day. You have to stick with it when the going gets tough. Like a good marriage, you have to be willing to hang around long after the love buzz is gone. Of course, this can lead to disappointment and an unbelievably high employee turnover rate. Hence, you have the bad reputation of the culinary school graduate.

Kitchen Tales _____

I got married shortly after I graduated Culinary School. We honeymooned in London and hung out a bit with some academic friends of my father-in-law, who was a university professor. My husband was attending law school at the time, a noble endeavor in the eyes of this cerebral crowd. And what did I do, they asked? "I am a chef." I fully expected the "oohs" and "ahs" I was accustomed to hearing in the States. But I didn't hear any of that there. I was clearly *The Help* and got the cold shoulder for the rest of the visit.

And let's not forget the financial impact of a culinary education. When you go to school, you spend money. Boy, do you spend money! The typical culinary student graduates in debt up to his neckerchief. Why? Because you not only pay tuition, but you also buy books and tools and uniforms. And if you're in school full-time, who's working? Okay, if you're of college age, maybe Mom and Dad will help you out. Or maybe you can find a rich widow to befriend. But I know many, many of you are career changers and you're paying the bills. The money is no small matter. Yes, student loans are available, but you'll have to pay them back eventually. Scholarships are few and far between. And what happens if you decide that this is not the career for you after all? I'll tell you what happens. You'll be out thousands of dollars.

As a culinary school instructor, I have had some great "A" students. They studied every night and practiced their recipes at home. But often, these high achievers imploded when they hit the real world because they were not nurtured at work the way they had been in school. In a culinary school, the teachers have an attrition rate hovering over their heads like a guillotine. Losing students reflects poorly on their ability as teachers, so they help you along. They make allowances. They give, perhaps, better grades than you deserve. So you should realize that out in the real world a chef doesn't care what grades you got in school. He only cares about what you can do in his kitchen and how fast you can do it.

Be aware that while every school teaches the same basic skills, they are not all equal. Some offer a thorough education, and some are more abbreviated. Some have a good faculty of dedicated teachers, and some are staffed with disgruntled former cooks. Some are committed to the success of the graduates, and some are all about the bottom line.

The Best of Both Worlds: Working and Going to School

By now you may have come to the conclusion, as many have, that the best course of action is to double your education by working while you are going to school. You'll get to practice what you are being taught. You'll get a true vision of what the business is like and how you might fit into it. And when you graduate, you'll already have something for your resumé and a string of contacts to go to for recommendations. Work will benefit your school life as well. Lessons become more interesting and less abstract.

But the combo is not for everyone. Going to culinary school and holding down a job can be very difficult. You'll be tired—really, really tired. You'll have no time for your friends and family. You will probably not be able to give either commitment 100 percent, which is a shame. You'll need to spend every spare minute studying because your grades will probably be lower than they would be if you didn't work. And low grades can mean you'll get less respect from your instructors, which will harm your network in the long run. Then again, you could be earning the instructors' respect. Students who work show a certain dedication, work ethic, and love of craft. It all depends on you and the effort you are willing to put into this experiment.

In culinary school, you will learn how to make a beef stock, why the bones are important, which bones are better, which vegetables go in it and why, which vegetables stay out and why, how hot the water should be at which stage and why, and what things the stock will be used for. Then, when you go to work, you'll be asked to make beef stock in a completely different way. It's okay, though, because this is how you'll begin to develop a sense of your own style of cooking. You'll take all the information you receive, mix it around in your brain, and decide for yourself what is best.

Don't forget that there are losers in every profession. There are losers who go to culinary school, and losers who try to learn everything on their own. Choosing one path over the other will not change your basic work ethic. The student who shows up tardy to class is the worker who gets to work late. The student who didn't do his homework is the worker who takes shortcuts. The student who cuts class is the worker who calls in sick when he's perfectly healthy. The student who thought he knew more than the teacher is the worker who butts heads with the chef. Those are the workers who never amount to anything. It is not the theoretical education that sent the reputation of the culinary school graduate into the gutter. It was the unprofessional attitude they exhibited once they got out.

The Least You Need to Know

◆ The traditional path of working from the ground up builds strong character and garners respect, but you will need to round out your education on your own.

◆ Culinary school teaches you a lot, quickly, but you'll need to work to overcome the negative stereotype and get on-the-job experience.

◆ If you have the stamina, to go to culinary school while holding down a cooking job is definitely the way to go.

Getting Ready for the Next Step

In This Chapter

◆ Developing stamina

◆ Working quickly and efficiently

◆ Becoming a valuable member of the team

◆ Showing enthusiasm for the craft

Before you launch into your culinary career, regardless of the path you choose, you should be prepared. Being a chef is completely unlike any other business and not as good in many ways. Workers have fewer creature comforts than employees in most other fields. As a chef, your employer won't be all that concerned about your happiness, comfort, benefits, or pay.

People don't expect a job that sounds so fun to be so hard. The most common complaint I have heard from chefs in the industry is that culinary students are not prepared for the physical and mental demands of a real restaurant. Don't let that be you! Cooking skills and theory are not enough. In this chapter I will tell you about the physical and mental traits you need to develop to make it in this business.

Stamina

Some jobs in the food service industry don't require stamina, but cooking isn't one of them. If you don't think you have stamina, you might look into food styling, take a job representing a distributor, or work the concession stand at the public pool. But if you want to be a chef, you'll need to be able to take the heat, both literally and figuratively.

Let's see if you can hack it. Think of your culinary career as the Tour de France. You are seven-time champion Lance Armstrong, chugging up and down the French Alps for a month. That is the kind of stamina you'll have to muster to succeed in this business.

Your day at work will be your mountain. Sometimes your shift will be an uphill climb. Business can be slow, and spirits can be low. You'll find yourself watching the clock. You'll desperately search for things to keep you busy, so your boss doesn't send you home to save payroll. Sometimes, though, you can coast down your shift, barely pedaling at all. When business is brisk and you have fun people to work with, everything clicks. Suddenly, the last order comes in, and you can't believe that eight hours have passed.

Cooking skills are your bike. Your skills are what push you to the top. Get a good bike, and it makes the climb easier. Ride a crummy bike, and you may have to get off and walk. Using and caring for your knives properly, organizing your *mise en place*, keeping your station clean—these are all skills that make the job easier. So does knowing what the difference is between whipping, folding, kneading, stirring, and beating; how to properly store and rotate product; what's in season; how to prepare it; and preparing it properly the first time. All of these things help you get to the top of the mountain and claim your yellow jersey.

You'll have to have a champion's attitude, too. Lance Armstrong pulled his bike out to train for the Tour in the rain and cold weather, when the other riders stayed indoors. You'll have to be willing to do what no one else is willing to do to succeed as a chef. You'll have to work weekends, holidays, early mornings, and late nights. You'll have to get filthy dirty, hot, and sweaty. You'll need to be the Lance Armstrong of the kitchen. You must *want* to gut the fish, slice the onions, and clean the grease traps. You must view every task as an opportunity to better yourself and your craft. You'll have to exceed all expectations, even your own.

Lance works hard, but you never hear him say, "My butt really hurts." You see him crash, tumbling on the pavement at 60 mph, skinning up an entire side of his body.

But then you see him hop back up on the bike. No one expects you to be pain-free after eight hours on your feet. But they do expect you to shut up about it. No one wants to hear that your feet hurt. Everyone's feet hurt. Grin and bare it. Same goes for the heat. Everyone is hot, so keep it to yourself. Hop back up on your bike and start pedaling.

If you don't have the stamina now, don't worry. You can do some things to make it easier, like eating right, exercising, and getting a good night's sleep (see Chapter 16). The job will get easier the more you do it. Eventually, you will develop the stamina you need, and your feet will no longer hurt, the heat won't phase you, and even the most disgusting chore offers up a challenge you are eager to accept. That's how you make it to the finish line.

Behind You!

Drink lots of water. When you sweat, it's important to replace the lost fluids. I have seen cooks faint in a hot kitchen more than once. The USDA recommends eight glasses for a typical day. Sweating in a hot kitchen in the summer is not, however, a typical day. You will need at least twice that amount as a professional chef.

Speed

Now pretend you are another seven-time champion, NASCAR driver Richard Petty, and you're racing at Daytona. Suddenly, in the final lap, A.J. Foyt passes you on the right, cuts in front, and heads toward the finish line. Would King Richard pull over and give up? Would he ask someone else to take the wheel? Absolutely not. He would step on it. A chef must have the ability to move quickly, all the while adjusting to obstacles. You must do whatever it takes to get the food out on time, make it look and taste right, and please the customer. If you can do that, you'll get the checkered flag. If you can't keep up, your career will crash and burn.

Speed is a critical skill of a successful chef. If you've ever had to wait a long time for a meal at a restaurant, you know what I mean. When you have to wait for your food, you will probably not become a repeat customer. The business lives or dies by the speed of its chefs.

Customers rarely understand the skill involved in keeping up with the orders on a busy Saturday night. Just as a driver watches the rear-views, his periphery, the speedometer, the road, and all the other cars, a chef needs to watch the tickets, the ovens, and ten different orders cooking at different stages on the grill. And besides monitoring his or her own station, a chef must know what every other cook is doing so that

def•i•ni•tion

Fire is not just a flame. When the expediter shouts "fire," it means to begin cooking a dish.

different parts of the dish come up at the same time. The chef has to know that the sauté guy has six pans going on the stove and five on deck waiting their turn. The chef also has to know which salads and appetizers have gone out and be ready to *fire* that table's entrées. Oh, and all the plates at the table need to come up at the same time. This is where the term multitasking must have originated.

Speed is clearly critical during the busy dinner hour, but it's just as important all day long, working up to that rush. Prep must be done as quickly as possible in the limited time available. If five o'clock rolls around, and your *mise en place* is not ready, you will quickly find yourself unprepared for the first orders. It's not office work, where you can let the files you didn't get to sit on your desk until tomorrow. If you don't get to it in a restaurant, the customer doesn't eat. And if customers don't eat, you don't work.

When the kitchen begins to decelerate, and someone's in trouble, a good chef knows how to help and doesn't wait to be asked. By the time cooks ask for help it's usually too late. A good chef can see the need coming and jump in to get it done. A good chef knows when to simply lend a hand and when to shove the cook aside and just do it. On a busy Saturday night no one has time to baby-sit the slowpokes. You deal with the ruffled feathers later.

A successful chef needs to think quickly, too. If a problem arises, the chef must be able to figure it out quickly and calmly. If a sauce is burned, a new one needs to be made. Is there a shortcut? Can it be done in two minutes? If an ingredient runs out, is there somewhere to get more now? A store? A friendly neighbor? The competition? If a customer is unhappy, is there a way to save his opinion of this place? A free dessert? A free meal? A personal table visit from the chef? (Anyone have a clean jacket?) A successful chef needs to be firing on all cylinders all the time.

Patience

A chef needs patience and perseverance. Like the Boston Red Sox, you can't expect to make it to the World Series right away. In fact, you may never make it. But you've got to want it enough to keep trying year after year.

Things aren't always going to go the way you'd like. You are not going to get your raise when you think you deserve it. You are not going to get the good shift when you want it. Your boss may not like your ideas or take your advice. But if you want to be a successful chef, you gut it out.

If you believe that what you have to offer is valuable, then take heart. Sooner or later you'll prove your worth, and someone will agree with you. After all, the Sox had to win for an entire season before they made it to the World Series. Game after game they had to prove their critics wrong. You'll have to work just as hard, and show your critics that you have the stamina and the speed to make it in the Big Show.

Like the Sox, you'll constantly have to overcome opponents and naysayers. Even on your own team, you're not always going to like everyone. It's a fact of life. There will be third-string players who never step up to the plate, leaving more work for you than they actually do themselves. There will be the players who want you off the roster. They'll cause problems for you, make your job harder. What will you do? Start a brawl? Kick dirt at the umpire? No! If you do, you'll be ejected! You have to handle it calmly, with professionalism.

Kitchen Tales

I once worked with a woman who was so incredibly nice that I thought she was faking it for the first three weeks I knew her. She was sweet to every single person on staff, including a smarmy waiter who continually made inappropriate comments within earshot for shock value. She was a smart player and knew that making a fuss would only fuel his fire. Eventually he got bored. Meanwhile, she earned the respect of everyone else.

Unworthy players eventually get traded. If the coach is an idiot, he'll be replaced, too. Making it to the Big Show is only half the battle. Only the strongest players have staying power.

Teamwork

In keeping with my sports analogies, work in the kitchen is very much about teamwork. There is no *I* restaurant.

Getting the food out is priority one. If you do not pull your weight, you'll get loud complaints. If you do not pull your weight, someone who does will replace you. A restaurant needs all its players in top form for every single game.

The team in question includes the entire staff. Everyone is connected. Cooks need the wait staff to collect and distribute the orders efficiently. Wait staff needs the cooks to cook quickly and skillfully. They need the bussers to schlep the stuff they have no time to schlep. They need them to clean tables, reset, refill drinks, and be the ears when the customer is in need. The bussers need the scullery to clean the plates, glasses, and silver quickly, so they have something to reset with. They also need the host to communicate clearly what tables they need to turn. The host needs to communicate with the chef, so that the chef knows how many more *covers* there will be, so that there is enough food, and enough time, to serve it all. This is just a snapshot of how the work flows on any given night.

If the chef, the cooks, the *line*, and the front-end staff are well organized, getting the food out is easy. But if one element is having an off night, it's *game over*. If the chef doesn't order enough or the cook doesn't prep enough, the night is doomed. If the waiters get bogged down or the bussers don't clear plates or refill water quickly enough, you'll never score a home run. All it takes is one screwup. And the consequence is? The customer waits, deciding never to return to or recommend this restaurant.

def•i•ni•tion

In the restaurant business, **cover** refers to a customer. If the restaurant did 200 covers, that means 200 people walked through the door, sat down, and ordered food.

def•i•ni•tion

The **line**, also referred to as the "hot line," is the cooking station in a restaurant where food is prepared to order. Cooks in that station are line cooks.

Being a strong team player can be challenging because none of us are in top form all the time. We get distracted or find ourselves under the weather. In the food business, the game doesn't stop for these complaints. A successful chef plays through the pain. Even if you've got a sprained ankle, the customer is still going to order off the menu, and pulling someone off the bench to replace you isn't as easy as you may think, especially if you have made yourself an invaluable player. You've got to be there. You made a commitment to the team, and you can't let them down.

Cheerleader

The best chefs I know are sincerely excited about their profession. They positively bubble over with enthusiasm for food and cooking and everything culinary. They are the cheerleaders of the profession.

The cheerleaders are so happy to be at work that they greet every single person with a smile, every day. They appreciate the work that everyone does and tell them so. When they try a new dish, they want everyone's opinion. They are enthusiastic about the food that their kitchens put out and are constantly thinking of ways to make it interesting.

Cheerleaders are so enthusiastic about a newly discovered cuisine that they get on a plane, fly to its country of origin, and try the real stuff. Cheerleaders are so thrilled every time a new fruit or vegetable comes into season that they drag the staff to the farmers' market to buy it. Cheerleaders are so happy to be cooking that they cook dishes on a whim just for the staff to eat.

Every restaurant needs a cheerleader, but not every restaurant has one. The genuine love of food is why so many people turn to this business. But that love of food doesn't always evolve into a love of craft. That's what happens to the cheerleaders. They take their love of food and turn it into a passion for excellence.

The cheerleaders also care about the profession and work to ensure that it moves in the right direction. They join other cheerleaders in organizations geared toward helping young culinarians find their way. They campaign for the quality of the ingredients we use, and they care about the way in which it is grown. They sponsor organizations that take our skills and use them to help those in need.

Go. Fight. Win!

> **Behind You!**
>
> Don't get the cheerleaders confused with the mascots. The mascots are the chefs with fancy titles, TV shows, and high-profile jobs. They could conceivably be part of a cheer-squad, but being a mascot doesn't automatically mean that you are shakin' the pom-pom.

The Least You Need to Know

- Your ability to stand the heat and stress will determine your level of success as a chef.

- Speed is critical to a well-run kitchen.

- Lack of teamwork will bring the flow of business to a screeching halt.

- If you have passion for your craft, spread the joy!

Part 2

Getting a Formal Culinary Education

Much good can be said for culinary school. It's a great place to be if you are interested in cuisine. Every single person you meet shares your interest. You'll be introduced to concepts and people that will change your life completely.

But it is school. Too many students forget this basic fact. Studying is important. Homework, tests, and projects all count. Your achievement in these areas will speak directly about you, your talent, and your worth to the industry. There is no sliding through for the successful chefs.

And be careful. Just like the restaurant industry, there is excess all around you. You can easily overindulge your way to obesity and party yourself into oblivion. Don't get distracted. Plot a course for your future, and stick to it.

If you don't have a definite goal in mind yet, then open your mind to everything and everyone you come into contact with. Take advantage of everything the school, faculty, and community have to offer. By the time you finish, you'll have a better idea of what lights your fire.

Chapter **4**

Getting Into Culinary School

In This Chapter

- Looking at the reputation and culture of culinary schools
- Reviewing the basic curriculum and the extras
- Finding out about faculty, class format, and credentials
- Considering financial aid and accreditation

If you are thinking about culinary school, it's probably because you have some notion of what they are all about. Either you have heard a chef talking about one, you've read about them, or you have visited one. Maybe you know a graduate of one. I'm sure you have some expectations, and you may even know which school you'd like to attend.

You're probably already aware of some of the most prestigious culinary schools. The Culinary Institute of America (CIA) is one of them. It is the mother of all schools, having been in the business of culinary education since 1946. It is widely thought of as the premier school of its kind in the country (at least by those who went there, go there, and work there). Johnson and Wales and the Art Institutes round out the top three chef factories. Another big-name school is Le Cordon Bleu. Even older than CIA, Le Cordon Bleu (LCB) in London and Paris are well regarded worldwide. Less prestigious schools have recently bought the right to carry the LCB name. For a full list of schools, and school directories, see Appendix B.

But before you pack your bags, let's do some investigating. The name, and even the reputation, does not guarantee a good education.

How to Find a School

To find schools, look on the Internet, in the back of food magazines, in the weekly food section of your local newspaper, and in culinary school reference books (for more ideas, see Appendix B). Make a list of your top five or ten school choices. Contact them, ask for information, which they will be thrilled to provide, and then start sifting through the info you receive.

How to Pick a Good Culinary School

In this chapter, I have provided some basic criteria for you to use as you evaluate your top picks. You will no doubt add some of your own criteria as well, like location. You'll probably want something close to your grandmother's house, the ski slopes, or the tattoo parlors (we all have our little hobbies). Available housing is something to consider, as is easy public transportation and proximity to city centers.

Kitchen Tales

I seriously considered culinary school after attending a food show at the California Culinary Academy (CCA), as a representative of the gourmet shop where I worked. One look at the dining room, and I was hooked. The building was a refurbished old theater. The dining room was where the theater seats used to be. There were kitchens above the stage on the second floor and along one side, all encased in glass so you could view the classes. As I watched the white hats scurrying back and forth to the dining room with trays loaded with canapés and petit fours, I heard my destiny calling.

Find Out About the School's Reputation

You already know that big school names are more recognizable and carry more weight, just like a degree from Harvard is generally worth more in the job market than one from a small state college. But keep in mind that the reputation of a college will not make you any smarter. It can, however, open doors for you that may otherwise remain shut; you will have to strut your stuff once you're inside the door.

If your heart is set on attending a particular school, find out what other folks have to say about its reputation. Do a little investigating. Start by asking anyone you know in the food industry. If there is a dream chef you'd like to work for someday, find out what he or she thinks of your dream school. It is my experience that people are happy to give their opinion and are even flattered to be asked.

Next, ask students and teachers at other schools what they think of your ideal school. You'll get a better sense of a school's general reputation from those who don't attend than from those who do.

Talk to Alumni

When you have a sense of the school's reputation, find out what it's like to be a student there. The best way to learn about a school is to talk to former students. Although current students also have a lot of good information, take it with a grain of salt. Probably due to stress and fatigue, they have a tendency to be cranky and disgruntled, no matter how great the program is. Graduates in the field will tell you how it helped and/or didn't help them. Current students may not see the big picture yet.

To find these people, contact the school. Some placement offices use graduates in high school outreach programs and job fairs. Since these graduates now work for the school, they tend to put a more (perhaps too) positive spin on their experience. Then again, if they have decided to work for the school, they must like it.

You can also find students on the Internet. There are dozens of sites dedicated to the culinary world (see Appendix A). You'll find blogs posted by individuals, chat rooms, and sites that rate schools and instructors. They are all full of opinions and advice, some useful and some ridiculous. The problem with the Internet is that you never know who you're getting advice from. It could be some whacked-out dude with a D average. But as you read more, common themes will emerge, and you'll begin to get an idea of what the school is really like.

No matter how you find them, ask these students about their experiences. Were the courses hard? Did they feel a lot of stress? Was the curriculum relevant? Did they make friends? Where do they work now? Has the education helped their career? What was their favorite and least favorite part of school and why? Who was their favorite and least favorite instructor and why?

Study the Curriculum

All culinary schools, from the Culinary Institute of America (CIA) to your local community center, cover basic topics because there is little variation on the proper way to chop a carrot or make *béchamel* sauce.

def•i•ni•tion

Béchamel sauce is one of the five *mother sauces*. It is often called a white cream sauce, which is a misnomer because, while it is creamy in texture, it is made with milk.

When you go school shopping, be sure they teach the following basic cooking skills. Refer to this list when you are talking to an admissions representative. If they don't know these topics or don't offer them, find someone who does, preferably at the next school on your list.

Course Title	Course Description
Safety and Sanitation	Preparation for and administering of the National Restaurant Association Education Foundation's ServeSafe certification exam
Knife Skills	Proper handling and use of knives, as well as the proper sharpening techniques
Stocks and Sauces	White and brown meat stocks, fish fumé, vegetable stock, all the mother sauces, and the derivative daughter sauces
Salads and Dressings	Vinaigrettes, emulsions, classic recipes, and identification of specialty greens
Egg Cookery	Egg composition, market forms, poaching, shirring, frying, French omelets, meringues, and custards
Meat, Fish, and Poultry	Identification, fabrication, market forms, proper handling, and classic recipes
Vegetables and Fruits	Identification, market forms, proper handling, control of pigment, textural changes, and classic recipes
Starches	Identification, market forms, proper handling of potato, rice, pasta, specialty grain, and classic recipes

Course Title	Course Description
Dry Heat Cooking Methods	Grilling, sautéing, frying, roasting, baking, with and without fat
Wet Heat Cooking Methods	Boiling, poaching, simmering, steaming, braising, and stewing
Baking	Yeast breads, quick breads, cookies, tarts, cakes, custards, frozen desserts, soufflés, puff pastry, and meringue

Once you find some schools that offer the basic cooking skills, start looking at the other course offerings. The more tuition you pay, the more extra courses will be available.

Look for a course in business, supervision, management, purchasing, or some combination of these. Having a solid grasp of management concepts can help you make informed career decisions. Even if you have no desire to be a boss, these classes will help you steer clear of poorly operated businesses.

Some schools require a dining room rotation where you learn front-of-the-house operations. For culinary students, this is often the most dreaded cycle. The common complaint is, "I didn't pay all this money to become a waiter." But you must understand how a restaurant operates if you plan on being a chef. If nothing else, it will allow you to better communicate with the wait staff once you start working in the field, and you'll come out of the experience with a greater sense of empathy for your colleagues in the restaurant business.

Your school will probably offer a course in nutrition, and it's a good idea to take it even if you don't plan on working in a hospital cafeteria. Not only will a basic understanding of nutrition give you the information you need to eat right and stay healthy (see Chapter 16), but it will also broaden your employment options. Clients often ask their personal chefs, corporate chefs, and caterers to focus on healthy food. For these jobs, a firm grasp of the principles behind the USDA Food Pyramid, popular and successful specialty diets, and the physiology of nutrition is a must.

Also a course or two in pastry is important, even if you don't plan on becoming a pastry chef. I have known dozens of chefs who couldn't afford to hire someone to make their pastries. In these cases, if they didn't know how to make a few desserts, they risked losing customers. You will be very valuable to some chef down the road if you

def•i•ni•tion

Laminate means to layer, and laminating puff pastry is the method in which puff pastry is made. The dough (*detremp*) and the butter block (*beurre de tourage*) are stacked and folded and rolled, over and over and over, until there are hundreds of layers of dough and butter. The moisture in the thin layers of butter becomes steam in the oven, causing the dough to puff.

Classic Cuisine

Anton Caréme, (1784–1833), founded French *haute,* or high, *cuisine,* which is characterized by complex preparations and a heavy use of rich sauces.

know how to whip up a soufflé, make a sorbet, or *laminate* puff pastry. It may even get you a job. It's very possible that you will be chosen over the guy who "doesn't bake." The more you know, the more employable you become.

Not every school offers a class on the history of food, but it's a good topic and worth your time to take if they do. Food history is an up-and-coming discipline, with societies devoted to the topic popping up in big cities and a handful of schools offering certificates in the field. That's because serious cooks know the origin of their craft. Knowing about Anton Caréme, his style, his age, his influences, and those he influenced will give you a new understanding of modern cookery. Even modern chefs play an important role in current trends. Michel Guérard, Paul Bocuse, James Beard, and Alice Waters are all famous names, but do you know why? Well, that's what you'll learn in a course in food history. These figures shaped culinary art as we know it. Understanding the philosophy driving their cooking will bring you closer to discovering your own style. If nothing else, you can win on *Jeopardy* ("I'll take Totally Obscure Culinary Facts for 500, Alex").

Enology, the study of wine, is an extremely important part of the culinary world. Naturally, wine courses involve alcohol, and I never taught or took a wine class that didn't include among its ranks (students or teachers) those who partook a little too much. It can make for an uncomfortable environment for students who really want to learn something without the distraction of giggling drunks. The schools that offer wine classes usually require it. So if you are concerned about alcohol consumption, you may want to look elsewhere. There are plenty of ways to learn the basics of wine and its culinary applications on your own.

International cuisine is important, especially if you plan to work in a large metropolitan area where culture and cuisine mix freely. In addition to classic French techniques and recipes, you should be exposed to Asian, Indian, Mexican, and Middle Eastern cuisines. The ingredients from just one of these regions could take an entire semester to understand. Of course, many, many more cuisines out there are worth learning.

Ask About Class Format and Size

As you review the curriculum, pay attention to the class format. In hands-on classes, you cook most of the recipes you learn. In demonstration classes, you watch the instructor do all the work. Ideally, a class should be a mix of both styles, with a chef demo prior to your getting your hands dirty.

Like restaurants, culinary schools are expensive to run. In order to make them cost-effective, there must be as much instruction with as little product output as possible. Demonstration classes are cheaper than hands-on classes. If a school offers hands-on classes, the students are often put into groups to save money. Be sure to ask about this. The bigger the groups, the less you will be doing yourself.

You'll want to ask about the student-to-teacher ratio as well. The higher the student-to-teacher ratio, the less individual attention you will get from the teacher. And when I talk about teachers, I mean actual chef instructors, not chef assistants. The assistants do not have the credentials or experience of the instructors. Because of this, the assistants sometimes give contradictory, even blatantly wrong, instruction. This is not always the case, but it happens often enough that you should look into it.

Interview Instructors

The faculty is the most important aspect of any school. Who are the instructors? Are they any good? Where do they come from and why are they here?

Many chefs turn to teaching because the restaurant business no longer suits them. They have grown tired of crummy hours, low pay, and lack of respect. Maybe they discovered that restaurant life just wasn't what they thought it would be.

Not all chefs enter teaching with a college degree other than a culinary school diploma. Of those who do hold a degree, few have a degree in education. This means that they arrive from the restaurant industry without any training in how to teach. Some schools make available seminars, workshops, and retreats designed to teach instructors how to teach. Ask the school what kind of training they provide for their faculty.

Behind You!

I have seen countless instructors hired specifically because they are European, despite lackluster credentials, simply for the draw of an "international" faculty. Believe it or not, there are crummy European chefs, with questionable ethics, just as there are here in the United States. A European pedigree should not be the criteria for choosing a school.

A teacher needs to nurture the stragglers and get them up to speed. Your instructor should have training in counseling, retention techniques, and basic encouragement. The principles of keeping students interested, knowing their names, caring if they show up to class, and monitoring their progress are traits that don't come naturally to chefs. Look for them in your future faculty.

How will you know if your teachers are any good? The school should allow you to come in and meet them. (If they don't, move on.) Bring a list of questions with you. Most teachers will have a prepared statement they have been asked to recite regarding the classes and the curriculum. They may not volunteer information about themselves. It's up to you to pry it out of them. Don't worry about their schooling or their credentials. What you really need to know is what they did before they taught and why they left that position to become a teacher.

Answers to the question, "Why did you become a teacher?"

A + answers:

- ◆ "I wanted to perpetuate the craft and share my knowledge with those that really want to learn it."
- ◆ "I enjoyed culinary school, and I always wanted to be a part of it someday."
- ◆ "I want to give something back."

If you get a response like these, sign up today!

B answers:

- ◆ "I wanted regular work hours, so I could be with my family."
- ◆ "I have back trouble that prevents me from working on a line."
- ◆ "The restaurant scene has ceased to fulfill me."

These answers indicate that this is a fall-back job. They'll probably do a good job, though, because it's a career move they chose with some thought and they probably have a love of food.

F Answers:

- ◆ "I hated my boss and was sick and tired of all the BS."

- ◆ "I wanted to make more money."

- ◆ "I couldn't get a job anywhere else."

These responses indicate that it is time to move on to the next school on your list.

Watch out, too, for responses that speak poorly of the school, curriculum, other faculty, or administration. If the teacher doesn't respect the company that writes his paycheck, why should he care about you?

Ask About Accreditation

To be sure your school is looking out for your basic needs, look for one that is accredited. Accrediting bodies monitor all areas of the school, making sure that the programs are fair, reasonable, and successful. They monitor course content, format, facilities, administration, faculty, and staff. The accreditation process is tough, and schools really jump through hoops to get it. Ask about accreditation if you do not see it prominently advertised. The accreditation documents should be available for you to see. Search the website of the accrediting body and find out more about the criteria they require.

A large number of accrediting bodies are out there, but only some of them are recognized by the U.S. Department of Education (DOE) as "reliable authorities as to the quality of education or training provided by the institutions … they accredit." (See Appendix B for links to accrediting bodies approved by the DOE.) This recognition is important because without the DOE approval, the accreditation does not enable Title IV financial aid benefits. In addition, certificates and Associate's or Bachelor's degrees from a non-accredited school are typically not transferable to another school's graduate program.

The process of getting accredited requires a school to carefully examine its program. It then presents a report to the accrediting organization's fact-finding team and is evaluated. Each accrediting body follows strict guidelines regarding curriculum, faculty, facilities, resources (i.e., libraries), program format, and staff.

Plenty of accrediting bodies are not DOE approved, and these accreditations are not necessarily worthless. A good example of this is the American Culinary Federation

(ACF; for more on the ACF, see Chapter 6). The ACF is the most recognized professional organization in the business and is the foremost certification agency for professional development. They sponsor trade events and competitions, assist members with employment and apprenticeship, and are very involved in education. But they are not recognized by the DOE. Still, a culinary school that carries an ACF accreditation has demonstrated high program standards recognized industry-wide, so much so that students attending an ACF-accredited school automatically receive an entry-level certification title upon graduation.

It is not uncommon for a school to be accredited by more than one accrediting body. Be sure to check them all out to see what you're getting.

Get Job Placement Data

Most schools offer some sort of placement service, whether a placement office with job counseling or a bulletin board in the hallway with current jobs scrawled on Post-it notes.

As you shop for schools, ask about placement statistics. How long do they monitor their graduates? If it's only for six months, the placement rate can be deceiving. With the limited tracking time, you could conceivably leave the industry, disgruntled after six months, which, unfortunately, many students do. (This is because they had unrealistic expectations, and they didn't read Chapter 3.)

I have known schools to hire their unplaceable students as teacher's assistants or some other lackey-type job. They work for the minimum tracking time required by the accrediting body, which then increases the school's placement statistics. As soon as the minimum tracking time is up, so is the gig.

The bottom line is that statistics are always going to reflect only the initial placement after graduation. Remember that as you interview schools. Don't let them woo you with placement statistics. Instead, concentrate on whether or not they help you with your job search and what kind of job contacts they have.

How to Avoid Getting Crushed by the Chef Mill

The culinary industry is booming, and schools are popping up everywhere. Is this a good thing? Well, if you're looking for a school, yes. Chances are that you will find one close to your home. But the sheer number of schools means that they are competing for your dollar. They want you and your money, and they'll say and do just about

anything to get you. Once you enter the
mill, they'll want to churn you out as fast as
possible to make room for the next batch.
It is, after all, a business, designed to make
money, just like a restaurant needs to *turn
tables* to make a profit.

Retention is as much a problem in culinary school as it is in any private school.
Students must stay in school if the school is
to survive. Because of the sheer number of
culinary schools, very few have the luxury of
a waiting list for admittance. Students who aren't admitted to one school will move on
to the next school on their list rather than wait six months. For this reason, very few
schools can afford to flunk students. It's bad for the reputation of the teachers, for the
reputation of the school, and for the bottom line.

> **def•i•ni•tion**
>
> **Turning tables** refers to moving
> customers through a meal and
> out the door to make room for
> the next party. This is accom-
> plished by promptly clearing dirty
> plates and delivering end-of-the-
> meal-hints, like dessert menus,
> coffee, and the check. See ya!

What this all means is that you are going to run into people in culinary school who
have no business being there. Some of your fellow students will have no interest in
becoming a chef. These people will be less likely to follow rules and won't care about
grades.

Clearly, these students will not do as well as the students who really want to be there.
Unfortunately, these students demand a lot of time and attention from the teacher,
who might otherwise be paying attention to you, the good student. As much as
instructors like to deny it, they do let students slide through, partly to get rid of them,
partly for retention, and partly because it's easier.

How do you avoid this? You can't. There will always be students who do not deserve
the attention they get. The best you can do is to choose the best school and try to
minimize the effect that the chef mill has on you (see Chapter 5). Identify the good
teachers who give you a reason to try harder.

Do Your Culinary School Credentials Matter?

Chances are good that no one will check your grade point average once you get out of
school. But the more honors and awards you can put on your resumé, the more likely
you'll get an interview. If you lack people skills or you're shy and scruffy, culinary
school credentials can give you an extra boost. But simply having a degree will not get
you a bigger paycheck (at least not initially). It will get you a few more options, but
you will have to back that degree up with your skills right out of the gate.

We use the term *credential* very loosely in the culinary world as it can mean several things. It can simply mean you completed culinary school. It can mean that you graduated with a degree of some sort. It can also mean that you applied for, tested, and passed any number of master certification exams sponsored by a professional culinary organization. Of this latter category, very few are available to students or recent graduates. Most are only attainable after you've worked a number of years in the industry.

The biggest thing a credential shows an employer is that you are willing to go the distance. A graduate of anything proves that he can follow through, and follow-through is a key trait that employers look for.

Certificates

For years the certificate of completion was the only thing you could get in a culinary school. A diploma, written in lovely calligraphy, had absolutely no meaning, other than proof that you had finished. Sometimes, if you went to a fancy school, you'd get a medal to hang around your neck.

> **Kitchen Tales**
>
> I once worked with a chef on faculty at a cooking school who was terribly proud of all his medals. He was so proud that he wore them to every school function open to the public. Once, the faculty decided to have a little fun at his expense, and we showed up to a food festival decked out in whatever awards we could find. There were swim team medals, horse show ribbons, piano recital certificates, even crossing guard uniforms. I wore my Girl Scout sash, laden with badges and pins I earned in the 1970s (including, of course, the cooking badge). It was the last time we saw his medals in public.

The simple fact that you have finished school will be enough for some employers, especially in entry level positions. But later in your career a degree may serve you better. If you choose to work for a large company, often the jobs higher up the ladder will only be open to those holding degrees.

Associate's and Bachelor's Degrees

Today, many culinary schools offer their students an Associate's degree or a Bachelor's degree. Both require a high school diploma or GED equivalent, but entrance exams such as the SAT and ACT are not typically required. Schools that offer degrees sometimes offer certificates in specialty subjects as well.

The Associate's degree will count toward a higher degree, but a certificate will not. When a culinary school offers a Bachelor's degree, it usually focuses on business, management, and finance, not cooking. Occasionally you can find a food science degree. You can easily find regular universities (not culinary schools) that offer degrees in nutrition, enology (the study of wine), and restaurant management.

It's possible that you may only find a certificate offered in your field of interest, not a degree. This is often the case with the pastry arts. If you have the means, it will serve you better to get a general degree in culinary arts than to get a specialized certificate. You will, in most cases, learn pastry as a part of your degree. Not only will a general degree teach you many other skills, it will also make you more employable and demonstrate that you can follow through. Once you're out of school, you become a better candidate for every job, including pastry. You can always learn more specialized skills, such as sugar pulling, once you get your degree. And if at some point you decide this career is not for you, a Bachelor's degree will serve you better as you shop for your next career.

How to Pay for School

We used to joke that the only admission requirement to culinary school was a checkbook and a pulse. Unfortunately, that's not too far from the truth. Admissions representatives do an outstanding job selling the programs, but they don't really need to. By the time most students call for an appointment, they have already made up their mind to sign on. They just need help figuring out how. Enter financial aid.

Most accredited schools offer the Federal Stafford Loan, which might or might not be subsidized (the government pays the interest), depending on your financial need. Parents can apply for federal loans, as well as the Federal Pell Grant, which you will not have to repay but for which you must demonstrate financial need. There is also a Federal Work Study program, Veterans benefits, and state-operated loan and grant programs. Myriad private loans are available, but beware of scams. (See Appendix B for web links to loan and governmental loan information).

Applying for financial aid requires interviews, counseling, testing, and tons of forms. But it's really not hard, and the school will help you. You can even do much of the paperwork ahead of time, online.

Please remember that while financial aid looks like free money, you will have to begin paying it back six months after graduation, most likely while you are working a $9-an-hour entry-level job.

The Least You Need to Know

◆ Talk to people in the industry about the reputation of a school and what it's like to be a student there.

◆ When interviewing schools, ask questions regarding curriculum, faculty, class format, student teacher ratio, and accreditation.

◆ To get a general culinary Associate's or Bachelor's degree is better than a specialized certificate.

Succeeding in Culinary School

In This Chapter

◆ Following rules

◆ Learning how to study

◆ Earning the reputation of a good student

◆ Benefiting from good grades

Here is your new mantra: "I am in school to learn." Repeat it over and over, as often as necessary. You are about to be challenged. You will be treated as though you know nothing because as much as you think you already know, there's a lot more you don't. No one cares what you did before now. You are all rookies, greenhorns, amateurs, neophytes. The uniform is a great equalizer. Get over yourself, and put on the hat.

Mise en Place Your Brain

Mise en place is a French term meaning literally "installation" or "put in some places." Chefs refer to it when getting all the ingredients for a dish ready before they start cooking. I knew a chef who purposely mistranslated the phrase as "a place for everything, and everything in its place." He knew it was wrong, but it helped his students understand that it's as important to prepare mentally as it is physically. The entire culinary school experience is going to be exciting and stressful, so get ready for it.

Open your mind to everyone and everything that crosses your path. No class is stupid. No class is useless. The school has decided what you need to learn, after much experimenting and experience. Take their word for it.

Follow the Rules

Think of culinary school as your test-run at a career. If you don't follow the rules, your grades will suffer, and by extension, so will your future career. Most of these rules are no-brainers, but I am including them because I want you to see the connection between your performance in school and your performance once you get out into the real world:

- **Always show up to class on time.** In the restaurant industry, if a customer has to wait for the entrée, do you think he cares that you were stuck in traffic? No. He is angry, and you've lost his business and any chance of advertisement by word of mouth. Reliability is the key to a successful career in the food business. Tardiness is not acceptable, and you will be fired if this is your habit. So figure out how to get yourself to class on time and never, never be late.

- **Never skip class.** If you think an employer will excuse unscheduled absences, you are mistaken. Legitimate or not, missing work means your job doesn't get done. Kitchen culture is a lot different from office culture. There are no sick days, there is no personal leave, and there are no doctor's notes. You miss work, you lose your job.

- **Dress with pride.** Wash your uniform regularly. Put your hat on the right way, with all your hair inside. If you need bobby-pins to hold the hat on, you're not wearing it right. No one cares how cute you look when they pull your hair out of the minestrone.

> ### Classic Cuisine
>
> The double row of buttons on the chef coat has a purpose. When the front of the coat gets dirty, it can be re-buttoned with the clean part facing out.

◆ **Don't take the food.** Most schools will not allow you to take home the food you produce on campus. There are a couple of reasons for this rule. Most importantly, they do not trust you to handle the food properly. The schools are afraid that you will leave it in the trunk of your car too long, someone will get sick from it, and then sue them. They are also afraid of school property being carried out along with the food.

◆ **Don't smoke.** Successful chefs know that smoking interferes with the ability to taste. But if you must smoke, follow the school's smoking policy. Stay in the areas they have assigned for this habit, so you impact others as little as possible.

◆ **Turn off your cell phone.** Unless you are a neurosurgeon on call, you do not need to be in constant contact with the outside world. If you have school-age kids or a sick elderly parent, put your cell phone on vibrate. Otherwise, leave it in your locker. This is common courtesy. The world will thank you.

◆ **Do your chores.** If you are going to be a chef, you might as well learn the right way to clean. You need to learn how to properly clean your station, haul mats, do the dishes, and mop the floor. No job in any kitchen anywhere lets you get out of cleaning. When business is slow, you'll have to clean out the most awful things just to keep from getting sent home and losing a day's pay. If nothing else, you'll learn the benefit of *Sheila Shine* and a clean side-towel.

def•i•ni•tion

Sheila Shine is a stainless steel cleaner and polish that removes grease and doesn't streak. Many restaurants use it to clean appliances and work surfaces.

Study

Fitting in study time can be hard, especially if you are working in addition to attending school. But the benefits of study far outweigh any inconvenience or unpleasantness associated with a little sleep deprivation.

Good grades bring the favor of your teachers. It's probably no surprise to you that they like good students better than poor ones. Even a student who gets mediocre grades but puts out the effort will do better in the long run than the student who blows off assignments. And the favor of your instructors is important because teachers who like you will recommend you. They may even write you a recommendation letter, which has real value.

def•i•ni•tion

Your **notebook** is the most valuable thing you will take away from culinary school. If compiled properly, it will contain every recipe, tip, term, technique, historical reference, and anecdote you have learned. Many students even include photographs. In short, the thing could probably get published as a textbook. It will become your culinary bible for the rest of your life.

Every school has different study requirements. Some schools will grade your *notebook*. Some will give written tests. Some will give practical exams. Many do all three. There are smart and easy ways to stay on top of your studies to easily meet these requirements.

It's essential that you keep up with your notebook. Recopy your notes after every class, every single day, while the information is fresh in your mind. A notebook is generally graded on content and neatness, so you'll need to rewrite or type it eventually anyway. Recopying your notes has two purposes. First, it gets them organized and legible. Most notes taken in haste, while the student tries to watch the teacher, are messy. Recopying will ensure that 10 years from now, you'll be able to read and understand what you were taught. Recopying also helps commit the facts to memory. Because writing something takes a little longer than reading it, the information sinks in a little deeper. And recopying your notes a little every night is much easier than all at once, all night long (a lesson I learned the hard way).

Start looking now for a sale on plastic sheet protectors, and buy lots of them. Culinary schools usually require them to protect your notes and recipes from smudges and spills. And while you're shopping the office supply stores, get a couple gigantic binders to build your notebook in. Look for the kind with the plastic sheet in the front, where you can slip a piece of paper in as a cover.

Take pictures of the food you make every day. When you are a successful chef of a high-profile restaurant in Manhattan with rich and famous clientele, you'll be glad you kept such a great notebook. Some society woman will request a Gateaux Saint Honoré, and you'll have only a vague recollection of it. But you'll remember you made it in school so you'll be able to grab your old notebook and look it up. Because you were such a great student, not only were your notes thorough and neat, but you also took a picture of the finished product. So now you know exactly how to proceed and what the finished product is supposed to look like, thus pleasing your fancy-pants client. She will be so impressed that she will offer to let you borrow her private jet for the weekend. It pays to study!

You will need to memorize some facts, such as the proper temperatures for rare, medium, and well, the lifespan of *Caréme*, or the number of medium shrimp in one pound. For this kind of study, nothing beats flashcards. Write your facts on index cards; then sit with a classmate and quiz each other. Carry them with you and study on the bus, in the dentist's office, or at the tattoo parlor.

Some classes will require a practical test, which means cooking. Some schools make you cook by memory, whereas others let you use recipes. But cooking with a recipe is no guarantee of success. If you learned a technique or recipe that was tough for you, make it again at home. Practice is the only way. Find someone to cook for. They'll love you for it! Or get together with classmates, split the cost of ingredients, and practice together. (See Chapter 7 for more information on cooking for guinea pigs.)

Kitchen Tales

As a teacher I was always stunned by the fact that 25 students using a single recipe would make 25 different versions of the same dish. Every cook is different. They all put their signature on it, for better or worse.

Teacher's Pet

Guess who you're in school for? You! Not your classmates. So who cares if they think you're a kiss-up? It will serve you better than sitting in the back row or gossiping with the slackers. Kissing-up is a time-honored tradition, but there is a right way and a wrong way to do it. Take it from the master. Kissing up is an art form, and if you can master it here, you can carry the skill into the field. Look out world!

First, being the teacher's pet doesn't mean complimenting him on his outfit. (Don't try that in a culinary school anyway. Duh! The outfit is the same as yours.) It means paying attention and asking relevant questions. Don't talk when the teacher is talking. The only thing worse than a student talking during a lecture is a student sleeping through one. Stay awake.

Regardless of what the teachers of your youth may have taught you, there *is* such a thing as a stupid question. The stupid question is the one that has already been answered and the one that will be answered shortly. Hold your questions until the end of the lecture, because the teacher may very well address your concerns within the lecture. And if you're not sure if your question has already been answered because you were talking, daydreaming, or legitimately distracted by furiously writing notes, write the question down and ask the teacher later, after class. Don't waste the time of the entire class because you were spaced out.

def•i•ni•tion

A **reach-in** is a refrigerator that you reach into, unlike the **walk-in,** which you must walk into. The reach-in can be tall, like a home refrigerator, or short, which is also known as a low-boy.

Being a teacher's pet means you offer to help. Offer to do the grunt jobs that no one wants, like dishwashing, mopping, or cleaning out the *reach-in*. When you are done working, instead of standing around waiting for someone to tell you what to do, ask, "Is there something I can do?" This is a key skill in the industry. As the McDonald's entrepreneur Ray Kroc said, "If you've got time to lean, you've got time to clean."

Most of all, being the teacher's pet means taking an interest in the subject. My favorite students were the ones who asked for more. I was always happy to give more information about the topic, more recipes, more history, or more of my experiences to anyone who really cared. Those students loved the craft. They were also the ones who got the As.

Making the Grade

The biggest reason to get good grades is not your grade point average. It's not to get on the honor roll or the dean's list. Those are fine reasons, don't get me wrong. But the number-one reason to get good grades ... drumroll please ... is winning the favor of your teachers.

Recommendations

Instructors will not give a recommendation to a middle-of-the road student. Why would they? Their reputation is on the line as much as that of the students. Can you imagine the phone call from the executive chef of the Hotel Swank when the kid you recommended decides not to show up on Friday night? It's not a happy phone call. Instructors know that recommending mediocre students and placing them into jobs they can't or won't handle will have a negative impact on their school's reputation. So chefs are extremely cautious. To get the coveted recommendations, which deliver the jobs, you need to get the grades. Yep, grades count!

To get a recommendation, you need to ask for one. Many chefs will happily offer to give recommendations, but when it comes to actually sitting down and typing a letter, they come up short. After all, they are busy people, and you are far down on their list of priorities. If you sense the promise of a recommendation letter is an empty one, offer to type up the letter yourself. The chef can edit it, and you can retype it before he or she signs it. I am always relieved when students offer this service. It means I get to be lazy and nice at the same time.

Networking

If your instructors like you, they'll become part of your network. They'll remember you and, years later, when you run into them, they may hire you or recommend you to a friend.

However, you need to nurture networks. Stay in touch with your chefs. Write them a postcard from time to time; let them know where you are and what you're doing. I can't tell you how fun it is, as a teacher, to hear from former students. And it is very disappointing when you lose touch with them and hear what they are doing through the grapevine.

Your network also includes your classmates. It pays to be friendly with everyone because you never know who is going to make it. Have you been to a high school reunion and seen those who have made it big? It's usually the geeks! Remember this before you turn up your nose at the classmate who tucks his chef coat into his *checks*.

While we're at it, everyone you come into contact with at culinary school could someday come in handy. The office staff, admissions representatives, and financial aid and placement staff all have contacts of their own in the business. Dishwashers and janitorial staff know hundreds of people in the industry. Purveyors and salesmen sell all over town. Make nice!

def•i•ni•tion

Checks is a slang term for the black-and-white pants worn by most professional cooks. The busy pattern hides the massive amounts of muck that spills on them every night. Your cutesy chili pepper pants do the same thing, with slightly less class. The traditional pattern is houndstooth, not an actual check. Tucking your chef coat into your checks is completely dorky. Don't do it.

Mentors

Your instructors are teaching you all about cooking. If you're lucky, you'll click with one who will teach you more. After all, many ins and outs of the business, idiosyncrasies of technique, and remedies for when the going gets tough aren't in the curriculum—you need someone to take you aside and tell you these things (see Chapter 15 on finding a mentor).

Being a mentor is not a job that a chef knowingly or willingly signs up for. And as a student, you can't exactly hold mentor auditions. But you'll know if you have a teacher who could potentially play that role. If it happens, work on the relationship. Ask questions, pay attention, and find out if the instructor has more to offer you. It could happen! After all, students who excel are worth knowing.

The Least You Need to Know

- ◆ Be prepared to study hard.
- ◆ Rules are in place for good reason, and breaking them will only keep you from your goal.
- ◆ Winning the teacher's favor can help you now and 10 years from now.
- ◆ Good grades will get you much more than a spot on the honor roll.

Chapter **6**

Enriching Your Culinary School Experience

In This Chapter

- Balancing work and school
- Joining professional culinary organizations
- Exploring your interests

Although a lot of thought and planning has gone into the curriculum at your chosen culinary school, the administration can offer only so much. The rest is up to you.

Endless learning opportunities will fill your culinary school experience. You will find activities on and off campus that can help prepare you for the real world. Some you shouldn't miss. Others you can definitely take a pass on.

Don't wait for the good opportunities to approach you. Seek them out. It's up to you to take advantage of them and get yourself the best education possible.

Working During School

Working at a restaurant while attending culinary school is an excellent idea. You will be able to put into practice everything you are learning and see how industry professionals interpret your lessons.

You Get to See Another Side

And working shows you another point of view. You'll learn that your teachers don't know everything, and neither do your employers (but don't tell this to either of them!). Seeing another point of view teaches you that there are many *right* ways to do anything. One method is not necessarily better or worse. Many instructors miss this lesson, too. They generate a singlemindedness in their students by telling them that theirs is the one-and-only correct way. Of course, their teachers probably taught them the same lesson, and so on and so on into the annals of culinary history. But the fact of the matter is, in some circumstances the rules don't apply. This is when cooking becomes artful. Being able to go with the flow and make something wonderful from whatever comes your way is a skill you can only get when you are out there, doing it every day in the real world.

> **Kitchen Tales** _____
>
> Hollandaise is thought to be one of the more difficult sauces to make, because it requires constant whipping of egg yolks over a *bain marie* (double boiler), as clarified butter is drizzled in ever so slowly. Once, I had a guest chef from Le Cordon Bleu in Paris demonstrate hollandaise for my class here in the states. You could hear the gasps a mile away as he combined all the ingredients in a pot, and whisked it nimbly over direct high heat. It was the best hollandaise we had ever tasted. I know of at least five other *right* ways to make hollandaise sauce. The advantage of each variation can be (and has been) argued for weeks.

You Can Apply What You Learn

Working while you are in school will not only make you a better cook, but it will also help you become a better student. Most students leave class wondering how the information they just learned could possibly help them in the real world. If you are working, you'll find yourself putting those puzzle pieces together during the lecture. The information will sink in deeper because it is more real to you. In cooking classes you will be comparing the instructor's methods to those of the cooks at work. During a class lecture on supervision, you will be wondering who at work knows this information and if they are applying it every day. Safety and sanitation instruction will make you aware of every sneeze and open sore; you'll be more mindful of the fridge temperatures and which cutting boards you should use.

You'll see every class come into play, from management to nutrition to your dining room rotation. And because you'll be exposed to more information, you'll be more aware when things go wrong. You will run across people who are working in an imprudent way. This is because most of the people in the restaurant business have had no formal training in cooking, business, or management. You will see their errors unfold before your eyes.

Behind You!

At work you can reflect on how the operation is run and how it could be improved. But unless you are extremely close with your bosses, keep your opinions to yourself. No boss wants to hear an entry-level culinary student explain that the business is being run improperly. File it away for future reference, and if need be, prepare yourself to deal with the fallout of the mistakes being made. No one likes a know-it-all, and you want the people at work to like you so you can add them to your network.

You Expand Your Network

Going to work will enable you to double your contacts. Add everyone you meet at work to your network, from the dishwasher, to the waiters, to the delivery guys.

A day will come when you will call on your network, just as you will get called on at some time as a part of someone else's network. You'll be asked who you know. Do you know anyone in pastry or anyone who could help on a catering gig or any good prep cooks for a new start-up? If you can help, you will, because this adds to your pile of good kitchen karma, which will come back to you tenfold.

Kitchen Tales

Networking is not just a catch-phrase. It's real. I have gotten jobs based on the recommendations of waiters and purveyors, and I have seen jobs denied based on the recommendation of the dishwashers.

You Can Find a Mentor

Working will also double your chances of finding a mentor. The more people you come into contact with, the more likely you are to find someone who inspires you. Keep your eyes and your mind open.

As I hope I've made clear, you can quite successfully work while in school. But before you apply for a job, think carefully. Working and taking classes is not going to be easy. You will essentially be working two jobs, one for grades and the other for money. Prioritizing the two can be tricky, especially if you actually need the money.

Make sure you understand that you'll be away from home for long periods of time. And when you are home, you will have to somehow fit your homework in. If you live alone, this won't be bad, but if you have people in your life who like having you around, they're going to miss you. Be sure to take into consideration their sacrifices as well as yours before you decide to work twice as hard. And be sure to fit them into your schedule so you don't lose them altogether. If you're sensible, you'll double your education, make money, and gain valuable experience that you simply can't get any other way.

Professional Organizations and Clubs

Since you're on your way to becoming a professional, it's time to start thinking about joining a professional organization. Many schools encourage their students to join these groups. If you can afford the membership fees, it's totally worth it. There are dozens of options, in various areas of specialization, and all have membership benefits.

The American Culinary Federation (ACF)

Founded in the 1920s, the ACF successfully elevated the job of chef from service status to that of professional. They continue to promote the professional image of American chefs.

The ACF is probably best known for its certification program, which is the most extensive in the United States. They offer 13 levels of certification designation, from the basic Culinarian (CC) to the prestigious Master Chef (CMC).

The ACF also sponsors culinary competitions all over the country, regional conferences, food shows, and an annual convention. The convention includes tryouts for the celebrated U.S. Culinary Team, which represents the United States in culinary competitions worldwide. Also at the convention are annual awards, including Chef, Educator, Pastry Chef, and even Student Culinarian of the Year.

The organization offers a monthly magazine and newsletter, dozens of scholarships, apprenticeship programs, high school certification, and accreditation for post-secondary culinary programs. They also sponsor a well-regarded child hunger prevention initiative.

Classic Cuisine

The American Culinary Federation's Culinarian's Code:

I pledge my professional knowledge and skill to the advancement of our profession and to pass it on to those who are to follow.

I shall foster a spirit of courteous consideration and fraternal cooperation within our profession.

I shall place honor and the standing of our profession before personal advancement.

I shall not use unfair means to effect my professional advancement or to injure the chances of another colleague to secure and hold employment.

I shall be fair, courteous, and considerate in my dealings with fellow colleagues.

I shall conduct any necessary comment on, or criticism of, the work of a fellow colleague with careful regard of the good name and dignity of the culinary profession, and will scrupulously refrain from criticism to gain personal advantage.

I shall never expect anyone to subject themselves to risks which I would not be willing to assume myself.

I shall help to protect all members against one another from within our profession.

I shall be just as enthusiastic about the success of others as I am about my own.

I shall be too big for worry, too noble for anger, too strong for fear, and too happy to permit pressure of business to hurt anyone, within or without the profession

---

The International Association of Culinary Professionals (IACP)

Begun as an organization of culinary educators, the IACP grew to encompass not only chefs but all areas of culinary arts as well. They offer continuing education and professional development, as well as resources and support systems for specified areas of the industry. Members can join any number of *interest sections*, which include educators, entrepreneurs, food photographers and stylists, food writers and publishers, chefs and restaurateurs, food historians, test kitchens, corporations, and one called *kids in the kitchen*, for those who want to focus on early childhood education.

IACP offers certification as a Certified Culinary Professional (CCP), and they award $150,000 in scholarships annually. They offer hunger relief programs, national conferences, regional events, monthly and quarterly publications, a job bank, business directory, competitions, and annual awards of excellence.

The Retail Bakers of America (RBA)

The RBA is a national resource for bakers and bakeries. Dedicated to education, the RBA provides education resources for schools and businesses, as well as certification for professionals. Certification levels include the entry-level Certified Journeyman Bakers (CJB), Certified Bakers (CB), Certified Decorators (CD), Certified Bread Bakers (CBB), and the all-encompassing Certified Master Baker (CMB).

The RBA hosts a formula database (a.k.a. recipes), vendor and member directories, and continuing education programs in marketing, business, and management. RBA has an annual convention that includes competitions and seminars.

The National Restaurant Association (NRA)

The NRA is the leading political voice for the food and beverage industry, with a strong presence on Capitol Hill representing and promoting this industry that employs 12.5 million people nationwide. They are also leading providers of current research and statistical information on the industry.

The NRA Educational Foundation is an arm of the organization dedicated to advancing the business through educational programs. They offer high school programs, mentoring, and scholarships, and their ServSafe program is the industry standard for safety and sanitation training. There is also a Food Service Management Professional certification program. Like all of these larger organizations, they provide weekly, monthly, and quarterly publications, as well as annual trade shows and regional seminars.

Kitchen Tales

Culinary organizations are not just places to get help. They are places you can lend a hand. Almost every organization has a cause they champion or links to groups that do. Chefs for Humanity is such a group. Founded after the Asian Tsunami in December 2004, they offer a place for food service professionals to roll up their sleeves and help, whether it is rebuilding homes for Katrina victims, partnering with UNICEF to teach nutrition, or hosting volunteer vacations for culinarians to feed the hungry overseas. Find out more at www.chefsforhumanity.org.

The James Beard Foundation

The late James Beard is often called the Father of American Gastronomy. His Greenwich Village brownstone has been preserved and houses the foundation that bears his name. The foundation works to promote America's unique culinary heritage and the appreciation of culinary excellence. It is best known for its annual awards, which honor all facets of the industry, including chefs, owners, journalists, authors, and restaurant designers. The house itself serves nightly dinners, prepared by the who's who of culinary art. And in it the extensive library and archive, available only to members, is housed.

The American Institute of Wine and Food (AIWF)

Founded by the industry's grand poo-bahs of food, Julia Child and Robert Mondavi, the AIWF is mainly about having fun with food and promoting education through social and educational events, such as wine seminars and food field trips. They offer scholarships to students of both culinary arts and enology.

Women's Organizations

A host of organizations are dedicated to promoting the achievements of women in the food and beverage industries. Les Dames d'Escoffier International was founded in the 1970s at a time when women were just beginning to make a name for themselves in a profession traditionally occupied by men. Its 25 chapters provide scholarships, mentor programs, and regional seminars. Similar organizations include the Roundtable for Women in Food Service, The New York Women's Culinary Alliance, Women Chefs and Restaurateurs, and the Women's Foodservice Forum.

And you can join dozens of other organizations, for instance, the National Ice Carving Association, the Bread Bakers Guild of America, the International Council of Cruise Lines, or the Research Chefs Association. There really is something for everyone. (See Appendix B for contact information.)

Campus Clubs

Some schools have an active student body, already undertaking the exploration of their special interests. But if your school doesn't, why not start your own campus club? It's a great way to enhance your education, learn new skills, and meet people with similar interests. Most schools have a Dining Club of one form or another. These groups go

Kitchen Tales

My extensive collection of menus has been a great source of inspiration through the years. Whenever I eat out, I ask the staff for a copy of the evening's menu. They are usually happy to make me a photocopy. Not only is it a fun way to remember special evenings, but it's useful when I have menu-block.

out together to sample the menus of local restaurants and critique them. This is a great way to start your menu collection.

Wine-tasting and wine-making clubs are also popular, as are brewing clubs. I have also seen sourdough clubs, cheese-making clubs, organic gardening clubs, and cookbook clubs. One of the most creative groups I've come across was a dinner club that took turns cooking meals for each other. The guests had to guess the theme of the meal based on the dishes presented. These guys were hard-core. The meal that really mystified me was the one in which each course represented a sign of the Zodiac. Pisces I might have figured out, but Virgo had me flummoxed.

Don't forget to look for food organizations within your community. Larger cities have food societies that offer lecture series and cooking workshops. Check your newspaper's food section for offerings in your area.

Bad Influences

At the risk of sounding like your mother, you are going to encounter some bad influences while you're in culinary school, and if you want to succeed, you need to avoid them.

No matter what school you attend, some students will not share your enthusiasm or dedication to the craft. Stay away from them.

You will also have to fend off the many temptations you'll encounter. The food business is full of excess. It's our bread and butter. But just because you're serving it up doesn't mean you should partake. Perhaps you've heard of the freshman 15—the 15 pounds many students gain during their first year of college. In culinary school it's closer to 30. And because wine and liquor play an important role in cuisine, it's everywhere, too.

I have frequently caught students with a coffee cup full of Grand Marnier, or a Coke can full of rum, boosted from the chef's cabinet. Culinary school is tough, but resist the temptation to let off steam by drinking during class, or while at work. Most schools will expel you if you're caught. And despite what you may have read about the confidential life of the kitchen, working under the influence is not tolerated anymore.

Pilfering is another all-too-common occurrence in the food business. I once caught a student trying to exit the building with a *burr mixer* down one pant leg. Why? Did he have a lot of chunky food at home that desperately needed to be puréed? No! He thought, "If I can steal it, why not try?"

A lot of theft in the food industry is less blatant than walking out with equipment down your pants. Eating food that was prepared for service is stealing, too. Eating ingredients is stealing. When someone goes into the walk-in and pours himself a glass of milk, food cost is increased and the supply is diminished. Just because there is a refrigerator doesn't mean you are free to snack on whatever you find. It's shoplifting. If you do that at work, the business suffers. If you do it at school, you pay for it in hiked tuition.

def•i•ni•tion

A **burr mixer** is also known as an immersion blender. Braun popularized the home version of this tool, which is basically a blender on a stick that can be inserted into a liquid. The liquid and food chunks are sucked into the blades, turning it to a purée. We lovingly refer to the industrial-size burr mixer as the bazooka.

The Least You Need to Know

◆ Working during school is tough but worth the sacrifice.

◆ Professional organizations offer extra training, certification, scholarships, and yet another way to network.

◆ Campus clubs are a fun way to accessorize your education.

◆ Avoid naysayers, sleazebags, partiers, and thieves.

Part 3

Learning the Trade on Your Own

Some of the best chefs in the world never stepped foot into a culinary school. They learned in real time, on the job.

Working in a professional kitchen is the easiest way to find out if the cooking scene is really for you.

Many people dream of leaving whatever cubicle they're in to find the job they're really supposed to have—the one that fulfills them and gives their life meaning. For you, it could be cooking. Or not. There is only one real way to find out. You need to go do it.

The benefit to learning the trade on the job is that you can quit it at any time, go back to your cubicle, and chalk the whole thing up to your experimental phase. If you conduct your experiment via culinary school, a lot more money, time, and emotion is at stake.

Learning to Cook at Home

In This Chapter

- Exploring the world of food
- Broadening your repertoire
- Trying everything
- Learning about classic French cuisine
- Keeping on top of your work

The first real recipes I remember making were with my maternal grandmother. I was only three or four years old, but I vividly recall making Puddle Cake. Grandma taught me to pour the wet ingredients into the center of the dry ingredients, making a puddle. I also remember going to the butcher when I was nine or ten and ordering thick pork chops so that I could stuff them, per a recipe I found in my Mom's *Gourmet* magazine. I made lots of Jell-O pudding with my other grandma, potato *lefse* at Christmas with my Auntie Violet, and a killer lasagna with my dad.

Unfortunately, not nearly as many families cook or bake as much as they did when I was growing up. Few families have the time or energy or even the know-how to cook for themselves. Because of this fact, the restaurant industry has boomed in the last few decades. Everyone is eating out. As happy as I am that my industry is doing well, I mourn the loss of families cooking together, passing on traditional recipes and favorite tricks and techniques.

Eating restaurant food or popping that frozen dinner in the microwave is certainly easier and faster, but you'll learn a lot more about food if you make your meals from scratch. If your plan is to become a professional chef, just say no to the curbside take-out and start cooking.

Get Cooking

If you want to cook for a living, the most important thing you can do is start cooking—a lot! Getting a job in the industry is, of course, important. But it's not enough. Most entry-level positions are going to be just that. You'll be given entry-level tasks and entry-level responsibility. You'll get really good at a few repetitive tasks, but not much else. To learn more, you're on your own.

def•i•ni•tion

Masa harina (dough flour) is flour made from dried hominy, which is corn soaked in calcium oxide. It is used to make corn tortillas and tamales, and to thicken soups, sauces, and stews. **Carnitas** means "little meats" and refers to shredded pork, cooked until tender, then browned until crispy. **Roux** is a thickener, made from equal parts of melted butter and flour

By cooking at home, I don't mean zapping a frozen enchilada in the microwave. Instead, figure out how to make enchiladas from scratch. Learn how to take dried beans, soak them, and cook them until they're tender. Teach yourself to make tortillas from *masa harina*. Figure out how to make *carnitas* and red chili sauce. You can even teach yourself to make cheese.

I really enjoy cooking this way. When I was just starting out, my then future husband mentioned that he liked tuna casserole. Being the show-off that I am, I decided to figure out how to make the dish from scratch. I bought fresh tuna at the fish market and grilled it to perfection. I made my own cream-of-mushroom soup, starting with a *roux*, and adding mushrooms and mushroom broth and cream. I shelled fresh peas. To top it off, I made my own crackers, which I then crumbled over my masterpiece. Did he like the casserole? Yes. Could he tell I had made it entirely from scratch? No. In fact, as I recall, he thought I was a little nuts to go through all that work as it tasted the same as the one his mom made with canned soup and chicken-of-the-sea. Little did he know that he was getting a taste of his future! Yes, of course, cooking like this takes longer. But you learn more. And when you are on the road to becoming a successful chef, you need to learn as much as possible.

Go Shopping

Do you wander the aisles of grocery stores looking for new and interesting foods? Do you buy ingredients with no clear idea of what you will do with them? If not, then now is the time to start.

Experiment with New Ingredients

Check out the produce section at your favorite market. Is there a melon or a leafy green that you have never seen before? Buy it. Figure out how to prepare it. Take a walk down the condiment aisle. See something weird? Grab it. Look it up. Eat it.

By moving out of your grocery comfort zone, you are going to increase your personal culinary glossary tenfold in no time. This sort of continuous culinary investigation is something the best chefs share. They are open to new tastes and textures. They don't turn their noses up at the unusual; instead, they embrace it and ingest it.

Do you have a local farmers' market? Find out when it is and go. Go every week. Get to know the purveyors and their products. They appreciate regular customers, and they probably like to talk about the products they sell. If you go regularly, you'll begin to understand the seasonality of food and in particular what your local area has to offer throughout the year. Keep these businesses in mind when the time comes for you to purchase ingredients for work. And don't forget that the contacts you make at the market, both purveyors and the other cooks you meet, also qualify as networking.

Get Some Good Cookware

Once you begin cooking in this manner, you will start accumulating cookware. Get yourself some good, durable pans. I use aluminum pots and pans almost exclusively. Aluminum is durable, conducts heat slowly and evenly, and cleans up easily. More expensive brands of cookware don't, in my opinion, cook any better than quality aluminum. My pots and pans must also be easy to clean. If I can't throw it in my dishwasher, I won't use it.

In my kitchen at home I use aluminum saucepans, sauté pans, a *sauteuse* for braising and big batches of stuff, and aluminum *sheet pans*. I have cheap

Behind You!

I don't recommend buying sets of cookware. They inevitably include things you'll never use. Buy piece by piece as the need arises.

def•i•ni•tion

A **sauteuse** is a frying pan with straight sides and a tight-fitting lid. **Sheet pans** are what the home cook would call cookie sheets or baking sheets. The professional aluminum variety come in half (the size that fits in a home oven) and full sizes (twice as big). They have an inch-high lip all the way around the edge.

spatter-ware stockpots, originally made for canning, an old stainless Revere Ware pasta pot with a missing handle, and several nonstick sauté pans that I use for eggs. I have other pans, too, but I hardly ever use anything else.

Try to resist the lure of gadgetry. There are a lot of unnecessary pieces of equipment out there, just waiting for someone like you. Even the tool kits handed out by the big culinary schools have a lot of needless junk.

When it comes to gadgets, you can usually find something you already have that will do the job just fine. Gadgets are expensive, usually good for only one thing, and take up space. Unless you have oodles of money and a ton of storage, leave the gadgets to the hobbyists. You're turning pro now.

Try Everything

Kitchen Tales

My favorite example of a useless gadget is the zester. This popular tool is designed to strip off the outermost rind of citrus fruit, called the *zest*, which is a common ingredient in all sorts of recipes. Zesters take the rind off in small channels, with space between them, leaving half the fruit unzested. What's more, the little worm-like strings of zest it produces aren't that useful. The strings inevitably need to be minced, either by hand with a knife or in a food processor, which you'll then need to clean. I don't typically have the time or inclination for these extra steps. Rather than use a zester, I use the finest holes on a standing box cheese grater.

Cooks who refuse to try something are a hundred times worse than kids or guests who do that. In no way can you be a chef if you don't know what food tastes like. As a chef, you will be asked to cook foods you wouldn't necessarily order for yourself. That means you'll need to know how it is supposed to taste and be willing to taste it yourself to be sure you have made it properly.

The vast majority of food dislikes stem from a lifetime of eating food prepared the wrong way. Fish is a great example of this. Many people cook fish until it is rubbery and dry. Yuck! As a chef, your goal should be to cook foods properly so that they show off their best qualities.

Let's stay with the example of fish. Go to the library and get yourself a good book on fish. Read about fish; then pick a recipe and try it. Then try another and another until you begin to appreciate and understand it.

A good chef understands the value of all food, and can cook it well when asked to do so, even if it is personally off-putting. The most common food aversions I have come across in a decade of teaching in culinary schools revolve around fish. Many students refuse to handle it and even more won't try the finished dish. (As you might have guessed, they did not get good grades for this sort of behavior.)

Behind You!

Don't give up if the first couple of recipes you try don't exactly thrill you. Move on to another recipe, or try another book. Just because a recipe is in print doesn't mean it's going to be great.

Fish phobias usually revolve around whole fish with their heads still on, or the weirder-looking bounty of the sea, such oysters, octopus, eels, sea urchin, and anchovies. The anchovy gets a particularly bad wrap. I happen to love them and welcome their presence on the occasional pizza because my grandpa used to give me anchovies and smoked oysters on Ritz Crackers as an after-school snack. But aside from pizza and cracker toppings, the salty, rich anchovy can really elevate a recipe, adding roundness and depth of flavor, without making it *fishy*. The best example of this is Caesar salad, which is not possible without my beloved anchovy.

Raw meat is off-putting to many people. Sushi is fairly common, but steak tartar is rarely seen on menus anymore. This is because people got all freaked out by a salmonella scare in the late 1980s and still haven't recovered. The fact is, food poisoning from raw meat and eggs is less common than acquiring it from cross-contamination of the bacteria onto cooked meat, fruits, vegetables, and tableware. Raw meat and eggs both have a long and illustrious culinary history. As long as they are handled properly (chosen good quality, kept cold, prepared on a clean work surface, etc.) nothing is risky about them. (For more on sanitation, see Chapter 22.)

Blue cheese is less popular as a cheese than it is as a dressing. Considered stinky to some, the blue veins (green in gorgonzola) are created by intentionally injecting mold into the cheese and allowing it to ripen and grow. Blue cheese is actually pretty far down on the odiferous scale, compared to limburger.

Some people think snails are gross. I think that even poorly prepared escargot is ter-

def•i•ni•tion

Charcuterie is the French term for a category of foods made from meat, such as pâtés, terrines, sausages, and other ground, seasoned, and molded meats known as force meats (because they are forced through a grinder and/or sausage casings). These products belong to the realm of the *Garde Manger* in a classical kitchen.

Kitchen Tales

Once, after a food festival, I sat in the kitchen with a fellow chef, chatting and nibbling on what was left on the bone of a roast. After about a half hour, I looked down and discovered I had been eating the brain of a suckling pig that had been roasted whole. It was pretty good!

rific. How can anything be bad when it is smothered in butter and garlic?

Offal (a.k.a. variety meats or body parts), is another source of disgust for many people in the United States although it enjoys wide popularity elsewhere in the world. Prepared properly, it can be quite delicious. Liver is the most common, but the category also includes heart, kidney, sweetbreads (the thymus gland of veal), tongue, and tripe (lining of beef stomach). Many of these parts end up in sausages and other *charcuterie*. Head cheese really uses parts of the head and is quite delicious when made properly.

Every culture serves foods that others would never think of putting on the dinner table, and I couldn't rightly call myself a chef if I didn't try them when given the opportunity. I've eaten fried grasshoppers, corn fungus, sea cucumber, fish heads, and chicken feet. No, I didn't like everything, but I tried it all, and I understand the significance of these foods in the context of the world's cuisines. Culinary art is not just about Jackson Pollack sauce patterns and a "bam" of garnish. It is about learning to appreciate the heritage of food and nourishment, respecting the ingredients, and honoring them with quality preparation. If you are going to be a successful chef, you must value everything.

Read Books Cover to Cover

To truly appreciate all foods, try making as many new and interesting recipes as you can. The more you cook, the better, smarter, and more efficient you'll become.

To start, pick a book that contains classic French cuisine, such as *Mastering the Art of French Cooking*, by Julia Child, Louisette Berthole, and Simone Beck, or *In Madeleine's Kitchen*, by Madeleine Kamman (see Chapter 8 for more suggestions). These are good choices because they cover classic French technique, which is the very basic information that every chef must know. Any book that covers stocks; the mother sauces; vegetable cookery; potatoes and grains; fabricating meat, fish, and poultry; dry and wet heat cooking methods; and basic pastry techniques will do, but get one from a reputable chef, preferably French (or one trained in France).

When most people buy and read cookbooks, they thumb through them until they find a recipe that interests them, and then they try it. What you must do, as a future professional chef, is read your book on French cuisine from page one until the end, including the introductions, the preface, prologues, all the sidebars, the glossary, and appendixes. This is important because these portions of the book, often missed by home cooks, contain much of the crucial information that you can really learn from. Contained in these often overlooked portions of cookbooks are explanations of the inner workings of recipes, the history, the background, experience and insight of the author, techniques, tricks, and tips that you might otherwise miss. By cooking cover to cover from such a book, you will be approximating every culinary school curriculum there is. If the experience doesn't change the way you cook and the way you view French cuisine, move on to another author and try again.

Why should it be French? Because French cuisine has influenced nearly all other western cultures. Let the Italians claim their influence (*Medici*, Smedici). France rules! Besides, isn't pasta from China? In France you can find every food imaginable. The regional cuisines of France, or *cuisine du terrior*, provide a wide variety of indigenous food, seasonings, and cooking methods. Look for books and recipes that feature the cuisine of Alsace, Pays Basque, the Loire Valley, Normandy, Provence, Burgundy, and Brittany. They each have a distinct climate and terrain, which makes each cuisine unique.

Typically, what most of the world thinks of as French cuisine is not what French people eat every day, but *haute cuisine* of the 1800s, and *nouvelle cuisine* of the 1970s. These composed presentations of refined sauces and elaborate garniture are influential, and should also be explored.

Once you finish with your exploration of French cuisine and you feel proficient in the classics, move on to another culture. Try Indian or Chinese or Italian. There are hun-

Classic Cuisine

Julie Powell created an Internet blog called *The Julie/Julia Project*, chronicling a year in which she cooked every recipe in Julie Child's *Mastering the Art of French Cooking*. It has recently been published in book form, *Julie and Julia: 365 Days, 524 Recipes, 1 Tiny Apartment Kitchen*, by Julie Powell (Little, Brown, 2005).

dreds of authors and topics for you to discover.

Find Some Guinea Pigs

Of course, with all this cooking comes an awful lot of eating. You may find that it's too much for you to handle on your own. And even if you think you can eat it all alone, you probably shouldn't. Besides, it's better to have input from others. You need some help! Call up your friends. Pick some who will really tell you the truth and give you an honest assessment of the meal, not what they think you want to hear. No polite ego stroking allowed.

I'm sure, if your friends are anything like mine, they'll eat anytime, anywhere. And if they are really good friends, they will try whatever you make, no matter how weird it is. When I was learning to cook, I was constantly feeding my friends. They were a unique bunch of miscreants, but they appreciated the finer things in life. The problem was that when I made something good, I kept getting requests for it, which moved me dangerously close to becoming a caterer. I tested their patience, however, the Halloween I decided to make fresh black and orange pasta. I had just seen how to make, roll, and cut the dough by hand. I didn't do a very good job, though, and my squid-ink and pumpkin pasta puffed up in the water to the size of cigars. My friend Lori proclaimed it inedible, and we went out to eat.

Don't be timid about cooking for people. You've got to jump in and not worry about their reaction. That will come later, when you do this for money. For now, you just need to get your feet wet. Your goal is to view the preparation of a huge dinner, like Thanksgiving, with the warm tingle of joyous anticipation, not the cold shiver of dread. The only way to reach that level of comfort is to practice. (How did the chef get hired at the restaurant next to Carnegie Hall? Practice, practice, practice.)

Learn to Love Cleaning

So many people avoid cooking for one reason. They hate cleaning up. I actually like cleaning, provided I don't have to do another 50 things at the same time. I have evolved to a point where I can cook and clean quickly and easily. In fact, I am so much better at it that I'd rather clean up myself than endure the agony of watching someone else do it in a less efficient manner.

Once you begin working in a professional kitchen, you quickly recognize that if you don't keep the mess in check, the job gets much harder. You hear the phrase "clean as you go" often in the restaurant business. That's because the typical workstation is pretty small, and there simply isn't room for a mess. Piles of dirty bowls and utensils, foods scraps, and spills will bury you in no time. By cleaning up after every task, no matter how small, you give yourself maximum room to complete every job, and you make the final cleanup quick and easy.

As you are cooking, put away your ingredients as soon as you're finished with them. This clears out usable space and gets the ingredients back where they belong. In the professional workplace, other workers in the kitchen need access to all the ingredients, too. It's not cool to hoard them at your station.

Your sink is your best friend when you cook. My habit is to fill one side of it with hot soapy water and to toss in the dirty pots and pans as they accumulate. The soapy water makes them easier to wash, which I do when the sink gets full. As you wash up, put the clean dishes away. This prevents you from wasting time sifting under piles of clean bowls and pots and pans looking for a small utensil when you need it.

I keep a wet side-towel next to me at all times and wipe up after every stage of a recipe. If I don't, the detritus from whatever I am making gets all over me, my floor, and everything else I'm cooking. Find a good, inexpensive cleaner that you can dilute with water and keep it in a squirt bottle. This way, cleaning and sanitizing bigger messes is fast and easy.

A broom and dustpan are always nearby, so I can sweep up as the flour flies. Keeping on top of the little spills keeps me from having to clean up a much bigger, ground-in mess when I'm finished. It also prevents me from tracking the mess all over the place.

A large, open garbage receptacle of some kind, out on the floor or on the counter, is a key feature of a well-operated kitchen. At home, most people keep the garbage under the sink or off in the corner of the kitchen.

Kitchen Tales

An auto parts store is a good place to find a lot of good, cheap side-towels.

But having to constantly open and close a cupboard or walk across the room with a pile of goop is time-consuming and inefficient. For big meals, I line a box or milk crate with a garbage bag and set it on the floor nearby or on the counter by the sink. With this, it's easy to toss in the goop and move on.

The Least You Need to Know

- ◆ Cook your own meals, from scratch.
- ◆ Expose yourself to the unusual foods.
- ◆ Try everything.
- ◆ Learn classic French cuisine by cooking from a classic book, cover to cover.
- ◆ Clean as you go.

Chapter 8

Getting Book Smart

In This Chapter

- ◆ Building a culinary library
- ◆ Improving your skills with classic cookbooks
- ◆ Getting smarter with reference books
- ◆ Broadening your repertoire with regional cookbooks
- ◆ Learning about others' love of food with essays and memoirs

Cookbooks may not be considered serious reading in the halls of academia. But if you are planning on becoming a chef, cookbooks are part of your core curriculum. However, sifting your way through thousands of cookbooks can be overwhelming.

In this chapter I have compiled a list of the most important books for any chef-in-training. These are just the beginning of your culinary library—if you are like most chefs I know, you will continue to add to it throughout your career. I have listed each category in alphabetical order, not order of importance. They are all important. Plus, I didn't want to hurt anyone's feelings.

Classics

Classics are called classics for a reason. The books in this section are indispensable resources for you to refer to time and time again.

The Good Cook series (Time-Life Books, 1980)

Those folks at Time-Life had it goin' on! This series is so detailed, so extraordinarily photographed and diagrammed that it should be required reading for everyone learning to cook. Twenty-eight books are in the series, which cover everything culinary, including all meats, eggs, sauces, soups, snacks, fruits and vegetables, wines and beverages, to name just a few, as well as a supplement on kitchen organization.

> **Behind You!**
>
> Many books listed in this chapter have had multiple editions, but you shouldn't feel compelled to rush out and buy the latest incarnation. The basic qualities that made them classics are there in every edition. That means it's okay to buy a used, older edition of any of these books. Saving money is important if you are trying to accumulate an impressive culinary library on a cook's salary.

> **Classic Cuisine**
>
> Jacques Pépin is best known in the United States as the host of numerous PBS cooking shows. He has authored numerous books, and is a dean at the French Culinary Institute in New York City. Before arriving in the United States, he was personal chef to Charles de Gaulle.

The Joy of Cooking by Marion Rombauer (Scribner, 1997)

When Scribner published a heavily revised edition of *Joy* in 1997, they came under a lot of criticism. Despite all the hoo-ha, I think it's a fine edition. They took out some recipes, added some others, but retained all the important stuff from the previous edition. It has some new and useful charts and diagrams, like a guide to chili peppers and a template for building a gingerbread house. Of course, it is missing some great stuff, too, like the possum and squirrel recipes in the game chapter. What I love about the old book—the concise writing style, and lack of fluff—is still mostly there.

La Technique by Jacques Pépin (New York Times Books, 1976)

I like this book for its clear descriptions and illustrations. Each step of each technique is photographed, which is great for beginners. I still recommend the book, even though the one and only time we met, Monsieur Pépin told me I was as big as a horse. I'm sure he meant it in a nice way. (After all, everyone must seem big to him.)

Le Guide Culinaire **by Auguste Escoffier (John Wiley and Sons, 1983)**

Originally published in 1903, several versions of this book exist. Escoffier himself insisted that it is not a book of recipes, but a useful tool, with guidelines but no detail. That is because you are already supposed to know how these recipes are made. It is an excellent reference for French *haute cuisine* nomenclature.

Mastering the Art of French Cooking **by Julia Child, Louisette Bertholle, and Simone Beck (Alfred A. Knopf, 2001)**

Originally published in 1961, this book began it all. Without it, there would have been no *French Chef* on PBS, which arguably began the whole celebrity chef phenomenon. It is a perfect collection of Classic French recipes and techniques. It rivals the most thorough culinary school textbook, probably because its authors opened a school (L'Ecole des Trois Gourmandes) and worked together as cooking instructors in Paris in the 1950s. Julia Child has written other books, and they are all good, but this one was her first, and it should be your first. Books from her TV shows, *The French Chef, Julia Child and Company, Julia Child and More Company*, and *From Julia Child's Kitchen*, are also great because they are organized by menu.

The New Making of a Cook: The Art, Techniques, and Science of Good Cooking **by Madeleine Kamman (William Morrow, 1997)**

Here you'll find a complete lesson in cooking. Madeline Kamman gives us the absolute best method and recipe for everything, according to Madeleine. Yes, she is a bit opinionated, but she has a right to be. She knows what she's talking about. She grew up working in her aunt's restaurant in the Loire Valley, attended Le Cordon Bleu culinary school in Paris, moved to America and became a chef instructor, opened her own school in Massachusetts (Modern Gourmet), opened a restaurant (the highly rated Chez La Mere Madeleine), starred in her own PBS television series (*Madeleine Cooks*), and has authored numerous books (including *When French Women Cook, Dinner Against the Clock*, and *In Madeleine's Kitchen*). Until recently she taught professional chefs at the really-hard-to-get-into School for American Chefs at Berringer Vineyards. This book is thorough, covering every culinary topic imaginable, and explaining the proper techniques. She also succeeds in explaining why the techniques work. This is

Classic Cuisine

Auguste Escoffier (1846–1935) is the father of modern French cuisine, the brigade system of kitchen hierarchy, and à la carte service. His partnership with Cesar Ritz at the Savoy and Carlton Hotels in London revolutionized service and gastronomy. *Le Guide Culinaire* was first published in 1903, and is still used as a standard reference by chefs worldwide.

important, because many chefs and authors simply repeat what they have been told without understanding why. Madeleine also covers the more mundane, but no less important, topics of sanitation and tools.

Reference

The following are great books to have on hand when you have a question. Some are good for troubleshooting, and some are just plain interesting. They will all contribute to your overall culinary awareness.

Cookwise **by Shirley Corriher (Morrow Cookbooks, 1997)**

When a biochemist explains the importance of fat in a recipe or the intricacies of an egg, listen up! This is a must-have book on the how and why of food and cooking. It is organized by category of food phenomenon, from fat and protein to the crystals in chocolate, sugar, and ice cream.

Culinary Artistry **by Andrew Dornenburg and Karen Page (John Wiley and Son, 1996)**

You'll turn to this book when you're stuck for ideas. It contains recipes and anecdotes, but I and many other chefs use it for the lists of interesting food and flavor combinations.

The Food Chronology **by James Trager (Owl Books, 1997)**

This is a chronological history of food, from pre-history to modern times. It covers topics including agriculture, animal husbandry, beverages, colonization, restaurants, art, and literature. A symbol denotes each topic and makes looking up specific information a breeze.

The Food Lover's Companion **by Sharon Tyler Herbst (Barron's, 1995)**

I have several copies of this book. I keep one in my office, one in my kitchen, and one in my car because I never know when I am going to need to know an obscure food fact. This is by far the best place to go to find out what a *flummery* (goopy fruit pudding) or a *shamogi* (Japanese wooden spoon for rice) is.

Gastronomique **by Prosper Montagne (Clarkson Potter, 2001)**

This book is more commonly known as *Larousse*, which is the French publishing house that first put it out in 1938. *Gastronomique* is by far the best culinary encyclopedia there is or ever will be. The esteemed Escoffier himself proofed the rough draft before his death, and he contributed the forward. First translated into English in 1961, it makes for great bedtime reading, although it is a bit heavy.

On Food and Cooking: The Science and Lore of the Kitchen **by Harold McGee (Collier Books, 1988)**

Harold McGee is the Einstein of the kitchen ($M=Ge^2$). If you want to know why blueberries are blue, what emulsification actually is, or how your olfactory cells work, McGee is your man. And if you want to be a successful chef, you'd better want to know these things. Buy this book.

The Professional Chef **by Culinary Institute of America (John Wiley and Sons, 2002)**

This is the mother of all culinary textbooks. I was taught in the Escoffier method, and I used Gisslen's *Professional Cooking* (see next entry) as a teacher, but I still own *Pro Chef.* It's a great place to go when you need a refresher on the derivatives of demi-glace or to know what the internal temperature of a *pâté de campagne* should be. Besides, other chefs refer to it all the time, and you don't want to appear clueless.

Professional Cooking **by Wayne Gisslen (John Wiley and Sons, 2002)**

This good and useful book is similar to *Pro Chef* but not quite as hefty. It covers everything *Pro Chef* does and also manages to squeeze in international cuisines, product identification, and presentation guides, as well as many helpful photographs and diagrams. Le Cordon Bleu has sanctioned the latest editions for use in their North American schools.

American Cooking

America, like France, has many regions that contain vastly different climates, crops, and traditions. It is worth exploring the food we eat from coast to coast for the culinary techniques alone.

American Cookery **by James Beard (Little, Brown, 1972)**

This book is a melting pot of important international recipes. Yes, there is much in it that is American, like grits and Boston Baked Beans and Lord Baltimore Cake. There is also classic French Boeuf de Bourgogne, German Sauerbraten, Swiss Fondue, and Egyptian Lentils. James Beard is often referred to as the father of American Cooking, and this book helps explain why. I am also partial to his book *Hors d'Oeuvre and Canapés*, first published in 1940.

Classic Cuisine

James Beard (1903–1985) is commonly thought of as the father of American gastronomy. Raised in Oregon, his family owned and operated a hotel, where he was exposed to great cultures and cuisine. He operated a catering company in New York City in the 1930s, appeared on the first televised cooking show, *I Love to Eat,* and wrote dozens of books and hundreds of articles on American cooking. He ran a cooking school from his home in New York, a home which today houses the James Beard Foundation and Archive, a nonprofit foundation promoting American Culinary arts.

Chez Panisse Cooking by Paul Bertolli and Alice Waters (Random House, 1994) and *Chez Panisse Menu Cookbook* by Alice Waters (Random House, 1995)

Alice Waters pioneered what the world now calls *California Cuisine*, which is fresh, seasonal ingredients, interpreted in innovative ways, using classic preparations. All of the Chez Panisse books are great. Even if I do not cook all the recipes, they certainly offer me plenty of inspiration. I also love the vegetable and fruit books and the superb *Chez Panisse Desserts*, written by Waters's pastry chef, the great Lindsey Shere. My copy of *Desserts* is dog-eared and smudged beyond recognition, especially the *Calendar of Fruit Seasons* in the back. (Also worth noting are the beautiful illustrations by every pastry chef's favorite artist, Wayne Thiebaud.)

Cooking Across America by Bernard Clayton (Simon and Schuster, 1993)

This terrific book chronicles a three-year road trip across the country, during which Bernard Clayton and his wife not only discovered the food of America but also the people who cook it. It is organized by region. Mr. Clayton penned several other cookbooks, including *The Breads of France, The Complete Book of Soups and Stews, The Complete Book of Pastry,* and *The Complete Book of Breads* (one of my favorites), which has recently been released in a thirtieth anniversary edition. He also wrote the hard-to-find *Directions to Building and Using an Adobe Oven,* a classic for anyone interested in artisan bread baking.

def•i•ni•tion

A **chaudière** is both the name of a cauldron and the chunky fish stew (which later came to be known as chowder) made in the cauldron by fishermen of the Northeast.

I Hear America Cooking by Betty Fussell (Viking Penguin Inc., 1986)

Fussell takes a historical look at the regions of the United States and what foods people eat in them, from the chilis and corn of native American tribes to the *chaudières* of the East Coast. If you have an interest in the indigenous foods of America, this is an excellent overview.

Louisiana Kitchen **by Paul Prudhomme (William Morrow and Company, 1993)**

If you live anywhere other than Louisiana, the only reason you know that jambalaya is a food, and not just a song, is because of Paul Prudhomme and the success of this book. Prudhomme was raised in Cajun country, descended from Acadians forced to migrate from Nova Scotia to French Louisiana in the early 1700s. When he tells you the difference between light brown and black roux, you'd better pay attention.

International Cooking

This collection is a good jumping-off point for investigating many other cuisines from around the world.

Celebrating Italy **by Carol Field (William Morrow and Company, 1990)**

With so many hundreds of Italian cookbooks out there, you probably already have your favorite. But Carol Field, who also wrote *The Italian Baker* (which I love), has managed to present not just recipes but their historical significance, which makes the food infinitely more interesting to me.

Couscous and Other Good Food from Morocco **by Paula Wolfert (Harper and Row, 1973)**

I love all of Paula Wolfert's books, including *Mediterranean Cooking* (1976) and *Cooking of South-West France* (1983). She is hands down *the* authority on Mediterranean cuisine. Wolfert single-handedly showed English readers the culinary importance of the Mediterranean region and made peasant food fashionable. Her recipes are all good and use authentic ingredients.

Foods of the World **series (Time-Life Books, 1968)**

This series is stupendous. Twenty-seven volumes cover the cuisine of 21 foreign regions, 8 American regions, plus supplemental recipe and kitchen guides. Each book discusses the regional cuisines of the country, with beautiful photographs and good authentic recipes. They are readily available at flea markets and garage sales.

The Modern Art of Chinese Cooking **by Barbara Tropp (Morrow Cookbooks, 1996)**

The late Barbara Tropp was best known as the chef and owner of the acclaimed China Moon Café in San Francisco and as one of the founding members of *Women Chefs and Restaurateurs*, an organization dedicated to promoting the education and advancement of women in the industry (see Chapter 6). Before she was a chef, she was a student of China, receiving her Master's in Chinese Literature from Princeton University. This book is great for first-time cooks of any Asian cuisine because it makes this complicated food accessible in a western kitchen. While the ingredients are not entirely authentic, the recipes are wonderful, and the instructions are clear and careful. Her *China Moon Cookbook* presents the nouvelle, California Cuisine–style of Chinese food served in her café.

A Taste of Mexico by Patricia Quintana (Stuart, Tabori, and Chang, 1986)

Patricia Quintana is the Culinary Ambassador of Mexico, and although you may never have heard of her, she's a superstar in her country. She studied with the greatest French chefs of the twentieth century, including Paul Bocouse, Gaston Lenòtre, the Troisgros brothers, Michel Guérard, and she founded the first culinary school in Mexico City, *Alta Cocina*. This is my favorite book on Mexican food because she breaks it down into specific regions, each with the most authentic recipes I have found. The ingredients are authentic, too, and may be difficult to find if you don't live in Mexico or the American Southwest. However, you can order them online. If you are serious about learning Mexican food, this book is a must. Chef Quintana taught me the best way to access a mango, which remains to this day one of my favorite techniques (see Chapter 17).

Kitchen Tales _____

The following online shops sell specialty ingredients:

- **Rancho Gordo,** www.ranchogordo.com, has everything you need for Central and South American cooking.
- **Dean & Deluca,** www.deandeluca.com, has everything under the sun, although it is a bit pricey.
- **Penzeys Spices,** www.penzeys.com, has the best selection of spices, with prices that can't be beat.

Special Disciplines

Here are some good selections for those of you looking to concentrate your talents in a specific area. And even if you don't particularly have an interest in these areas, the books are excellent to have on hand. You never know when you'll need to whip up a pâté. Again, these are only meant to get your collection started.

Baking and Pastry

The Fannie Farmer Baking Book by Marion Cunningham (Alfred A Knopf, 1984)

Not the mom on *Happy Days*, Marion Cunningham was a friend and colleague of James Beard. In 1979 she edited the twelfth edition of the *Fannie Farmer Cookbook*, which itself was an 1896 revision of the *Boston Cooking School Cookbook*. I use this for basic baking recipes because they are straightforward and consistently good.

Great Desserts by Maida Heatter (Andrew McMeel, 1974)

It was difficult to pick just one Maida Heatter book to recommend. I also love *Cakes*, *Great Cookies*, *Chocolate Desserts*, *Pies and Tarts*, and *Great American Desserts*. As a pastry chef, her huge repertoire was incredibly helpful to me. And everything I ever made out of her books lived up to its promise. Not every book can deliver that!

The Professional Pastry Chef, 4th Edition by Bo Friberg (John Wiley and Sons, 2002)

Bo Friberg was my first pastry instructor, and I apprenticed with him as part of my externship at the California Culinary Academy in San Francisco. The first edition of this book was our textbook, and had a mere 265 pages. The most recent edition weighs in at over 1,100 pages, and it has a sequel, the *Advanced Professional Pastry Chef*. These books cover every pastry technique imaginable, and include all of Bo's great charts, designs, templates, and food styling, not to mention the world's best puff pastry recipe.

Professional Baking by Wayne Gisslen (John Wiley & Sons, 2004)

This is another comprehensive textbook, with excellent explanations enhanced by illustrations. Like its counterpart, *Professional Cooking*, the latest edition has Le Cordon Bleu's fingerprints all over it, with more trendy recipes, colorful sidebars, and pretty photographs. The drawings are still there, thankfully, as are the more basic techniques you need to know.

The Secrets of Baking by Sherry Yard (Houghton Mifflin, 2003)

This is a great book, and not just because I helped write it. Okay, that is why it's great. Sherry helped, too. The chapters are divided by "Master Recipe," with thorough explanations on the "how and why" of each recipe. It then lists dozens of variations that can be made from that one master recipe. It's a master baking course.

Healthy Food

Cuisine Minceur **by Michel Guérard (William Morrow and Company, 1976)**

def•i•ni•tion

Spa cuisine is a healthy, upscale cuisine, first served at health spas for patrons trying to lose weight.

Cuisine Minceur translates from French to *The Cuisine of Slimness*, and what Monsieur Guérard did here was start a revolution. From *Cuisine Minceur* came *nouvelle cuisine*, which further evolved into *spa cuisine*. Today, we take reduction sauces for granted, but in the 1970s the idea that French food didn't have to be fattening was groundbreaking. Incroyable!

Nutrition for Food Service and Culinary Professionals **by Karen Drummond (John Wiley & Sons, 2003)**

This book is in its fourth edition, and you can tell it's been updated because they added the word "culinary" to the title. Get any edition you can find, because it's really only the basic information on general nutrition—not the recipes—that is useful. It's a good explanation of how fat, carbohydrates, protein, and vitamins effect the body, what nutrients occur in food, and how to get the most out of your food nutritionally.

Fish

Fish: The Complete Guide to Buying and Cooking 70 Kinds of Seafood **by Mark Bittman (Macmillan Publishing Company, 1994)**

This wonderful book contains recipes as well as buying tips, market forms, common names (fish often have aliases), and illustrations showing the trickier stuff, like cleaning. It's written with both novice fish cooks and seasoned professionals in mind.

Behind You!

Many foods have more than one name, and as a chef, it is important to know what's what. Seafood is a great example of this. The popular *orange roughy* is also known as *slimehead*. Which one do you think sells better? The scary looking *monkfish* is also an *angler*, and in French it's called *lotte*. *Red fish* is *perch*, *dogfish* is *rock cod*, and *flounder* is *halibut*. These annoying aliases are not solely the territory of seafood. A *New York steak* is also a *New York strip steak*, a *Kansas City steak*, a *top loin*, and a *club sirloin*. Also, the *kiwi fruit* is a *Chinese gooseberry*, and a *filbert* is a *hazelnut*.

Wine

The Oxford Companion to Wine **edited by Jancis Robinson (Oxford University Press, 1994)**

This 1,000-plus page encyclopedia contains everything you'll ever want or need to know about wine. It covers wine from around the world, not just France and California, and provides detailed regional maps.

The New Wine Lover's Companion **by Ron Herbst and Sharon Tyler Herbst (Randon House, 1995)**

Well written and informative, this encyclopedia is less daunting than Oxford's version but no less useful. Like the *Food Lover's Companion*, this is not at all dry.

What to Drink with What You Eat: The Definitive Guide to Pairing Food with Wine, Beer, Spirits, Coffee, Tea—Even Water—Based on Expert Advice from America's Best Sommeliers **by Andrew Dornenburg, Karen Page, and Michael Sofronski (Bulfinch, 2006)**

Authors of *Culinary Artistry* and *Becoming a Chef*, these guys are the masters of taste, and they're who the professionals turn to for advice on pairing food with the beverage of your choice.

Just a Good Read

The Physiology of Taste **by Jean Anthelme Brillat-Savarin, translated by MFK Fisher (Heritage Press, 1949)**

Originally published in 1875, this collection of meditations on food is a cult classic for foodies and culinary snobs, covering everything from the senses, taste, appetite, thirst, and even obesity. It is insightful and often funny.

Tender at the Bone **by Ruth Reichl (Random House, 1998)**

This is a sweet and funny memoir of growing up with interesting people and food, by a woman who eventually became the restaurant critic of *The New York Times* and editor-in-chief of *Gourmet Magazine*. The sequel, *Comfort Me with Apples*, was published in 2002.

The Gastronomical Me **by MFK Fisher (Harper and Brothers, 1939)**

I discovered MFK Fisher when her books were re-issued in 1989 by North Point Press. The beautiful prose in this and her other volumes (*Serve It Forth, An Alphabet of Gourmets, Consider the Oyster, How to Eat a Wolf*) recount a lifelong love of food.

The Jungle **by Upton Sinclair (See Sharp Press, 2002)**

Published in 1906, *The Jungle* recounts the horrors of the Chicago meatpacking houses and the lives of the immigrants who worked in them. Sinclair's book prompted the federal government to enact the *Pure Food and Drug Act* and the *Meat Inspection Act*. That's a powerful book.

Fast Food Nation **by Eric Schlosser (Harper Collins, 2002)**

This book will change your life. First read *The Jungle*, then this book, then watch the film *Super-Size Me*. You'll never look at the drive-through the same way.

Kitchen Confidential **by Anthony Bourdain (Harper Perennial, 2001)**

This is a gritty, no-holds-barred look at the restaurant world. It's not always pretty, but it is fairly accurate. Anthony Bourdain also has some TV series companion books that are entertaining: *A Cook's Tour* (Bloomsbury, 2001), and *Nasty Bits* (Bloomsbury, 2006). Check out his fiction, too, which includes *Bone in the Throat* (Bloomsbury, 2000), and the historical *Typhoid Mary* (Bloomsbury, 2000).

> **Kitchen Tales**
>
> Anthony Bourdain lived a slightly wilder existence than I did. He came up through the ranks in the 1970s, a decade before I did, and the times were certainly different. A friend of mine, 10 years my junior, thought *Kitchen Confidential* was ridiculous, with a totally inaccurate portrayal of sex and drugs in the business. It seemed pretty close to me, but obviously the industry varies between location, and era (just think about the culture changes alone throughout the 1970s, 1980s and 1990s). Don't make general conclusions about the industry based on the book. Just enjoy it for what it is: a peek into the life of a chef.

The Least You Need to Know

- The key to a successful career as a chef is a well-rounded culinary library.

- Classic, regional, and specialty cookbooks are important for continuing your education.

- Reference books are not just for the inquisitive. They can spark an interest and explain the how and why of a recipe.

- Recreational reading can show you how other people view food and the culinary arts.

Chapter 9

Learning on the Job

In This Chapter

- ◆ Understanding the difference between apprenticeships, internships, and externships
- ◆ Learning how and why to volunteer your skills
- ◆ Finding easy, entry-level jobs

Historically, learning on the job was the only way to become a professional chef. You (or your parents) approached a chef whom you respected and were given a position as an apprentice. Your duties would include all the cruddy jobs that no one else wanted to do. In exchange, you were fed and given a corner of the shop to sleep in. You watched what went on around you, you learned, and eventually you were entrusted with increasing responsibility.

Although nowadays you won't have to bed down in a corner of the kitchen, as a budding chef you can still learn the craft on the job.

A Job by Any Other Name ...

Apprenticeship, *internship*, and *externship* are all terms that denote on-the-job training. Each term refers to a different type of training, but the meanings vary depending on your location. What is termed an apprenticeship in one part of the world can mean something completely different in another. Internships are commonplace in most vocational training programs but are practically unheard of in the culinary world. And while an externship is a standard part of most culinary school programs, the format this training takes is by no means universal.

Internships

An internship is typically a full-time, temporary job placement that lasts anywhere from a couple of months to a couple of years. The duties are real-life responsibilities, and the applicant is paid. The position becomes a line on the resumé, and often the applicant is hired on as a full-time employee when the internship is finished. In the restaurant business, internships are pretty rare.

Externships

Culinary schools know that the best way to learn anything is by doing it. They also know that no matter how thorough their education is, it is no substitute for working. For that reason, an externship is a required component of most culinary school programs. It is similar to an internship, but with some significant differences. It is essentially a short-term job placement, in which the student may or may not get paid. Because it is a part of the culinary school's program, the student pays tuition during his or her externship rotation.

An externship can take place anywhere that the school sees fit, including restaurants, hotels, clubs, and bakeries. Each school maintains its own policies regarding placement and monitoring of its externs. Some schools test and evaluate periodically, while others let their students fend for themselves.

Behind You!

Many top-end restaurants no longer accept externs. Despite the free labor, the reputation of arrogant culinary students is more than some employers are willing to risk. You'll have to prove yourself if you want to get into places like that.

The businesses have varying policies as well. Some rotate the extern through all the stations, providing a full experience. More commonly, however, an extern is placed in the traditional role of an apprentice, that is, in the corner of the prep kitchen, peeling carrots. While this experience is not without merit (you gain speed at peeling, not to mention humility), it usually comes as a shock and disappointment to the extern. After all, a culinary student has more training than a traditional apprentice does. Plus, the student is shelling out a ton of money for the experience. And only a small percentage of externs are hired on when the externship is over.

Apprenticeships

Although you can still find places that will exchange room and board for lackey work, the apprenticeship system has changed, both in the United States and in Europe.

Today, apprenticeships are commonly monitored by a governing board of some kind. Completion of such an apprenticeship results in a certificate, title, or designation of some kind, depending on the country. A certain amount of working time is required, usually 6,000 hours, or three years. The progress of the apprentice is assessed periodically, and some countries also require additional education.

It is possible to find a traditional apprenticeship in the United States, either on your own or under the watchful eye of an accredited organization. Small colleges, in conjunction with the American Culinary Federation (ACF), offer such programs (see Chapter 7). Participating ACF chapters place candidates into ACF-approved local businesses. An apprenticeship lasts three years, during which time the apprentice is required to complete coursework. The class schedule varies, but is usually part-time, one or two days a week. Upon completion, the apprentice is awarded the first ACF designation, Certified Culinarian (CC). Tuition and material fees may or may not be sponsored by the participating business. Depending on the state, academic credit hours may be transferable to other colleges. The benefit of this program is ACF oversight, which guarantees strict educational standards and provides the organization's benefits, including educational seminars, outreach programs, and networking opportunities.

Volunteering Yourself

Of course, you can still beg a chef to take you in. More along the lines of a traditional European apprenticeship is the practice of volunteering yourself. This usually involves doing something for nothing, and many people balk at such an idea. Why should you work for free? Because it's a good way to get your foot in the door of a well-respected establishment where you wouldn't otherwise be qualified to work.

Some places will hire you to do entry-level work. But if you have your sights set a little higher, consider starting your own little externship program. Offer yourself up to a chef, and see if he or she would be willing to let you come in to help one or two days a week. Most restaurants are used to the extern phenomenon and welcome the free labor. And because you are approaching them on your own, without the help of a school, you're demonstrating your commitment to learning the craft.

Kitchen Tales

I have strongly encouraged many of my students to do volunteer work at restaurants. And in almost every case, the gig turned pro within a year. It is a student's dedication to craft that really turns an employer on.

How do you go about getting a volunteer position when you have little or no experience? Start by identifying your dream job. Even if it is at the hottest spot in town, chances are they will jump at the chance to get stuff done for free. Find out when the chef is in, and stop by during off hours. Do not go during the lunch or dinner hour. Even showing up too close to that time is a no-no because there will be furious prepping going on. After the lunch or dinner hour is ideal. Write up a resumé (see Chapter 11) and a letter of your intentions. State your available hours, (the more flexible you are, the better) and explain what you hope to get out of the experience. Make it clear that you hope to wow the chef with your talent and eventually be put on payroll. This is important. You don't want to get taken advantage of. Be sure to throw in a bunch of glowing compliments about the restaurant, the food, and the chef's style and philosophy of cooking. (You should actually know about this stuff. You may need to do a little research.)

Kitchen Tales

Having worked in restaurants throughout high school and college, I couldn't understand why I had to pay tuition for three months while I went out to work for free. For that reason, I opted for an in-house apprenticeship, during which I was basically the chef-instructor's slave. It was fun and turned out to be a good prelude to teaching.

Wait a couple of days, and then follow up with a phone call. If the follow-up call doesn't seem promising, move on to the next restaurant on your list. You'll probably find that volunteering is easier than looking for a paying job. This is because very few chefs can resist the offer of free labor coupled with compliments.

When you are invited in, be sure to work as hard as you possibly can. Show them why they should hire you. Pay attention to the comings and goings of employees, and be ready to submit your resumé for consideration as soon as a paying position opens up. If you have been a volunteer for six months and haven't heard a peep about being hired, ask. If the answer is "not now," it's time to consider moving on.

Baby Steps

Not everyone has the luxury of working for no pay. Many people actually have bills to pay and families to care for. It can be hard to justify taking time away from them and any chance of earning money. For those of you who fit into this category, consider these entry-level jobs you are certainly going to be qualified for.

Catering

Catering is an excellent way to network, hone your skills, and make money, especially if you live in or near a big city. Best of all, it's a pretty easy business for a beginner to break into. All catering companies need bodies, especially during their busy seasons, which vary from company to company, but usually revolve around the Christmas and wedding seasons. Even if you have no real culinary experience, they still need people to peel the apples, shrimp, or carrots. (I didn't say it was going to be fun, just that you were going to get paid to do it!)

Small catering companies tend to feed weddings, birthday and holiday parties, or business meetings. The larger ones cater large corporate events and special events like the Oscars and Rolling Stones backstage parties. I live in Southern California, where there are caterers galore. There is even an entire subcategory of movie-set caterers called Craft Services. All types of caterers tend to pay the same, which is about $7 to $9 an hour for a beginner. Some operations also allow tipping.

The type of catering company you choose should depend on where you are heading with your career. If your goal is to start your own shop, a smaller caterer could be a good place to learn about business. If you want to learn how to cook a high volume of food, choose a larger company. All caterers require *the schlep*, that is, carrying everything, sometimes including the kitchen sink, to a job site. I never particularly cared for schlepping, but I certainly did it enough times to have a true appreciation for caterers and high regard for those who make a success out of it.

Kitchen Tales

Catering can be fun, especially when the sites vary with each event. I have catered at zoos, the Natural History Museum, fancy homes, and city halls. I'm not a fan of music festivals, though. I once worked a Kenny Loggins show, and that *Caddy Shack* song was stuck in my head for weeks.

How do you find the catering company that's right for you? First, decide on the scale of event you're willing to attempt; then get on the phone. Call wedding and event planners and ask who they use. Look in the yellow pages for catering advertisements. Local specialty food stores and culinary schools may also have job postings. Or go to the movies and look for the Craft Service credits at the end.

Entry-level positions in catering vary widely. Often one crew of cooks prepares food prior to an event, and an entirely separate crew works on-site. The jobs roughly mirror a restaurant kitchen, with *prep cooks*, *pantry cooks*, pastry cooks, and line cooks. Cooks can be stationed at a grill all night, at a cold buffet, or as a runner, constantly re-stocking a buffet or line. Usually a cook is not placed in one job exclusively. The position is determined by the event, and you must be flexible.

def•i•ni•tion

A **prep cook** is a preparatory cook or one who readies all the ingredients for the night's dishes. This usually involves a lot of chopping, portioning, and pre-cooking.

A **pantry cook** works mainly with cold ingredients to prepare cold dishes, including salads, sandwiches, and cold appetizers.

Behind You!

I have one word of caution about catering. Often up-and-coming chefs will attempt catering on their own or with a colleague. It is relatively easy to get started, cooking for friends and friends of friends. If, however, you find yourself branching out much beyond that circle, be aware of local business laws and health department codes. Most counties in the United States don't allow you to cater out of your home. The first time your client finds a cat hair in his cheese puff, it'll be curtains for your little venture.

Bakeries

If dessert is your thing, you are probably thinking about becoming a pastry chef in a restaurant or hotel. I bet you've already got a subscription to *Pastry Art and Design Magazine*. However, you might want to think instead about starting out in a bakery. A bakery produces similar products but without as much pressure. In a restaurant, one menu item will include elements from several different stations of the kitchen that must be brought together at the same time. In a bakery, recipes are prepared and sold one at a time. Bakery jobs are no less skilled, but they are somewhat less hectic. Local bakeries offer a great opportunity to perfect recipes, techniques, and skills through sheer repetition, which is the best way to become an expert at anything. Here, too, is a small environment to learn about running a business.

Another reason to choose a bakery over a restaurant is the bread factor. Few restaurants make their own bread these days. Most buy from large production artisan bakeries.

In a bakery you may be asked to work very early or very late, because most baking is traditionally done for morning customers. As with all culinary jobs, you must be flexible, especially when you're a rookie. Some bakeries will start new employees with simple tasks, such as measuring and mixing various stages of recipes.

Kitchen Tales

I had an early morning job at a muffin shop when I was in culinary school. The muffins were very popular, but not, perhaps, as popular as the owner thought. The jobs were divided by stages of the recipes. One person was entirely responsible for mixing dry ingredients. Another person mixed the wet ingredients, and still another combined the two. I was a baker, so I simply scooped out the prepared batter, baked it, and sold the muffins to eager early birds. The owner was clearly afraid that we would steal the whole recipe and sneak off to open our own muffin shop. With all those precautions, you would have thought we were spinning straw into gold. I still get a laugh out of this because the shop was only in business a short time. They were, after all, only muffins.

A novice baker may be put in charge of simple recipes. You may also be given a try-out to determine your skill level. Certain tasks are considered extremely delicate, like folding egg whites and making custards. You will have to prove yourself before you are entrusted with them. If you have an artistic flair, you may become a finisher, glazing and piping and fussing over all the goodies.

To find the bakery of your dreams, start in your own town. Where do you go to buy bread and cakes? Approach the owner with your resumé in hand. If you get your baked goods at the grocery store, why not check it out? Many large supermarkets have bakery departments. There, you'll not only improve your skills, but you'll probably also have the added bonus of working for a large-scale union operation with benefits galore. I often wished I had worked at a grocery store bake shop. Have you ever watched them pipe roses? They are frosting superstars, able to create 20 to 30 flowers a minute!

If grocery stores aren't your thing and you can't find a bakery nearby, try wedding and party planners. They will have lists of bakers they rely on for wedding and celebration cakes. Large caterers may also have their own baking departments, which are great for learning to bake at a high volume.

Kitchen Tales

When I took my Master Baker examinations, I was the only restaurant chef in the running. Everyone else came from bakeries. There were guys from family-owned bakeries, large chain bakeries, and even a couple of guys from Pillsbury. While I felt prepared for the test, those bakers knew a lot that I didn't. There is another entire subculture of bakery bakers, and it's cool! They speak a slightly altered culinary language. They use formulas instead of recipes and are constantly concerned about the protein content and ash count of flour. It's fascinating. Best of all, they are not corrupted by the glamour of the restaurant scene or haggard from the stress of the line. They are real artisans.

Delicatessens

If pastry is not your forté, but a small shop appeals to you, think about a small deli or specialty food shop. Sandwich making may not seem like a challenge to you, but trust me, it is. When you find yourself at noon with a line out the door of hungry type A junior executives demanding their turkey on rye, no mayo, no onions, you'll be dangerously close to living the line cook experience. A deli is a terrific place to test your stamina and learn efficiency. Of course, all shops are different, but on the whole, getting in the door is relatively easy. It's a good place for a novice to gain experience doing easy prep work.

Besides the obvious cold-cuts, shops also specialize in cheeses from around the world, specialty pâtés and terrines, salads, wines and beers, picnics, high tea, take-out or eat-in. Many such places need a trained chef, not only to prepare the foods, but also to choose, buy, and market foods and cookware from around the world.

The Least You Need to Know

◆ Apprenticeships, internships, and externships all provide similar experiences.

◆ Volunteering is an easy way to get your foot in the door.

◆ You are qualified to work at many entry-level positions right now.

Part 4

The Job Search

Once you get yourself adequately trained, you'll want to put all that knowledge to work. Most people go for what they know. But there is a whole wide world of culinary opportunities you may not be aware of. You should consider all your options before you commit.

Figuring out what kind of culinary job you want is hard enough, but actually looking for a job can be a total drag. It is scary and stressful and not at all fun. And the odds are against you. For any one position in food service, dozens of people apply. How can you convince potential employers that you arc the best choice? By using my guidelines, you will increase your odds at every interview.

And once you're hired, you'll need to look like you know what you're doing. I'll help you by sharing a few tricks of the trade that I've picked up along the way.

Entering the Field

In This Chapter

- ◆ Mastering your trade
- ◆ Looking at your employment options
- ◆ Entering the culinary workforce

For those of you looking to enter the culinary field today, getting started can be daunting. Part of the problem is the public's perception of the trade. Few people even think of it as a *trade* anymore. Many think of it as art. Some think of it as performance. The vast majority of workers think of it simply as a means to a paycheck. While it can be all of those things, it is first and foremost a trade and one at which you must be adept before it can evolve into other things.

Where to Begin?

Historically, mastering the trade has been a lifelong endeavor. Auguste Escoffier, arguably the most important culinary figure in history, not only defined French cuisine as we know it but also created the *brigade* system of kitchen hierarchy. This system, based on a military model, still defines most European-style kitchens. In the brigade, you enter the field as an apprentice. You then work your way up through the ranks until you find your niche. When it was introduced in the mid-1800s, this system streamlined the kitchen, eliminated redundancies, and allowed a huge number of complicated meals to be prepared in an efficient and organized manner.

Escoffier's Brigade System—La Brigade de Cuisine

French Title	English Title	Job Description
Chef de Cuisine	Head Chef	The Big Boss
Sous Chef	Second Chef	Second in Command
Chef de Partie	Section Heads	These chefs are the bosses of their particular area of expertise
Le Garde Manger	Larder Cook	Commands the cold areas of the kitchen
Le Chef du Froid	Cold Work Chef	Works under the Garde Manger, specializing in cold centerpieces, cheese and meat platters, pâtés, terrines, and all cooked meat that is served cold
Le Hors d'Oeuvrier	Hors d'oeuvre Cook	Works under the Garde Manger, preparing bite-sized appetizers, served prior to the main entrée
Le Boucher	Butcher	Works under the Garde Manger fabricating (breaking down into specific cuts) all meats
Le Saucier	Sauce Cook	Prepares all sauces, with the exception of dessert sauces
Le Rotisseur	Roast Cook	Prepares all large cuts of meat, historically on a rotisserie
Le Poissonnier	Fish Cook	Prepares all fish
L'Entremettier	Vegetable Cook	Prepares all vegetable dishes
Le Potager	Soup Cook	Prepares all soups, including all stocks, bouillons, and broths

French Title	English Title	Job Description
Le Patissier	Pastry Cook	Prepares all sweets and desserts
Le Bolanger	Bread Cook	Prepares all breads
Le Tournant	Relief Cook	Relieves staff in all areas of the kitchen
Le Communard	Staff Cook	Prepares staff meals
Le Chef du Nuit or Le Chef de Garde	Night Cook or Duty Cook	Watches over the kitchen and the food cooking in it through the night
Le Chef du Petit Dejeuner	Breakfast Cook	Prepares breakfast dishes.
Le Trancheur	Carver	Carves all meat for presentation
Le Grillardin	Grill Cook	Cooks anything on the grill
Commis	Assistant Chef	This is the entry level to a section. A commis must rise from third to first commis before becoming a Chef de Partie
L'Apprenti	Apprentice	The workers just starting out in the trade. They get all the cruddy jobs that the commis can't be bothered with.
Aboyer	Kitchen Clerk or Announcer	In America this position is commonly called the *expediter*, and his or her job is to call out the orders, make sure everything is going together properly, and ensure everything goes out to the dining room in a timely manner.
Plongeur	Scullery	Washes all dishes.

Of course, the mid-1800s were very different from today. Entry into this life occurred at a very young age, usually 12 or 13, at the discretion of the adults. You may not find this system appealing in today's world. Can you imagine apprenticing your 12-year-old today? What's more, only males entered the system. While female chefs did exist, they were outside the brigade and pretty rare.

But, in many ways, Escoffier's brigade system would make life a lot easier. There would be much less confusion in determining how to get started in this business if everyone continued to follow it. It is still in practice in European kitchens and in those run by European chefs around the world. But on the whole, kitchen hierarchy in America is only loosely based on the brigade and varies widely from place to place.

Classic Cuisine

Born in 1846, Auguste Escoffier entered the kitchen at age 13 and worked his way up through the ranks. He is most famous for his partnership with Cesar Ritz at the Savoy Hotel in London, where together they revolutionized the hotel and dining industries. He simplified menus of the time, which consisted of multiple dishes served all at once, (what we think of as *family style*) and created what is now called the *à la carte* menu. Escoffier was a prolific writer, and *Le Guide Culinaire*, first published in 1903, is a standard reference still used by all those serious about French and international cuisine (see Chapter 8).

To master the trade today, you'll need to take matters into your own hands and make training your priority. Try to enter the culinary workforce in a place that will teach you as much as possible. If you are interested in the art, gravitate toward an establishment that values innovation and imagination. If you have a particular interest, such as bread, then surround yourself with experts in that area.

Ultimately, your skill level will determine where you enter. Wherever this turns out to be, it is *your* responsibility to accurately assess your skill level and represent it honestly. Go ahead and aim high, but be prepared to back it up.

My first job after graduation from culinary school was for a renowned chef who had come for a week as an adjunct instructor to teach us about Southwest cuisine. He ran a restaurant in Berkeley that was very popular at the time. His pastry chef was recruited to open a restaurant for Wolfgang Puck in San Francisco, and I applied for her old job. I'm not sure why, but I was hired. Looking back, I realize my menu ideas and sample desserts were not that great. It's more likely that the chef saw in me someone he could mold. Either that or he was desperate. Needless to say, I was in way over my head. I struggled mightily, was read the Riot Act on more than one occasion, and clashed repeatedly with long-time employees who should have had my job. Eventually I had some success, but if I had it to do over again, I would do things differently. Instead, I'd look for a job working for another pastry chef who would mentor me and bring me up slowly.

Entry Levels

There are hundreds of culinary jobs out there—so many that you probably have no idea where to start. You're wondering what the protocol is. Who do you contact first? What jobs do you dare try for? The good news is that it's easy to get a job in the culinary field. Building a long and fulfilling career, however, is a little harder.

Getting a job is easy because in the United States, there really isn't much more protocol than common sense. No secret handshake gets you in the door. To get a good job and keep it, you must be competent. But this in itself will take some work on your part. You have to learn the necessary skills, practice and perfect them, and work your way toward a goal of some kind.

If you are just starting out, a good way to begin your quest for knowledge is to widen your opportunities. Spread your resumé around and try a variety of jobs. This will improve your chances of landing your dream job in the future. It will broaden your education, and ultimately make you more employable. As an employer, I was far more likely to hire a line cook who had some experience in a butcher shop over someone who had only ever been a line cook. And a pastry cook with some experience on a line cooking something other than sweets is much more valuable to the chef. The more well-rounded you are, the easier you will get work.

> **Behind You!**
>
> If you are like most potential chefs, you dream of working in an exciting, trendy, well-regarded restaurant. In these spots the culinary arts are truly appreciated. The critics pay attention; the public pays attention; and other chefs pay attention. These spots are not, however, the best place to enter the culinary workforce. These jobs are harder to come by and can be too intense for cutting your teeth. What's more, if it doesn't work out, for whatever reason, you'll begin building an unfavorable reputation. If you're still a novice, it's better to work on your reputation in a place with a lower profile.

Many interesting options are available, especially for the up-and-comer. Keep an open mind, and remember that opportunities present themselves in unexpected places.

Personal Chef

This is a rapidly growing field, mainly because people are too busy to cook these days. Many families have two working, exhausted parents. No one learns "home economics" in the schools, and many parents are too busy to teach their kids to cook. Because of this, personal chefs are in high demand, especially in big cities and luxury communities. But even Joe Schmoe is hiring a personal chef today for frozen dinners he can stockpile in his freezer, or special menus that make it easier to stick to his Zone diet.

Personal cheffing is certainly not limited to working for one family. People with means will often take along a personal chef when traveling. People with boats often hire a personal galley chef for excursions. Athletes hire chefs to maintain a proper diet while on the road. I am a big fan of the Tour de France, and I know that all the teams have a chef and crew cooking nutritionally specific foods at every stage of the race. Think of all the sports, all the teams, all the athletes that need to stay healthy. Eating at McDonald's is simply not an option for them. If you're interested in nutrition and health, this is a great area to look into. (Note to Team Discovery … call me!)

There are also facilities that require a live-in (or out) chef. A good friend of mine in college cooked for a fraternity. She knew when all the best parties were. Unfortunately, she had to work most of them. Think of all the college campuses in your area.

For the unattached, the seasonal employment of a resort is an opportunity worth looking into. Many restaurants in ski villages, beach resorts, and summer camps have trouble finding good help willing to return year after year. If you're outdoorsy, this could be a golden opportunity. You could conceivably have employment year-round if you're willing to travel.

Getting a personal chef gig in someone's home is not as easy as some of the other options. Networking is definitely helpful here. Openings are sometimes posted in the paper or online, but they are usually snatched up pretty fast. In some areas placement agencies deal with personal chefs. Look for domestic placement or service placement agencies. In big cities you may even find an agent specializing in cooks.

The Military

While the food is not *haute cuisine*, the military is a terrific training ground for the culinary arts. The cooks I've met in the service have been the fastest, cleanest, smartest, most sensible, and most considerate professionals I have ever known. (If I could bottle their work ethic, I'd make a mint!) It's not Beetle Bailey anymore. Military cooks are highly trained, and many strive to compete in world-class culinary competitions for their armed service team. Cooks in the military are regular enlisted members of the armed forces. Once boot camp is completed, you undergo specialized culinary training for several weeks before being posted to your first assignment. Main training facilities include Lackland Air Force Base in Texas for the Navy and the Air Force and Fort Lee, Virginia, for the Army and the Marines. There you get a basic culinary education, including classic culinary techniques, nutrition, sanitation, and management.

Cooks are called Food Service Specialists in the Marine Corps and Coast Guard, Food Service Operations Specialists in the Army, Service Specialists in the Air Force, and Culinary Specialists in the Navy. The positions have different titles in each branch, but the duties are similar to any restaurant chef, including creating menus, food preparation, administration, procurement and storage, records, finances, distribution, and serving. Just as in the civilian food service world, more-experienced cooks eventually take on administrative roles.

In the service, cooks have one added duty that civilian cooks don't. They are responsible for personnel morale. Let's face it, a lot of morale boosting is needed in the service, especially in deployed locations. Food is a great conduit for happiness. Imagine all the warm fuzzy feelings food arouses in you. Now imagine having that feeling in a camp somewhere in Afghanistan. If you're a sailor on a ship or a sub, you are stuck in tight quarters all day and night. In situations like that, you can either look forward to a meal or dread it. It's infinitely more satisfying feeding these folks than serving caviar to the swanky folks of Beverly Hills. It's a recipe for good karma.

Kitchen Tales

A submarine chef is thought to be the toughest culinary gig in the military. The space is so small that only one cook can be on duty at any time. And unlike the rest of the service, everything is made from scratch. I tried to get assigned to a sub through the Navy's Adopt-a-Chef program, but alas, no girls allowed! There's no room for separate women's facilities on a sub. There is talk of an all-women's sub in the near future. Sign me up!

Bases in the United States typically contract outside catering companies, with one or two enlisted personnel overseeing the operation. In deployed locations, the soldiers run the show. You may be asked to pick up a service rifle from time to time, but your main job is keeping the troops well fed. Informal cooking contests are commonplace. Don't underestimate the importance of bragging rights for the best chicken fajitas. Chefs in combat experiment with cuisine just as much as any other cook does, often sneaking in special ingredients from care packages to improve a marinade or a sauce.

For the talented chefs, there are official competitions as well. Each branch of the service sponsors annual competitions to recognize the best food service operations.

Classic culinary techniques are judged, as is field cooking. These competitions are often co-sponsored by culinary organizations such as The National Restaurant Association (NRA) and The American Culinary Federation (ACF). Chefs also compete for coveted spots on culinary teams, like the US Army Culinary Arts Team and the All Navy Culinary Team. These teams represent their branch of service and the United States in events such as the International Culinary Olympics, held annually in Erfurt, Germany.

> ### Kitchen Tales
>
> In May of 2006, I was graciously welcomed onboard the *USS Salvor-ARS,* a U.S. Navy rescue and salvage vessel, as a civilian Culinary Specialist. We sailed for three weeks, towing an old Coast Guard ship from Pearl Harbor to Guam. My assignment was to train the galley crew, but I ended up learning way more than they did. Sure, I spiced up their fajitas, showed them how to garnish their baked fish, and how to make a little cake-box magic. But they showed me what hard work really is, what pride in a job well done means, and what it means to serve your country. I can't wait to go again!

The Navy in particular has a reputation for taking care of its chefs. They have several training facilities, including one at Pearl Harbor. In ports across the United States and overseas, local civilian culinary talent is routinely brought on board for special training. These civilian chef exchanges improve the quality of the product and keep the military cooks up to date on the latest culinary trends. You'd be hard pressed to find chipped beef on toast any more.

Many military assignments include duties other than cooking. For instance, in addition to ships and subs, the Navy culinary specialists run the Vice President's house. They perform valet services and must be proficient in areas of protocol and etiquette. The uniform is a tuxedo as often as it is a chef coat. The Navy also staffs the White House Mess, located in the West Wing, just below the Oval Office.

Hotels

Getting into a hotel job is a bit tougher for the beginner than starting in a small restaurant. Hotel cooking requires a higher level of skill, and the jobs are more demanding. But paying your dues in a well-established three- or four-star hotel is a ticket to ride anywhere else. Even less-acclaimed hotels are excellent training grounds.

You usually need to pass through the gauntlet of the human resources department. Most good hotels won't even look at you unless you are applying for a specific job opening. Due to the high volume of applicants, resumés are not typically kept on hand in a "just in case" file as they often are in smaller restaurants. Dropping by with your resumé won't work either. Job postings in the paper or on the hotel's website will have very specific instructions on how to send your resumé and to whom it should go. These postings are updated frequently, so it's a good idea to check them often.

> **Behind You!**
>
> If you get to the interview stage, don't be surprised if you are subjected to background checks, drug tests, and health exams. These are rare in small restaurants, but common in hotels. Hiring the wrong person for the job is an expensive mistake for an employer, and good management understands this. Smaller restaurants don't go to such lengths because these procedures are expensive. Pass this phase, and you've already begun to prove yourself worthy.

Getting through human resources leads you to the chef. There will be skill tests and tryouts, and you may actually be put to work for a period of time. If you pass, you will likely be put into something like the pantry station, which is a cold salad and sandwich type of assignment, or some sort of swing station, which rotates you through several positions, like room service, buffet service, or a pizza station. Your shift will probably be the least popular to start out. You've got to be willing, if not eager, to take whatever they offer. I cannot stress this enough. Be eager! That's how you move up the ladder.

Another reason to consider working in a hotel is union membership. In most independent restaurants, union involvement has a negative connotation. It often means that management failed and the union was called in by disgruntled employees. In hotels, however, union membership is a given, and it's considered a perk. The unions provide benefits that are otherwise unheard of in the restaurant business. Workers are eligible for all sorts of services, including credit cards and credit counseling; educational and personal loans; auto, health, and life insurance; mortgage and real estate assistance; layoff and disability assistance; and legal resources.

Cruise Ships

I was always told that cruise ships are a super place to train. In school, many of my chef instructors had a cruise ship background, including Bo Friberg, one of the chefs I apprenticed for. He always told us about life on the ships as he demonstrated his swift techniques of twisting Danish, rolling croissants, or modeling marzipan. I thought it was such a great idea. It seemed like the perfect environment to learn in. I would be trapped, working ungodly hours and super long shifts. I could really perfect these techniques. I thought a year or two like that would make me a super-chef.

I applied to all the cruise lines and was rejected by them all. At the time, I couldn't understand it. I was an honor student with years of restaurant experience already under my belt. When I told Bo, he explained it to me in the delicate and sympathetic manner we had come to know and love. "Well, of course! You're a girl!" Apparently, ships of foreign registry were not accountable to the type of equal employment opportunity laws as businesses in the United States are. So I kissed that idea goodbye. Today, things are much different, and many women are filling culinary positions on the high seas.

Like hotels, the application process for cruise ship employment is very specific. Some lines have employment links on their websites where they post current openings. Others require you to send in your resumé to their corporate offices regardless of openings. Follow the instructions precisely if you want to be considered. When you pass the initial stages, be prepared for drug tests, physicals, and background checks.

Entering a ship-board kitchen also mirrors the hotel industry. Because many of the executive chefs are European, cruise lines frequently follow the *brigade* system. If you have no experience, but some solid training, you can begin as a cook trainee, a garde manger trainee, a patisserie trainee, or a commis. You can apply for other positions if you have a minimum of three years experience. At Carnival Cruises, the Corporate Executive Chef interviews every single qualified applicant himself. This ensures that he will get the type of employee he's looking for. This is not the kind of job you want to quit or lose mid-contract. It's a long way to shore for the disgruntled or disappointing employee, and it's hard to find replacements when you're in the middle of the ocean.

The lure of exotic places is the big draw of cruise line employment, but note a few things before you sign up. The job is long. Most lines require you to sign a contract for four, six, or eight months, during which time you will be working seven days a week. There is no pay between contracts, and if you decide to quit mid-contract, you'll have to get home on your own. You must be in good health for such a job, and you will be required to take a medical exam. If you are prone to seasickness or are claustrophobic, forget it. You will work in all kinds of weather, and you'll share windowless quarters with several roommates.

Of course, there are certainly positive aspects to the job as well. You are allowed to go ashore and see the exotic sights occasionally because, like all good employers, they want their workers to be happy. It is a real collegial environment. The people on board are there because they are really into their jobs. You'll get excellent training and have the potential to master your trade. Best of all, you'll get free room and board, so you can save the money you earn.

Chain Restaurants

Jobs in chain restaurants are relatively easy to get, and while they don't hold the kind of prestige an independent restaurant has, they more than make up for it in job security and benefits. The management systems in these places really work. The fact that they're chains and have successfully expanded is proof of that.

Chain restaurants have systems in place for everything from making salad dressing to dealing with disgruntled customers. It's all compiled in neat manuals, and there is little question as to what your job is. There is not a lot of room for creativity, and the quality of the product is not always the greatest. But it's an excellent place to learn speed, basic skills, and business. The opportunity for advancement is also much greater in a chain. One can conceivably work up from a dishwasher to a regional manager within a few years. These jobs offer more stability, too. Chain restaurants stick around much longer than independents, and the companies are usually eager to transfer their good employees if need be.

> **Kitchen Tales**
>
> I worked at chain restaurants all through college. When I went home during break, the companies always transferred me to a job in my hometown and helped make the transition relatively painless.

The benefits available in large, corporate-owned restaurants are nothing to sneeze at either. The health insurance plans are much more comprehensive than what the corner shop has to offer. There are strict rules regarding work hours, overtime pay, and vacations. Also, retirement packages are available, which is rare in the independent restaurants.

One night, while out to dinner with my dad, we waited for a table at a local chain restaurant for over an hour. When we were finally seated, the staff was courteous and the service was prompt. But they screwed up the order. As soon as we reported the mistake, apologies were made by all involved, including the manager, who quickly fixed the problem and then presented us with free dessert. This kind of customer service, on such a busy night, at a place that obviously didn't need our business, is all too rare. I was so impressed by the display of professionalism that I invited the manager to come speak to a Culinary Supervision class I was teaching at the time. The students rolled their eyes with typical culinary student snobbery, but the presentation was fascinating, and it cut them down to size. The customer truly is always right if you want to stay in business. This kind of restaurant can really teach a beginner how to succeed.

Independent Restaurants

Jobs at independent restaurants are often the most coveted because it is here that a chef can make a name for himself or herself. Let's face it, few chefs became stars after a 20-year career at the local HoJo. The hard truth is that the number of independent restaurants far outnumbers the famous chefs that emerge from them. For that reason, jobs in a neighborhood restaurant or trendy hot-spot may not necessarily be the best long-term bet. An all too common problem at these places is poor management, which leads to a high turnover rate of employees and a short period of success. Most of the independent restaurants I have worked at have gone out of business.

Classic Cuisine

HoJo is Howard Johnson's, a national restaurant chain begun in 1925 in Massachusetts. It was the first establishment to capitalize on the traveler's need for something familiar far from home. The orange roof and colonial architecture of the HoJo meant you knew that inside you could find your favorite home-style dinner (fried clam strips and macaroni and cheese) and the famous 28 flavors of ice cream, with the oval HoJo wafer on the side. In the 1950s, when the interstate highway system was constructed, HoJos acquired property at the off ramps and created the *motor lodge*. In 1965 HoJo sales exceeded that of McDonalds, Burger King, and Kentucky Fried Chicken combined. After the death of founder Howard Dearing Johnson, the popularity of fast food grew, and HoJo fell out of favor. As of 2005, only five original HoJo franchises remain.

There are a number of reasons why good management is hard to find. Many owners love food but have no restaurant background or business sense. Poor hiring practices are another culprit. Cheap, inexperienced labor, hired without a sound screening process, leads to problems. And a lack of adequate supervision spells disaster. Inexperienced chefs and owners often refuse to acknowledge and adjust to a changing market. Even if things go well, early success often breeds premature expansion.

Working in a shop that ignores these problems or doesn't recognize them can leave employees disenchanted and soured toward the industry as a whole. You may easily find yourself, as many have, hopping from job to job. Unfortunately, short stints at several different restaurants are hard to explain on a resumé. Employers do not want to see that you stayed at your last job only two months. If you leave it off your resumé, the gap of time looks suspicious. It's a lose-lose situation.

However, if you insist on ignoring these warnings and you really want to go to work in one of these hotbeds of controversy, do your homework! Find an independent restaurant with a good reputation. Talk to current employees. Talk to former employees if you can find them. Research the chef and the owner to see what kind of successes (or failures) they have had before now. Then, consider what your goal at this establishment would be. Is it simply to be associated with it and get it on your resumé? Is to learn all you can from the chef? Is it to work in a busy trendy environment? Regardless of your goal, you should plan to stick it out as long as you can. Two years would be the minimum commitment for a good-looking resumé.

Entry levels here will vary with your training and skill. No experience whatsoever will land you in the prep or dish station. Minimum experience and willingness to learn could get you a pantry job, or cook position, probably during a slow shift. Don't expect to be a line cook unless you've done it successfully before.

The Front of the House

If you have your sights set on a particular restaurant job, but you are unqualified or they're not hiring, it could be well worth your time to look into a dining room job. I know you are not reading this book because you want to become a waiter. But don't discount the value of dining room experience. The benefits are numerous.

First, as a waiter with kitchen training, you'll know more about food preparation than other waiters. This will lead to more knowledgeable presentations to diners, and in turn, more tips. Speaking of tips, in nearly every restaurant I ever worked, the wait staff made *way* more money than the cooks. Best of all, once you're in, you'll know when your ideal kitchen job opens up.

Once you become a cook, you'll have another advantage. You'll have empathy and patience for the wait staff and the complete ability to see through the BS. You'll know exactly what it takes to do the job, and you won't settle for less. Having the respect of your fellow cooks is one thing. Having the respect of the entire restaurant staff puts you on another level entirely.

I have waited tables at good and bad places (mostly bad). I have lived through the hell that is Mother's Day brunch on Fisherman's Wharf. I have worked the counter at a

Colorado truck stop at 5:30 in the morning. (I still can't stand the smell of eggs and Tabasco sauce, a delicacy favored by all the best truckers.) I have tipped an entire tray of Long Island Ice Teas onto a customer. I have completely ignored tables for hours at a time, which continues to be my anxiety dream of choice. I am convinced that it all made me a better chef. I know what it is to have the pressure of the customer, the kitchen, and the dining room manager on you all at once. Waiters get such a bad rap, especially in Los Angeles (where, rumor has it, they're all really actors). Yes, there certainly are bad waiters, just as there are bad chefs and bad doctors and bad gas station attendants. The good ones have real talent and deserve as much respect as any good line cook. (And they deserve a good tip.)

Make Your Choice

Finding a job is hard, and sometimes we find ourselves in a position of having to take what is available. But taking the first thing that comes along is risky. If you don't have a plan, you'll end up bouncing around from job to job.

Cooks that skip from job to job are immediately suspect by potential employers. More often than not, when an employee leaves a job, it is because he quits, not because he is fired. If an employer sees job hopping on your resumé, he's going to assume you'll be hopping out of his place, too. Employers want long-term workers who will stick around when the going gets tough.

Look for a place where you will learn the most and get the most bang for your buck. Take your time, open your mind, and think long-term. You'll be less likely to end up with a job, a boss, or a commitment that you can't live with.

Sometimes, the lure of a title can get you jazzed about a job. But beware. Do some research. Find out what you're getting yourself into. If they are willing to hire a relatively inexperienced cook as the *chef*, it's probably because they don't want to pay for a seasoned veteran. Chances are you'll have a lot less creative freedom than you'd like, a lot less money than you'd like, and a lot less respect than you'd like.

In the long run, employers are more impressed with longevity than sexy titles. You'll be more likely to get the job of your dreams if you have spent several years working your way up in a quality establishment.

The Least You Need to Know

◆ Honestly represent yourself and your skill level.

◆ Keep an open mind, and think long-term.

◆ Look for a job that will enrich your career and one you can stick with for the long haul.

◆ It's better, in the long run, to be a dishwasher at a great establishment and work your way up than to start at the top of a crummy joint.

Chapter

11

Looking for a Job

In This Chapter

- ◆ Writing your resumé and cover letter
- ◆ Using references and reference letters
- ◆ Finding job leads
- ◆ Following up

After reading Chapter 10, you probably have some ideas about where you want to start. Now it's time to get an interview.

Your job search strategy should follow a few basic steps.

1. Get your resumé in order
2. Check in with your network
3. Browse job leads
4. Research employers
5. Contact employers

So let's take it from the top.

Get Your Resumé Ready

The first thing food service employers look for is dependable workers. Entry-level applicants should be easy to train and enthusiastic. Other commendable traits include honesty, initiative, leadership, good communication skills, and loyalty. If your previous work experience demonstrates these traits, include it on your resumé. Otherwise, stick to your food industry experience.

Resumés for the food service industry should be short and sweet. You should fit as much information on as few pages as possible. One page is by far the best. Use two pages only if absolutely necessary, which, for entry-level positions, usually isn't. Give no lengthy explanations. Use proper grammar, but keep it simple.

Heading

The heading is you. List all your contact information, including all phone numbers and e-mail addresses. You want employers to be able to find you when they're ready to offer you the job. If you are a student living away from home, list your local address, not your parent's address.

Some resumés list the title of the position being sought at the top as a bold headline. This is a good idea if you are applying to a big operation that is constantly hiring for many jobs. The less the employer has to sift through papers to find you, the better.

Objective

The objective is your immediate professional goal, such as line cook or entry-level pastry cook. It is the job you are going after here and now. Don't list your future aspirations of owning your own shop or becoming corporate executive chef. The people reviewing your resumé want to know what you are willing to do now, for them.

Education

List your highest, most recent degree first, even if it isn't related to the culinary field. A degree in anything shows that you can follow through. If you have attended college but don't have a degree, list the years you attended and mention the major and/or minor subjects you studied. Do not list high school unless you are a recent graduate or have not been to college. List your grade point average if it's good. Only list honor societies, leadership awards, clubs, or extracurricular activities if they demonstrate leadership skills. If you tested out of high school, list the name of the test and the date you received your high school equivalency documentation.

Work Experience

This is the tricky part for those with no experience in the industry at all. You need to demonstrate that you are a reliable worker and that you're not going to leave the minute the job gets tough. If you have worked in the field, list the jobs you've held, starting with the most recent. When you list the dates, it's customary to list only the month and year (October 2005–February 2007). No one expects the exact date, nor do they really care.

Briefly describe each position you held. Don't get into too much detail, unless you think the tasks performed are crucial to the position you're going for. If you were a pantry cook, you can say, "prepped and prepared a variety of cold menu items." If you were a prep cook, you can say, "prepared *mise en place* for all stations of high volume Mediterranean restaurant." Spend time on the wording here, and play up your experience.

If you have never worked in the industry, but you have been to culinary school, play up the relevant classes you took. List all relevant extracurricular activities you participated in, including professional organizations, clubs, and competitions. If you worked in the dining room of your school's restaurant, be sure to mention that, too.

If you have no experience and no culinary training, you'll need to list experience that shows you have a professional attitude. Employers will hesitate to hire someone with no actual kitchen experience, so you'll really need to sell yourself. Use phrases like *fast learner*, *willing to learn*, *reliable*, and *trustworthy*. The chef wants to see evidence that you're not going to leave when the work gets hard. Include a section that highlights your skills. Your ability to wield a chef knife, your expertise at stock preparation, your ability to properly fold egg whites and roll out pie dough is all good, and it's stuff the employer should know.

Behind You!

Limit your resumé to *relevant* information. If you're just starting out, list every culinary-related job you've ever had. But as you become more experienced, start dropping the less impressive gigs. For instance, today I leave off my stint behind the fountain at Farrell's Ice Cream Parlor serving up Hot Fudge Volcanoes when I was 17. The only jobs people care about today are the jobs I've held at the professional-chef level. But when I was starting out, I listed all my jobs in food service. You need to show that you know what it means to work in the food business, regardless of the job titles.

Additional Information

This section can easily fall under the heading of TMI (too much information), so include it only if you really think the information will make you look more attractive as a candidate.

Any skills that will directly influence your performance on the job you're applying for should be listed first, such as additional languages. Spanish, or whatever the language of the largest immigrant population in your area happens to be, is especially relevant. If you aren't fluent, you may want to put, "comprehension of basic Spanish," or "basic understanding of kitchen Spanish." This shows the employer you are willing and able to learn to communicate with everyone.

In the old days, we used to put "computer literate" on the resumé, to show that we knew how to operate one. Today, everyone knows how, so it's no big deal. And because it's not really related to a prep-cook job, I wouldn't bother. If you are looking at a management position, however, that's another story. You will need to show that you can organize schedules and inventory, so you might list the relevant programs you know, such as Microsoft Excel.

This is the section to list any professional affiliations you may have, if you haven't already listed them under *Experience*. This means food-related affiliations, not your membership in Little Orphan Annie's Secret Society.

Listing hobbies is weird, unless it directly relates to food. For instance, if you are an amateur brewer or cheese-maker, a chef will find that interesting. Leave off your love of knitting. Sport hobbies are cool if they show that you care about staying fit. The fact that you are keen on BASE-jumping will only show the employer that you take unnecessary risks and one day may not show up to work.

References

Expect to be asked to supply references. Any employer who fails to check references is a fool. There is never enough room to add references to a resumé, so type them up on a separate sheet, and have it with you when you apply for the job or go to an interview. Add *References Available Upon Request* at the bottom of your resumé. Include both professional and personal contacts. List their name, the context in which you know them, how long you've known them, their profession, and their contact information.

Jill Jones
111 Main Street
New York, NY, 11111
212-515-1212
jilljones@email.com

Objective
Seeking a position as full-time, entry-level pastry cook.

Education

Sept. 2001–May 2003	American Foodological Institute Associate's Degree, Culinary Arts Honors Graduate
Sept 1997–May 2001	Wassamatta University Bachelor's Degree, Art History

Work Experience

Sept. 2002–Present	Morning Prep Cook The Chum Bucket, Bikini Bottom, FL Prepared mise en place for 200-seat waterfront cafe
Aug. 2001–Sept. 2002	Fry Cook Mel's Diner, Phoenix, AZ Prepared and served regional specialties for a busy neighborhood lunch destination
June 1999–June 2001	Bartender Mo's Tavern, Springfield, FX Served cocktails for busy college town hot spot

Additional Information

- Fluent in Spanish
- Member American Culinary Federation (ACF) and Retail Bakers of America (RBA)
- Marathon runner

References Available Upon Request

Sample resumé.

Letters of recommendation are a good idea because they show the employer that it's not just you who thinks you're great. At least one other person does, too. If you're a graduate of a culinary school or other college, get every instructor you can to write a letter of reference for you. Get one from every employer you've had and anyone else who can vouch for your work ethic. Have copies of your letters of recommendation ready.

Behind You!

Be sure to proofread the recommendation letters you receive. Bad grammar will only be overlooked if the person writing the letter is very important. If someone who wrote you a poorly worded letter is not such a big deal, you may want to reconsider using it.

Cover Letter

Your cover letter is an important part of your resumé, especially if you are mailing it. It should give a brief explanation of who you are and what you want. If you know the name of the person doing the hiring, address the letter to that person. Do not repeat information that's already on your resumé. When I receive long cover letters, I usually don't bother to read them, and I usually don't bother to look at the resumé either. It shows me that the applicant is unfamiliar with professional protocol.

Jill Jones
111 Main Street
New York, NY, 11111
212-515-1212
jilljones@email.com

To Chef Wilhelm Knickerbocker,

Thank you for taking the time to review my resumé. I am seeking an entry-level position as pantry cook. I have excellent knife skills and a thorough understanding of classic cooking techniques. I am anxious to join the team at Knickerbocker's Smorgasbord, where I hope to learn as much as possible about smorgasbord cuisine.

Sincerely,

Jill Jones

Sample cover letter.

Write a separate cover letter for each employer. Personalizing the letter is not only courteous, but it also shows you are serious about wanting to work at their establishment. Save one generic copy of your cover letter as a template on your computer, and then tailor it for the specific job you are applying for. Find out the name of the chef or the person who will be doing the hiring, and fit the name of the business into the text.

Behind You!

Be sure to proofread your personalized cover letters, making sure that you use the correct restaurant and chef names.

A Few Words of Caution

Never lie on a resumé. Always assume that whoever is hiring you will confirm everything you put on your resumé. My friend Dave, who owns a Southern California placement agency, says, "your resumé is your fingerprint, and it can be traced."

If you were fired from a job or you quit after only a short time on the job, it's okay to leave the job off your resumé, but be prepared to explain the gap in time. The decision of whether to include the job depends on whether the time you spent there speaks well of you and your skills. If asked, you can simply state that it didn't work out. No need to get into the nitty-gritty. Chefs don't want to hear you bad-mouth other chefs.

Kitchen Tales

When I was in culinary school, we had visiting chefs all the time, including former White House chef Henry Haller. Through him, one of my fellow students landed an externship at the White House. I thought that sounded great, so I promptly sent off my resumé, inquiring about a job as pastry chef. Needless to say, I didn't get a job. Instead, I got a very curt letter in response, which basically laughed at me for even thinking of such a thing. I still have the letter, despite how embarrassed I was to receive it, because it's so cool. The return address has no actual address on it. It simply states THE WHITE HOUSE.

Finding a Job

Once your resumé is in order, you are ready to submit it. But where do you send it, and to whom? You should know what kind of job you want by now. The next step is to find one that's available.

All of the following methods of job hunting should be a part of your search. Don't choose just one. The most successful hunter sets traps all over the jungle. He doesn't just dig one pit and then hide behind a bush waiting for a tiger to fall into it.

Call Upon Your Network

They say that 80 percent of jobs available never get advertised. I'm not sure who *they* are or how *they* gather these statistics, but having been an employer, *they* make sense to me. I much prefer hiring someone recommended to me by a friend to dipping into my resumé file. There is a higher success rate because someone I know is vouching for that person's ability.

Building a network is easy and free. But it's not something you can just go out and do. You will be building it throughout your career. Now is the time to contact your network, keeping your eyes and ears open for job leads. While you are searching, remember that the network is a two-way street. You may be called upon during your search to help out someone else on theirs. Don't turn them away. You need all the good karma you can get.

You never know where you'll run into someone who could help you get a job. Here are some tips on building your professional network:

- Join professional organizations
- Visit job fairs and trade shows
- Post on Internet message boards and chat rooms
- Talk to salespeople
- Talk to neighbors
- Talk to other patients at the dentist's office
- Talk to other parents at the little league game
- Volunteer your time in the community

Read the Classified Ads

The easiest way to find job openings is to open the newspaper. Most of the jobs advertised there are entry-level positions, which at this stage of your career is probably where you should be focusing.

Look under as many headings as possible. Don't limit yourself to looking under *cooks*. You should also check *bakers, caterers, chefs, craft service, culinary, food, food service, hospitality, hotel, kitchen, pantry, pastry, prep, restaurant,* and *service*.

Do an Internet Job Search

The Internet has revolutionized job hunting. Now you can e-mail your resumé to hundreds of employers with the click of a button. Tons of recruiting sites are out there. Stick with large, reputable ones, of which there are many. You don't want to randomly send your personal information into the world of cyberspace alone. The large companies charge a hefty fee to the employer for accessing applicants' information, which helps to weed out the wackos.

The first step is to set aside a good chunk of time to browse and gather information. What sort of key words are getting you the most hits? What sites have the most to offer you? What sort of format must you send your resumé in? How many versions of your resumé will you need?

You may need more than one browse session. Setting aside specific time to browse is important because it's easy to lose track of time when you're surfing the Internet. Keep in mind that the Internet is not your only means of gathering job leads, so be careful not to waste too much time here.

After you've identified suitable job postings, you're ready to submit your resumé. Resist the temptation to surf, and limit yourself to 15 minutes for each response to a job advertisement.

Check Out the Placement Services

Placement services (a.k.a. headhunters) can be mighty helpful. For employers, they have the ability to tap into an enormous labor force and can help fill positions of all kinds. They represent a wide range of companies with dozens or even hundreds of jobs that need people. The best part about these agencies is that the service is free and confidential to the job seekers. The employer pays the fee. If you come across an agency that wants to charge you, keep moving.

Look for placement agencies that specialize in the hospitality industry. They're out there, and they represent all aspects of the business, including contract food services (like Aramark, a company that staffs everything from ballparks to hospitals), restaurant groups and chains, grocery stores, corporate offices, research and development firms, personal chefs, and independent restaurants.

Be aware that many search firms deal mainly with applicants who have some sort of management experience. This is because employers pay big bucks to use the placement services. If all the employer needs is a pantry cook, it is cheaper and easier for them to hire the dishwasher's cousin. That being said, it never hurts to try. By submitting your resumé, all you have to lose is a piece of paper. My headhunter friend Dave staffs lower-level jobs for free to his clients, just to keep, what he calls, the "love connection." I call it good karma.

A good headhunter will talk you out of a job for good karma, too. If you're not suited for a particular job, you'll leave it sooner than later, and it would be a waste of time for everyone involved.

> **Kitchen Tales**
>
> Here are a couple resources I have found particularly helpful:
>
> DD Factor—Professional Culinary Recruiters
> 2615 190th St., Suite 221
> Redondo Beach, CA 90278
> 310-376-0870
> factorjobs.com
>
> Riley Guide On-line Job Placement
> www.rileyguide.com

Waiting for Something to Happen

If nothing that's advertised appeals to you, it doesn't mean your dream job isn't out there. I bet you already know where you want to work. Why not go there? Eat there. Talk to the chef. If you are too shy to meet with the chef in person, submit a formal resumé and cover letter. Maybe they don't advertise job openings. Maybe they're hoping someone like you will walk in off the street. You never know.

Once you've submitted your resumé, don't forget to follow up. It shows employers that you are really interested. Many times I have had trouble deciding between two candidates and ended up giving the job to the one who called to check back.

Another reason to follow up is that too many places recruit, hire, then leave the remaining applicants hanging. Call once a week and politely remind them that you have submitted your resumé and you are inquiring about any openings. They will either tell you that the position has been filled, or they'll call you in. If you really want to work there, ask them to keep your application on file, and then call them back in three or four months to inquire about further openings. They'll either get sick of you and tell you to quit it, or they'll remember you and call you when the time comes.

The Least You Need to Know

◆ Your resumé should be short, accurate, and informative.

◆ Send a short, personalized cover letter along with your resumé.

◆ Your network is your most important job source. Use it.

◆ You can find jobs in the culinary field posted in newspapers, on the Internet, and through placement services.

◆ Following up on a job application is just as important as a good-looking resumé.

Chapter 12

Making the Most of Your Shot

In This Chapter

- Preparing for your interview
- Nailing your interview
- Showing off your skills
- Handling the first day

Congratulations! Either by answering an ad or walking in bravely off the street, you've gotten an interview. Now let's turn that interview into a job.

Prepare

Simply showing up at the designated time is not enough in this job market. For every job posting, especially in big cities, dozens of applicants appear. You are going to have to stand out from the pack—in a good way!

The first thing for you to do is to learn as much as there is to know about the place you intend to work. They are definitely going to ask you why you want to work there. You may have been dreaming of this job for years, and you have a long list of reasons you want the job. Great! But on the off chance that you have never heard of the joint before you saw an ad in the paper, you need to discover why you want to work there. The chef does not want to hear that you need the money or that you've been turned down everywhere else. Chefs want to hear how much you admire their work. And this may take a little homework on your part.

So do a little research on the restaurant. Find out how long they have been in business. Is it a relatively new start-up, or do they have a loyal following? Learn about the owners. Is it a sole proprietor, or is there a parent company? Have they had success in the business before? Who is the chef? Is this his first year on the job, or did he inherit the position from his dad? These details are important to the people who work there. They are proud of their history, and they'll want to tell you all about it when you arrive for your interview. If you show up knowing all about them, it will speak well of your desire to work there.

Research the food style, too. You should know what they serve and where it comes from. Study their menu. Learn about the cuisine. If you know someone on the inside, find out who designed the menu and why they chose to do it in that particular way. You could even make an anonymous phone call and ask a few questions about the restaurant's culinary philosophy.

If you have never eaten at the place, do so before your interview. Familiarize yourself with the food. Observe the service, the ambiance, the presentation of the plates. Is it busy and loud, or is it quiet and slow? If the meal or service is not to your liking, file it away in the back of your mind for future reference. However, don't bring up any problems during an interview.

One of the most important things to research before you have your interview is salary. Find out the going rate for the position you are applying for. You can do this on the Internet or simply by asking around. Do you have friends in the business? Ask them. If you know what other businesses are paying, you'll know what kind of salary range is acceptable.

What to Wear

Dressing for a job interview should be like dressing to meet your future mother-in-law. You want to appear clean-cut, upstanding, conservative, and neat. Just as you want your future mom-in-law to want you as a future member of her family, you want the restaurant staff to welcome you into their culinary family.

Do not dress to shock or to make a statement. You can show off your tattoos and piercings later, once you're getting a regular paycheck. Wear no jeans, no shorts, no tank tops or Sex Pistols t-shirts. (The possible exception to this is if you are look-ing for work at a punk rock club. If you've done your homework, and you know your audience, playing to their taste is fine.)

Make sure your clothing is clean and pressed, with an absence of pet hair. You should smell clean, but not perfumed. Fragrance interferes with the ability to taste. And for goodness sake, brush your teeth. Nothing is more off-putting than bad breath.

Women should wear a suit with slacks or a skirt. Don't wear a skirt that is too short, heels that are too high, or a neckline that is too low. Your hair should be neat and out of your face. Make-up and jewelry should be minimal.

Men should wear a suit and tie or nice slacks with a belt and a shirt with buttons down the front, tucked in. Wear nice shoes with socks. Shave.

Nothing is wrong with being stylish, but there is a fine line between stylish and trendy, and not every employer is going to appreciate trends.

What to Bring

Bring your knives with you. You may be asked to demonstrate your skills. Tryouts are commonplace, and you never know if they will schedule one for another time or ask you to hop up and show them what you've got.

Behind You!

> Should you wear your chef coat to the interview? Not unless you have been requested to do so. It can appear arrogant, and you don't want a piece of that. Worse than that, it's dorky, especially if you wear your thermometer on your sleeve. However, you should have a chef coat and apron with you, just in case. Be sure they're clean. You can keep them in your car or fold them neatly into your knife roll.

Have at hand several copies of your resumé, cover letter, reference list, and recom-mendation letters. Bring them in a neat portfolio of some kind or a clean manila enve-lope. It doesn't matter if you have already sent them a copy. They may have mislaid it. Bring any menus you have designed, articles you have appeared in (or written), and anything else that will demonstrate your skill and talents.

Don't forget to have a couple pens and pencils and a hanky in case you sneeze. You may be asked to produce a driver's license, identification card, or Social Security card. Have them with you. If you get hired, the employers will need copies of them for your file.

First Contact

Unless you are told otherwise, enter through the front door. Smile, say hello, give the person at the front desk your name, and say that you are here to see so-and-so for an interview. You'll be told where to wait. If you are offered a beverage, decline politely. You don't need to deal with spills.

Now it is time for you to enter the fishbowl. From here on out, everything you do and say is noticed and noted. So sit up straight, calm down, and don't pick your nose. It's survival of the fittest from now on.

It is common for employers to ask applicants to fill out an application. It is an excellent way for them to screen out idiots. Even though you have your resumé, fill out the application. Don't write *See Resumé* on it. Part of the reason they are asking you to fill out an application is to see if you will follow instructions. They are also checking to see if you are neat and organized, so read the instructions carefully and write legibly. They will check the facts, so be sure the information you write matches your resumé.

When your interviewer comes in, stand up, shake hands, introduce yourself, say "it's nice to meet you," and please remember to smile! Don't forget, you're enthusiastic about working here!

Now you're halfway home. Keep up the good work.

Nailing the Interview

You may be surprised to learn that most employers detest interviewing because it is unpleasant, time-consuming, and often fruitless. If you are not directed into a private, quiet area, do your best to stay focused. The interviewer may or may not use standard interviewing practices. You may be asked formal questions from a *patterned interview*, a style of interview in which each applicant is asked identical questions. Or the chef could take a very casual attitude and get chatty with you. You should be asked open-ended questions, but if you are not, offer up a little more. If they ask "Did you like your last job?" what they mean is, "What did you like about your last job?" They should try to find out as much about you as they can.

Be very careful not to offer up any opinions on politics or religion. Stay away from hot or obscure topics, and focus on the food. They want longevity, loyalty, and hard work. Everything that comes out of your mouth needs to be focused on communicating to them that you are the employee of their dreams, not a daydreamer.

Keep smiling throughout the interview, and remember your body language. Sit up straight. Don't cross your arms in front of you. Don't slouch in the chair, with your arms and legs spread out. Scratching your face or keeping your hands in your pockets suggests you are nervous, shifty, and possibly hiding something. Looking away or fidgeting shows that you are not really interested in the interview. You need to smile, and look the interviewer in the eye. Stay engaged, and listen to what he is saying. And don't interrupt. The minute you say "huh?" the interview may as well be over. If I sound like Miss Manners, that's because manners matter, especially in a job interview. You must show the employer that you are the best candidate.

At the end of the interview the chef may ask if you have any questions. If he hasn't told you up front how much they are going to pay you, you'd better ask. You need to know the hours they are expecting you to work, what benefits, if any, they offer, and the salary. And if they ask you how much you want, be prepared by knowing the going rate for your level of experience. The number you offer should show that you are serious about the position and that you understand your own market value.

> **Behind You!**
>
> It is common for applicants to undervalue themselves, so know in advance what you're willing to settle for.

You should have some other questions ready, too. Find out what they expect from employees. Do they routinely promote from within? Do they have goals to expand the business? What are their busy seasons? Who is their fish purveyor? You don't really have to care. Just ask something to show them that your brain cells are functioning. Remember, you want to stand out from all the other applicants.

Tryouts

It is standard procedure to test cooks for their positions. How this testing takes place varies widely. Some will ask you to stay and cook right then and there, so you should be ready and willing to do so. If this happens, it is a good sign. It means the interview went well, and the employer is impressed with you.

It is possible that the employer will wait and weed through the applications before bringing people in for a tryout. The tryout can be the equivalent of a second interview, but it is by no means a lock. Trust me on this. I have denied a job to many based on the tryout, and I have been denied as well. As a young pastry chef wanna-be, I got as far as the tryout in one job, during which I mistakenly used salt instead of sugar in a very large and expensive batch of cheesecakes. Setting aside, for a moment, the fact that they had an applicant make such a large and expensive batch of anything, it was a good lesson on why you need to taste everything as you're making it.

At your tryout they may ask you to do simple tasks, like chopping, to judge your knife skills. They might put you on for a whole shift and have you shadow another employee (who will probably give you the most hated tasks). They could also give you a recipe to follow, and judge how it comes out.

It is important that whatever they ask you to do, you do it their way. They may ask you to do simple recipes from memory that they expect you to know. This type of test judges your understanding of technique. If they give you a recipe, follow it. Don't wing it or go from memory. The chef is not interested in your style. He wants to know if you can cook in his style and follow his directions.

Your work habits will also be scrutinized. Are you neat? Do you clean as you go? Are you organized? Easily flustered? Are you chatting a lot with the other employees? All of this is crucial information to an employer. What they want is a fast, clean worker, with strong skills and a friendly disposition, who enjoys the work and keeps at it for a long time.

It is possible that the employer may test you on specific skills that are outside the norm. For instance, I worked with a great pair of chefs once who were sick and tired of repeating everything to their cooks. They decided to judge new applicants on their ability to pay attention and remember what they were told. During a tryout they would throw a dozen tasks out in a specific order and see which ones actually got done. The cooks who got hired were the ones who took out a pencil and wrote it all down.

When you apply for an upper-level job as a chef, sous chef, or pastry chef, you will probably be asked to create and present a menu or a few menu items. This *tasting* could take place at the restaurant or at some other venue away from the commotion. Sometimes you will cook everything at the site, and sometimes you will be asked to bring it in fully prepared. You may have to bring all your own ingredients, or they could offer to provide whatever you'll need. It is even possible that they will give you a *mystery box* test, in which you will have to create something fabulous from whatever they have on hand. All of these scenarios are commonplace. Don't worry. By the time you are at that level in your career, it will be an easy performance.

After your interview and callbacks, be sure to follow up if you really want to work there. They may tell you that they'll be making their decision within a couple days or weeks. When that time has passed, call and politely ask if the position has been filled. If it hasn't, keep the dream alive. If it has, move on to your next conquest.

> ### Classic Cuisine
>
> My favorite French dessert of all time is the *Gateaux Saint Honoré*. This fabulous tart-shaped pastry consists of a disc of *puff pastry*, with a spiral of *pâte a choux* (cream puff batter) piped on top. The two are baked together until crispy and golden. Then the space between the spiral is filled with *crème chiboust* (pastry cream and Italian meringue folded together), and decorated with *crème chantilly* (sweetened vanilla whipped cream) piped in a specific pattern using a pastry tip made exclusively for this dessert. Then, as the crowning glory, cream puffs filled with pastry cream are dipped in caramelized sugar and glued around the rim. You can imagine that this concoction takes a bit of skill to create. No wonder! It was conceived as a test for young pastry chefs.

Your First Weeks

If you successfully navigate the interview and tryout, you may very well find yourself with a job. So don't panic! It is, after all, what you've wanted all along.

Most employers cover themselves by putting you in some sort of probationary period for the first several weeks. This is, in essence, an extended interview. During the designated time, usually 30 or 60 days, you can be terminated with or without cause. After the probation period, you will be eligible for whatever benefits are offered, and the employer must, of course, have a good reason to fire you.

The first couple of days will be weird and awkward. Expect it, and go with the flow. Do what they tell you, and you'll be fine. Try to make friends, or at least avoid making enemies. Keep smiling, and keep being polite. You could conceivably get teased, tested, hazed, or sabotaged by the current staff. Just roll with it. It's all in good fun (hopefully).

Always remember that cooking at home or in culinary school is not like cooking for a living. At home, you can take your time, listen to your favorite CD, and cook what you want. In culinary school, you spend all day working on one dish. If you mess it up, you can try again. If you get tired, you can take a little break, have lunch, and chat with friends.

Working in a real restaurant is completely different. In a real restaurant speed is critical. No one wants to hear your Dire Straits CD. No one cares that you have a bad back or a hangover or that you don't like to touch fish guts. There's a job to do, and if you don't do it, someone else will be happy to earn your measly paycheck. Remember that, and you'll do fine.

The Least You Need to Know

◆ Show up to your interview prepared.

◆ Dress for success.

◆ Stay focused, engaged, and smile!

◆ The tryout is just a callback, not a guarantee.

Chapter 3

Tricks of the Trade

In This Chapter

- ◆ Staying cool and comfortable
- ◆ Working quickly and efficiently
- ◆ Ordering, storing, and working with your products

You learn tricks from books; you learn tricks from class; you learn tricks by seeing them in action; and you figure out tricks on your own. In this chapter, I've saved you a little time by compiling some good tricks for you. You can thank me later.

Tricks for Comfort and Happiness

It's hot. You're sweaty, tired, and sore. So let's try to keep you from getting grumpy, too.

Drink Plenty of Water

People should drink eight glasses of water a day to stay healthy and hydrated. That's on a regular day. Professional chefs working on their feet in a hot kitchen need twice that amount. When you get dehydrated, you not only feel thirsty, but you also get tired and cranky. Extreme cases of dehydration lead to headaches, dizziness, and eventually unconsciousness, which is kind of a drag.

Kitchen Tales

At one restaurant where I worked, the chef kept a 5-gallon bucket full of water infused with whatever fruits or herbs were plentiful that time of year. In the summer it was melons or peaches or berries. In the winter it was lemons and oranges. The refreshing water kept us all energized and hydrated. We felt loved, too.

Keep a plastic cup or bottle next to you at your station at all times. (Never use glass. If it breaks, you need to empty and clean every container of food in the proximity.) A plastic bottle with a lid (like a sports bottle) will help you avoid spills.

Coffee is not thirst-quenching, and neither is soda. As a matter of fact, one can of cola contains nearly a quarter cup of sugar. Sugar is hydroscopic, which means it absorbs water, and that absorption makes you thirsty. So use your head, and drink water.

Also, don't eat too much during your shift. Working on a full stomach is awful. It slows you down and makes you thirsty, too.

Protect Your Hands

Many restaurants require their food service workers to wear gloves when handling food for public consumption. The main reason for this policy is to protect customers from your cooties. But gloves are also useful for protecting your hands.

For instance, many foods, including beets and cherries, contain pigments that can stain your hands if you don't wear gloves when handling them. I learned this the hard way a week before my wedding. I got a great price on a few cases of cherries. My plan was to pit them all and then freeze them for use later in the fall. I started with a pitter, but that quickly became uncomfortable, so I just ripped the cherries in half by hand to remove the pit. My hands turned purple, but I wasn't worried because I figured the color would just wash off. To my horror, it didn't. The next day, my hands began to fade from purple to gray, with purple still lingering in the creases of my skin. The next day, the color was still there. I washed my hands repeatedly and scrubbed them raw. Finally, as a last resort on the night before my wedding, I soaked them in a bleach solution.

Hot chilies are another case when gloves come in handy. The *capsaicin* that produces the pepper's heat is transferred by touch. It originates at the center membrane of the chili, to which all the seeds are attached. So the seeds are super hot, as is anything they touch. The oil doesn't really burn the skin on your hands unless your skin is dry.

Dry or sensitive skin is extremely suscep-tible to the heat, as are your eyeballs, lips, and other delicate body parts. I mention this only because I have witnessed some extremely unfortunate incidents. One very macho cook I knew refused to wear gloves as he de-veined jalapenos. He knew not to rub his eyes. But when he completed the task, he went to relieve himself in the employee bathroom. The customers in the dining room could hear his screams.

If the establishment doesn't provide plastic or rubber gloves for its employees, you can easily get yourself a box at any large warehouse-type restaurant supply store.

Clothing

On really hot days, you'll willingly try any-thing to keep cool. I wore a neckerchief as a student and a teacher but never when I worked in restaurants, unless it got really hot. On those days we would dig out our neckerchief or find a bandana, dampen it, and toss it into the freezer. Now *that's* refreshing. We always had two—one to wrap around our neck and one on deck in the freezer, ready to switch.

def•i•ni•tion

Capsaicin is the compound that produces the biting heat of a chili. It is measured on a scale, which a scientist named Wilbur Scoville created in 1912. Scoville Heat Units (SHU) are measured in increments of 100, with sweet bell peppers at 0, hot pepper sauce around 5,000, and the habenero chili at around 100,000.

Kitchen Tales

The constant handwashing necessary in the food service industry leaves hands very dry and scratchy. I always have lotion with me to put on after work. There is no point using it during your shift because it gets washed right off, and, besides, you don't want your food to taste like lotion.

A chef's clothes are light and comfy for a reason. They keep you cool. Wearing jeans in the kitchen may look cool, but it's actu-ally not cool at all. Denim is much hotter and heavier than the cotton most checks are made out of. And don't buy polyester checks. That's just crazy.

Shorts are not good either. You could spill something hot, or drop something sharp, and that would hurt. And sanitation is another reason shorts are bad. One hot summer in Berkeley, California, I thought it was brilliant of me to wear shorts to work. I wore a knee-length apron, and at the end of the night, when I took the apron off, it looked like I had been lying in the sun all day. The exposed skin was brown, but not from tanning. It was pure filth. Grease, food, smoke, flour, and everything that was made that night was on my legs from the knees down to my sock line, in a thin film. I got some nice looks on the train home that night, and some spare change.

Comfy Feet

Good shoes are essential. The comfort of your footwear determines the comfort of your feet, and the comfort of your feet has a direct impact on your overall happiness at work. Finding the footwear that's right for you may take a while. Like all rookies, I started with clogs because it was cool and chef-y. But they weren't comfortable to me, and, in fact, they hurt the top of my foot. Sneakers were fine, but anything with a rubber sole rots quickly from floor grease. I also went through a plastic gardening-clog phase. Because they were bright red, I was routinely accused of moonlighting as a clown, but they were durable and easy to clean. I have since found that leather lasts longer, and good workman's boots have become my favorite shoe for work.

First Aid

Every restaurant is supposed to have a first-aid kit, and most do. However, as Murphy's Law would have it, the kit is often empty when you need it the most.

You can hire a service to come and replenish the kit on a regular basis, but it never seems to be regular enough. It's not that so many injuries occur, (although there are more than in most other jobs, given all the sharp knives and fire and such). It's that employees routinely stock their home medicine chests with supplies from the first-aid kit. Many times I have cut myself, only to find no bandage or *finger cot* in the kit to stop the gushing blood. In that case, I am resigned to using masking tape and plastic wrap, which is a terrible solution and not the tip I was planning on giving you. My tip is this: carry your own first-aid kit in your knife roll. And don't tell anyone you have it, unless someone else is gushing blood and heading for the masking tape.

def•i•ni•tion

Open sores pose a real health hazard because several nasty sicknesses can be easily transferred from your goop to the food, where the warm, moist, inviting protein causes it to breed and spread. A **finger cot,** which is simply a rubber finger covering, like the finger of a rubber glove, must cover a bandaged sore.

Tricks for Expediency

Don't get caught flustering around with the easy stuff. Figure it out quickly, and get back to work.

Measuring

There are measuring cups for dry ingredients and measuring cups for wet ingredients. Each holds the same volume. The wet cups are clear and have a handle and a spout so the wet stuff can be poured. They usually come in cup, pint, quart, 2-quart, 4-quart, and 2-gallon sizes. A dry measuring cup is an actual cup that holds exactly the volume indicated, either 1 cup, ½ cup, ⅓ cup, or ¼ cup. The contents are meant to be heaped in and then leveled off for an exact measurement.

In an ideal world, you would use dry cups for dry ingredients and wet cups for liquids. However, if restaurants have measuring cups at all, they are usually the wet kind, and you need to make the best of what you have. To measure liquid in dry cups, hold the cup directly over the bowl or pan, so spills end up being used. To use the wet cups for dry ingredients, shake the cup and level out the dry stuff as best you can.

In professional kitchens, butter comes in one-pound blocks, not the quarter-pound sticks you use at home. No little measuring marks on the side tell you how much one tablespoon is. You just have to know. Copy the following *Butter Table* onto an index card and refer to it often. I can't tell you how frustrating it is to see cooks trying to cram solid butter into a measuring spoon. Trust me, you can eyeball it. If your recipe needs to be precise, the recipe will list the measurement by weight.

Butter Table

Ounce	Cup	Tablespoon
16 oz (1 pound)	2 cups	32 TB
8 oz	1 cup	16 TB
4 oz (1 stick)	½ cup	8 TB
2 oz	¼ cup	4 TB
1 oz	⅛ cup	2 TB (6 tsp)

Here's how to eyeball it:

Cut a pound of butter into four equal sticks

Each stick is 8 tablespoons or 4 ounces

Cut the stick in half for 4 tablespoons or 2 ounces

And so on ...

Equipment

The best purée comes out of a bar blender, not a food processor. The smaller cavity whizzes the food much closer to the blade and many more times through it. The food processor has a bigger bowl, which sends the food to the outer edge, like a centrifuge, further from the blade and fewer times through it.

def•i•ni•tion

Robo-Coup is the brand name of a heavy-duty food processor made with professional food service in mind.

Towels make great shims if you lose a foot off your *Robo-Coup*. And if your mixer whip doesn't quite reach the contents of the bowl, jimmy it up with a towel. However, if you use a towel, don't leave these appliances unattended; towels aren't a part of the standard design for a reason.

The coffee grinder has long been requisitioned for use as a grinder for whole spices, but it's also good for grinding fresh herbs. Grinders do a good job of pulverizing rosemary needles and thyme leaves, and using the small appliance is much easier than chopping the herbs by hand. Grinders typically chop the herbs into smaller particles, which allows them to be distributed in a recipe more evenly. Don't forget to clean your grinder before you use it for coffee. Better yet, just get a separate one for spices.

When grinding toasted nuts in a food processor, completely cool them first. If they are a little bit warm, the oil they contain will exude during processing and turn the whole batch into nut butter. I like to spread nuts out on a cool sheet pan and toss them into the freezer for ten minutes before I grind them. If, on the other hand, you want nut butter, then be sure to process them piping hot.

Handling

I consider food handling the most important aspect of food service. If it's not done properly, you're in the doghouse. Here are a few tips the textbooks don't mention.

Defrosting

The proper way to defrost everything is slowly, in the refrigerator, at 41 degrees. This takes planning. But even if you are hyper-organized, you might need to defrost something on short notice.

You can submerge frozen meat in cold, running water (70 degrees or lower). The water should be running and draining so that nasty microorganisms do not collect, breed, and migrate. Running hot water on frozen meat does not defrost it significantly faster, but it does begin cooking the meat on the outer surface, while the inner meat stays frozen. This is both gross and dangerous. Also, you can cook frozen meat while frozen, as long as the internal temperature gets to where it's supposed to be.

Behind You!

Defrosting meat in the microwave is fine for a single hamburger patty at home. But large pieces of meat do not thaw evenly, and they get partially cooked in random spots. This leads to poor preparation and even bacteria growth.

You also can submerge frozen fruits and vegetables in cold water, as long as they are in the original sealed plastic packaging. Don't try it with a zipper bag. They leak. If the fruits or vegetables are frozen but loose, they will defrost quickly at room temperature, spread out on a sheet pan in a single layer.

Never place frozen pastry by a heat source. The butter in the dough will melt and ooze out. Frozen cookie or tart dough can be defrosted quickly by cutting it into small chunks with a chef knife and leaving it at room temperature for 10 to 15 minutes. You cannot defrost frozen *filo dough* quickly. If you try to rush it, it will fall apart.

def•i•ni•tion

Filo (or phyllo) dough is tissue-thin pastry dough used in Greek and Middle Eastern pastries, most commonly baklava.

Cooling

Most of the cooling that takes place in a kitchen should be done rapidly, especially when it involves protein. Meat stock, for instance, must be cooled before it is refrigerated. If it goes in the fridge hot, it will warm the entire refrigerator to an unsafe temperature (see Chapter 22). But if the stock sits too long at room temperature, microorganisms will move in and set up house. To cool stock quickly, use an *ice bath*.

def•i•ni•tion

An **ice bath** is a bowl full of ice water used to cool hot foods down quickly. Common foods that are cooled in this manner are stock, soups, and custard sauces. The hot food is poured into a second bowl, which is placed in the ice bath and stirred until cool.

The liquid being cooled should be in a metal container if possible, rather than plastic. Plastic is an insulator and slows the process down.

Trays of hot foods are cooled on a rolling rack, which is a cooling rack on wheels, roughly the size of a tall filing cabinet. It has shelves every few inches that a sheet pan can slide into, with space in between for air to circulate. To speed this type of cooling, transfer the hot food to a cool pan so you only have to wait for the food to cool and not the pan, too. The same is true for hot stuff in saucepans and sauté pans.

Kitchen Tales

Many kitchens have ice wands, which are large hollow plastic paddles filled with water and frozen. They are used to stir hot liquids, drastically reducing cooling time.

If you leave a hot pan out to cool, be courteous to your co-workers and drape a towel or pot holder over the edge in plain sight. This is the international signal for *hot pan*. If you have ever firmly grabbed hold of a scorching hot pan, you'll appreciate that tip.

Save Everything

It's hard for me to waste anything. I wash and reuse zipper bags, for cryin' out loud. If I have perfectly good food with no immediate use, I find a way to save it until I need it. Fruits of all kinds freeze well, but prep and ready them for use first. This means washing, peeling, cutting into pieces, and pitting or seeding as necessary. Citrus zest can be frozen, grated, or peeled thinly with a peeler.

Freeze grated fresh coconut and pre-toasted nuts. They are easy to defrost and can be quickly added to any recipe.

Any kind of juice freezes easily. I like to wash and reuse cardboard milk cartons for this, as they fit together neatly in a freezer and stand up nicely to defrost.

I also use milk cartons for stock scraps at home. When I have a carrot end or an onion skin, I toss it in the freezer milk carton. When it's full, I can peel off the box and plop the frozen scraps into a stockpot.

Surprisingly, many kinds of cheese freeze really well. Grated is the easiest to use, but you can freeze chunks, as long as you defrost them slowly in the fridge.

Food Tricks

Try these handy tricks on for size:

- For a superior sifted powdered sugar, wrap a cup or so of the stuff in a double layer of cheesecloth, like a *beggar's purse*. Shake it back and forth for a delicate dusting of fine powder.

- The perfect peeled kiwi is skinned, not with a peeler but with a spoon. Cut each end of the kiwi off to expose the green inner flesh. Insert a spoon, bowl side facing the flesh, into the kiwi between the skin and the flesh. Push the spoon all the way up so that it is visible on the other end. Holding the spoon still, rotate the fruit, separating the skin from the flesh. The fruit will pop right out of its skin, with a perfectly smooth, round edge.

def•i•ni•tion

> A **beggar's purse** is the name given to any little bundle of food. It probably originally referred to Chinese *dim sum*, but now it refers to anything wrapped in a thin sheet of dough, crepe, noodle, won ton, or even a leaf. The edges are gathered up at the top, and the dough is either twisted or tied together.

- The best way to remove the flesh from a mango was taught to me by Patricia Quintana, whose official title is Culinary Ambassador of Mexico. First, cut the mango in half lengthwise. The pit stands upright in the middle, so this requires two cuts, one on each side of the pit. Some flesh will be left around the pit, which you can easily remove with a knife or save for a snack. Now, take a half mango in your hand, and using the largest spoon you can find, preferably with a bowl the size of the mango, scoop out the flesh, scraping the spoon as close to the skin as possible. If it is ripe, this job is easy, and you are left with a perfectly smooth, rounded, glowing orange mango half, which you can then cut into perfect fanned slices.

- When you mince garlic, sprinkle a little kosher salt on the board. The coarse grains help cut the garlic down, and the salt brings out the water, which softens the garlic into a paste.

◆ To neatly slice an onion into a dice, follow these directions: slice the onion in half from stem end to root end. Peel off the skin. Lay one half flat on the board, with the stem end facing the knife (root end facing away). Hold the onion by placing your palm on the top of it, and stretch your fingers up and out of the way. Now slice parallel to the table, ½ inch up from the table, all the way back until you reach the root. Do not cut through the root. Keep the root intact.

Now remove the knife and move it up another ½ inch and repeat another parallel slice. Remember not to cut through the onion's root. You need it in place to hold the onion together. Repeat the parallel slices every ½ inch until you reach the top of the onion. Now cut perpendicular to the slices you just made, slicing down from the top of the onion, from just in front of the root to the stem end, still keeping the root in tact. Repeat this cut every ½ inch all the way across this hemisphere of the onion. Next, turn your knife the right way (like you do for regular chopping) and slice every ½ inch from the stem to the root. The onion will fall apart into a beautiful dice.

Kitchen Tales

Cheer up. Onions make everyone cry. Some people wear goggles or sunglasses. Some people say to cut next to cold running water. Some say you should use hot water. Some people say to cut with a piece of bread in your mouth, sticking out to catch the onions fumes. (Personally, I think this is a prank. A culinary hazing. "Let's see if we can get the rookie to work with bread sticking out of his mouth!") The only method I know that works is to cut well-chilled onions. The oils are more solidified and thus less likely to escape into the air. This, however, is problematic because cold onions contain more sugar than room temperature ones. More sugar means they will burn quickly when heated. So plan ahead, chop them cold, and then let them come to room temperature before cooking. Or get in touch with your sensitive side, and give yourself permission to cry.

◆ *Concassé* is a French word that means to crush or chop. But in Chefspeak it means to peel, seed, and chop a tomato. To remove the peel, cut a small "X" at the bottom of the tomato. Drop it in boiling water for about one minute. Promptly remove it from the boiling water and drop it into ice water. This temperature change causes the skin to contract, pulling away from the flesh of the fruit. The ice water also stops the cooking process. Gently remove the peel. Next, slice the tomato in half, along its equator. Take each half and gently squeeze out the seeds, as if it were an orange you were squeezing for juice.

To chop your peeled, seeded tomato, lay the flat side on the cutting board, and begin by slicing as you would for a *julienne*. The tomato is rounded, but because the seeds are gone, it will flatten out once it's sliced. Then, turn the julienne, and cut it into a dice.

> ## def•i•ni•tion
>
> **Julienne** is a thin, matchstick-shaped cut.

The method used to peel tomatoes also works for peaches and other stone fruits. It works to loosen the skin of pearl onions, too, but don't bother to cut an "X" on the onions.

Organizational Tricks

Mise en place is good, but sometimes it takes too long. You can always get some food cooking while you prep the rest! For instance, you can put water on to boil, toast nuts, or get bones roasting while you chop your vegetables. If you wait until everything is prepped before you start cooking, you'll be there all night.

Store the knives and other tools you repeatedly use during your shift in a tall bucket filled with water. Kept at your station, it is easy to access, keeps the knives clean, and keeps them safely out of the way. Change the water periodically during your shift.

A wet side-towel or paper towel under your cutting board keeps it from sliding around on the counter as you chop.

Be sure to label everything you put in the fridge and freezer, with the date and contents. It's sometimes impossible to figure what's in a frozen package, and it takes too long to open everything in search of what you need. Make your label on masking tape, using a sharpie. Masking tape won't stick to anything cold or damp, so stick it on the container before you freeze it. The tape is cheap and sticks forever. Best of all, you can remove it when you empty the container, which can then be reused and relabeled. Don't send the empty container to the dish station with the tape on it. They'll leave it on, and the tape will fuse to the container in the heat of the dishwasher.

Cleanup Tricks

Spills in a kitchen are dangerous. Although the floors at each station are probably covered with rubber perforated mats, floor lies between them, usually tile or cement. One slip, and down you go. Unfortunately, when spills occur, you don't always have time to get the mop.

Oil spills can be temporarily handled by a light sprinkling of kosher salt. The salt creates a little traction to get you through until the mop arrives. It's important to alert all your co-workers that the spill exists, so they can proceed with caution.

> **Kitchen Tales**
>
> Always keep a wet side-towel by your station during your shift. Fold it over several times so it is a neat package. It's a quick way to clean up any little messes, and by folding it, you can unfold and refold to expose the clean sides throughout your sift.

Eggs are another nasty, slippery mess. The easiest way to clean up an egg is to scoop it up with a wide hamburger flipping spatula or a pastry chef's plastic rubber scraper and then wipe the floor with paper towels to soak up any additional egg before mopping. The spatula/scraper scoop-up is really the best way to get any thick mess off the ground quickly. Be sure to wash it before you resume its intended duties.

I always reserve (stash or hide) a clean side-towel to use in cleanup at the end of my shift. Nothing dries and shines a stainless-steel countertop better.

Purchasing

Fruits and vegetables have USDA grades based on size, appearance, and overall quality. Just to make things difficult, each type of fruit and vegetable has its own grading scale. The best could be Extra Fancy or Fancy, #1's or A's. The largest could be Jumbo or Extra Large.

The produce you find at the large chain grocery stores will be the best quality and the best looking. Sorted by size and appearance, all the tomatoes, for instance, in a case of #1's will look beautiful and identical. This is important to the produce manager at the market, because if the tomatoes look wonky, no one will buy them. However, the chef making marinara sauce knows that the tomatoes are going to get mashed up anyway, so who cares what they look like when they come in? For less money he'll buy #2's, which will be a mish mash of sizes with perhaps a bit of bruising, but will have the same flavor.

#3's are an even better deal, often too ripe for use raw, but perfect for cooking down.

> **def•i•ni•tion**
>
> **Caprese salad** is fresh tomatoes sliced and layered with basil leaves and slices of fresh buffalo mozzarella, drizzled with olive oil. *Caprese* is Italian, "in the style of Capri."

As a pastry chef, I routinely bought the lowest-grade berries for sauces and sorbet. (Find just a hint of mold? Toss it into the berry vinegar bucket, or freeze it for jam.) If the chef tells you to make tomato sauce, don't let him catch you chopping up the #1's he bought for *caprese salad*.

While ground herbs and spices are available, it's worth knowing that spices quickly lose their flavor and aroma when ground. Unless you use your ground spices up quickly, it's more cost-effective to purchase the whole spice, toast it in a dry skillet, and grind it in a coffee grinder.

Storage

When new shipments come in, you must rotate the product, with the oldest in front so it's used first. This is a little thing we in the business like to call FIFO (first in, first out), which means that the first product that came into the shop needs to be used before subsequent deliveries are opened.

Green, leafy vegetables are delicate things, which can be easily overcooked, easily bruised, and easily wilted. They should be kept moist and stored loosely so air can circulate. (Think about how they are stored at the market.) Salad greens can be washed and stored loosely in a covered plastic bin, and smaller quantities can be wrapped in moist paper towels.

Root vegetables and onions you should keep cool, but do not refrigerate. The sugar content of these foods increases under refrigeration, which can be problematic when the time comes to add heat. Sugar burns more easily than starch, and so, if the potatoes were stored in the fridge, your fries come out of the deep fryer too dark and a little bitter. This effect will reverse itself if the foods are left out at room temperature for a couple of days.

Fresh herbs should be stored like salad greens. I wrap them loosely in damp paper towel and keep them in a bin in the refrigerator. I've known chefs who store them in water in the fridge like a bouquet of flowers, and others who like to hang them like laundry from a line in the walk-in with clothespins. Do not chop them until you are ready to use them, because they begin to discolor when bruised by the knife.

Foods containing oil can turn *rancid* if left on the shelf too long. If they are not used up quickly, store them in the refrigerator to prevent rancidity. This is true of any food containing oil, including nuts, nut butters, whole wheat grains and flours, and (naturally) oils.

def•i•ni•tion

When fats and oils have been exposed to oxygen, light, and heat for too long they turn **rancid,** meaning that they take on a disagreeable taste and odor. Typical exposure depends on the specific food, but in general, store fats and oils in the refrigerator if they are more than three months old.

The Least You Need to Know

◆ Drink lots of fluids and wear proper clothing to stay cool.

◆ Proper food handling is essential in the restaurant business.

◆ Knowing certain tricks for preparing food will make you much more efficient in the kitchen.

◆ Proper purchasing and storage can make or break a restaurant.

Part 5

Being a Successful Professional

Once you're working, it doesn't get any easier. There will be a new culture to assimilate, new hours, new skills, and new pains. On top of all that, the job may turn out to be completely boring. Then what do you do? If your goal is to become a successful chef, you need to look around for things that spark your interest.

Getting along with your co-workers is key to being successful at anything. Listening to the advice of those who know more than you do, which at the beginning of your career is practically everybody, is also important. Look around you. Who seems happy and fulfilled? Pay careful attention to those people, and ignore the naysayers.

You should never reach a point in your career when you stop and say, "that's it, I've made it." Always strive to learn, know, and do more. But it will be an effort on your part. No one is going to hand you the knowledge. You've got to go out and get it. Lucky for you, plenty of organizations, publications, and destinations are available to help you learn more.

Chapter 14

Building Restaurant Relationships

In This Chapter

- ◆ Learning important communication skills
- ◆ Dealing with negativity
- ◆ Avoiding the swelling ego
- ◆ Following rules of common courtesy
- ◆ Developing common sense
- ◆ Maintaining relationships with ex-employers

One of the hardest things to do, no matter what your profession, is to get along with everyone you work with. Your co-workers, supervisors, and customers come from all walks of life. They all have different expectations and different agendas. The key to success in the workplace is to find a way to coexist peacefully with all types. This is not easy, but it's possible.

Communication Skills

Communication is probably the most important aspect of getting along with others. One of the most overlooked aspects of good communication is understanding how others perceive what you say and do.

Most workplace communication fails when something someone says is mistakenly interpreted as a threat. People get defensive when they feel threatened. If you can resist the temptation to be defensive, you'll be more successful in the long run.

As an example, consider a common occurrence in a busy, high-stress restaurant. It appears that someone has stolen your *mise en place*. You look around, see that everyone has theirs, and think you spy the culprit, a co-worker who came in late, but now is fully prepped and ready for service.

How you decide to handle this says a lot about your ability to communicate. The typical reaction includes a little yelling, some accusations, and perhaps the re-theft of said *mise en place*. Some folks never say a word but fume about it all night, and end up harboring resentment. Others may complain to the rest of the staff rather than deal directly with the accused.

Rather than reacting in any of these ways, why not take a deep breath and respond with composure? Yes, this person probably did take your *mise en place*, but instead of throwing a fit, try to find a solution. Deal directly with the co-worker first, rather than complaining to the other colleagues or snitching to your supervisor.

Solutions could include asking if the accused knows what happened to your *mise en place* or asking if the accused could help you prep, as he seems to have the time and yours has disappeared. You could offer to help the accused prep the next time he comes in late. He may react negatively to any of those scenarios, but at least you gave the peaceful resolution a shot.

The key in this type of situation is to react directly and courteously. Don't get caught up in the anger. Focus on the job at hand, and make the job your priority. Always start by treating everyone with respect. Whether they end up earning that respect remains to be seen.

You should go to work each day with the intention of resolving every issue that may come up, not always proving yourself right. The kitchen is part of a business, and your priority should be to make that business run smoothly. You should listen fully and respond positively to criticism. This shows that you are flexible, adaptable, and have the best interest of the business at heart.

Negativity

Any high-stress job is difficult. The service industry is no exception. Most people have no idea how enormous the pressure of working in a restaurant can be. Unfortunately, many people don't know how to handle the stress, and rather than feed off of it for energy, they wallow in the difficulty of it. I bet you know the type. No one and nothing is ever good enough. You get the feeling that they truly believe their complaints make them more important, more legitimate.

Watch out for these guys, because occasionally you may find that you agree with their negative assessment of the situation. Don't get swept up in their pessimism. The responsible thing to do is to gracefully back out of any negative conversation. Remember that your priority is the job at hand and any negativity only makes the task more difficult.

> **Behind You!**
>
> I have known many terrific cooks who had no capacity to deal inwardly with stress. But because they were terrific cooks, we put up with them. The key to survival if you find yourself working with someone like this is to keep your distance.

You're Not a Chef Yet

Nothing is more exciting than being referred to as a chef for the first time. When I graduated from culinary school, our executive chef ended the ceremony by asking the audience to "congratulate the new chefs." I remember looking at my instructors and our guest speaker, Chef Dean Fearing, and thinking how far out of their league I was. I never felt chef-worthy until I began teaching, a decade later.

> **Classic Cuisine**
>
> Dean Fearing is a great practitioner of modern Southwest cuisine. He is the long-time executive chef of The Mansion on Turtle Creek in Dallas, Texas. He wears cowboy boots in the kitchen and plays guitar in a country-western band. But more importantly, he helped put Southwestern ingredients, techniques, and style on the culinary map. I'm a fan.

Unfortunately, some people feel that a culinary education or a respectable apprenticeship buys them the right to the title. This attitude is a recipe for trouble. If you can't keep your ego in check, you will not win any friends or impress any supervisors.

The single biggest complaint I hear regarding rookies is that they think they are already chefs. They know it all. I hear this time and time again from chefs who are desperately in search of good employees. Fewer and fewer employees seem to be willing to work hard and pay their dues.

So when you start working, you need to control your ego. To do that, you must show your co-workers the proper respect. When you start your first job, everyone there has been in the business longer than you. Respect them for the job they do, whether they are the executive chef or one of the busboys. Every employee is vital to the team.

Next, work diligently, keep your mouth shut, and mind your own beeswax. If they want your opinion, they'll ask for it.

Help out whenever you can. Don't ask whether help is needed. Just help. The greatest chefs I know just jump in and help. If you ask if someone needs help, especially someone with a touch of insecurity, the answer will probably be no. By the time a cook realizes help is needed, it's usually too late. At that point, pride takes over, and the help is more humiliating than the weeds she discovers herself in. So don't wait to be asked.

On the flip side of helping when needed is trying to do everything yourself. If you think you are better and faster than everyone else, you probably aren't. It's just your budding ego. You can't handle everything yourself, so don't even try. Accept the help when it's offered. Your ego is no good for the business, and the business is where the main focus should be.

Don't brag. It's a loathsome habit. Instead of talking about yourself, find out about everyone else you work with. Discover their opinions, especially when they think differently than you. Ask for feedback, and accept criticism. Be honest with yourself and your co-workers about your strengths and weaknesses. If you say you can handle it, you'd better mean it. There is a fine line between believing in yourself and self-importance. Pride grows easily into arrogance.

Kitchen Tales

I once worked with a chef who was so sick and tired of being questioned that she had a t-shirt made that read *Yes, I AM sure!*

Don't grab the credit, and don't shirk the responsibility. Passing the buck is an all-too-common trait, and is most unsavory. What you seldom see is someone accepting blame and facing his mistakes.

Don't second-guess or openly question your supervisors. If you have legitimate concerns, ask to speak with your supervisor in private. Openly criticizing authority is highly disrespectful.

Common Courtesy

I drill proper manners into my children. They must say "please" and "thank you"; they may not begin eating until everyone is served; they must refer to adults as "Mr.," "Mrs.," or "Miss"; they must ask to be excused; they may not play with their presents until they write thank-you notes; and they must sit quietly in the theater and not speak until the show is over. Why? Because sometimes it seems like society has lost the ability to distinguish between courteous and offensive behavior, and I want to be sure they don't end up like the rude people I run across every day.

If your plan is to make a success of this career, you must care about your co-workers, care about the success of the operation, and follow these basic rules of common courtesy:

- **Rule #1. If it's not yours, don't take it.** This is just as relevant in reference to staplers in an office as it is to knives, side-towels, and *mise en place*. Even a quick snatch of a paring knife to open a bag of flour is considered dishonorable among cooks. Always request and receive permission first.

- **Rule #2. If you make a mess, clean it.** Plenty of messes happen in a kitchen. Until you see someone running up with a mop, consider it your problem. In a kitchen, we are talking not only courtesy, but safety. A puddle of water, oil, or eggs on the floor can conceivably mean a bad fall, loss of personnel for the night, and a workman's compensation claim.

- **Rule #3. If it's empty, fill it.** It is such a burn to find the bin of flour, the well of ice, or the milk dispenser empty during a busy shift. Refilling it takes little time, unless you have no time, and then it takes forever.

- **Rule #4. If it's broken, fix it.** If you do not possess the capacity to repair the piece of equipment, at least alert the staff that it is broken. Don't leave it to become someone else's problem.

- **Rule #5. If you don't know, ask.** No one cares if you are embarrassed. Don't proceed in ignorance, thinking you can figure out how it's done. If you screw it up because you really had no idea, you've wasted time and product. Remember, product equals money.

- **Rule #6. If it's not your turn, wait.** This is just as true in the lunch line as it is in line to use the Robo-Coup. If you see that someone is getting ready to use a piece of equipment, wait until that person is done. Cutting in front is outrageous. In no way can you justify it. Everyone's task is of equal importance in a restaurant, and I guarantee that you can find something else to do while you wait. And don't shove someone's pan off the burner, either. Sheesh!

◆ **Rule #7. Share the space.** It may be your workstation, but it's shared territory, and there is shared equipment in it. The sooner you relinquish command of your region, the sooner your neighbors will become allies.

◆ **Rule #8. When you've finished using an ingredient or a piece of equipment, replace it.** Nothing is more frustrating than spending 10 minutes looking for something that is not where it should be.

◆ **Rule #9. Don't waste people's time.** Don't be too chatty. No matter how well intentioned, excessive talking is not welcome when there is work to be done. Save your lame jokes and oh-so-amusing anecdotes for after the rush.

◆ **Rule #10. Always remember to say "please," "thank you," and "excuse me" at the appropriate times.** It's nice to be nice. Why be rude? An agreeable demeanor greases the wheel of restaurant relationships.

Common Sense

Many people believe that common sense is a thing you either have or you don't. I don't buy that. I think common sense can be learned, if you're motivated to do so.

What is common sense? Common sense is the ability to see the big picture and the ability to see what's missing from the picture.

Understanding where you fit into an organization and why what you do matters is the key to happiness on any job. Job apathy grows in the absence of that understanding. It's a "Why should I try? No one cares, no one notices" attitude. As an employee, your job is to discover your place, the way you fit into the whole, and then to do the job to the best of your ability. When you do this, the jobs that are connected to yours can be done properly. Understand the connections, and you can easily find the breakdown during a crisis. Understand the connections, and you can improve the efficiency and the quality. Understand the connections, and your job suddenly matters a lot more and starts to get interesting.

You can only see what's missing if you can see the big picture. A good waiter knows that an order of iced tea is not just a glass of iced tea. It's also a lemon, sugar, a straw, and a long spoon. A good host knows that six chairs fitting around a table don't guarantee that the party of six will be comfortable there. A good cook knows that the best techniques in the world don't matter if the plates are not clean and warm.

Following through, finishing what you start, understanding what you need to do and doing it is all common sense. An employer looks for people who don't have to be told what needs doing. They just do it. Helping get things done and being willing to pitch in are traits that people notice.

Burning Bridges

Sometimes, no matter how hard you try, restaurant relationships don't work out. If you have followed my advice, then it's through no fault of your own, and you can take heart in knowing you tried your best. When bad things do happen, your initial reaction probably is to rant and rave and try to get the anger off your chest. But such actions are not necessarily the right course for your career. Throwing a fit may make you feel better, but it probably won't do you any good in the long run.

If you have been let go, any move you make toward placing the fault anywhere but at your own feet will be regarded as proof that getting rid of you was the right thing to do. Don't prove them right. If you are fired, don't place the blame on others, especially your superiors. Management and supervisors stick together. Instead, admit your mistake and move on.

Behind You!

Never threaten your employer. Threats of litigation will probably backfire. Threats of physical violence or extortion will land you in jail. The damage you'll do to your career will be much more severe than any embarrassment you face now.

The cool thing to do is to mend as many bridges as possible before you leave. Make finding your replacement as easy as possible for your employer. Offer to help fill the position or train the new hire. A good reputation can follow you just as easily as a bad one, and if you leave on a high note, that's what they'll remember. Professionalism will outweigh poor performance in the end.

If you decide to quit a job, you must follow a definite protocol. First, before you tell anyone that you are even thinking about leaving, tell your supervisor. (If she hears it through the grapevine, your chances of a good recommendation are greatly diminished.)

Tell your supervisor first, in person, and write a resignation letter, too, for your personnel file. Do this at least two weeks before you plan on leaving; a month before would be better. The more time she has to find a replacement for you, the easier her job is and the better you come across.

If possible, make yourself available to train your replacement and offer to answer any questions she may have once she has taken over. Organize your station, and return any equipment, ingredients, or recipes you may have.

If you do all this, you will be remembered with fondness and recommended by your peers, and you will maintain a very useable network.

The Blacklist

I bet you have one. It's a mental list of the people you would refuse to help out if asked. They have insulted you, ignored you, or taken advantage of you. They are the people who burned the bridge.

Surprisingly, when the time comes for you to deny services to a person who appears on your blacklist, you'll find little pleasure in it. Revenge is not at all sweet, and in fact, it often backfires.

People on the blacklist conjure up memories for you of the incidents that got them there. But they don't always know they've been blacklisted. Even though it may sound fun to deny them a table, a job, or a letter of recommendation, it's really just mean, and you end up looking like a jerk. Shine it on.

The Least You Need to Know

- Go to work each day with the goal of resolving every issue that may come up.
- Avoid negative people and negative situations.
- Check your ego at the door.
- Be nice to everyone.
- Use your head, and see the big picture.
- Let go of your grudges.

Chapter **15**

Finding a Mentor

In This Chapter

- ◆ Finding a mentor
- ◆ Choosing mentors for different aspects of your career
- ◆ Making the most of your mentor
- ◆ Mentoring others

You've gotten an education, either on your own or in a school, and now you have a job doing what you've always wanted to do. You're out there alone, with nothing but your wits to keep you alive. Don't make the mistake of thinking you are at the end of your journey. Never stop learning, and never stop trying to be the best chef you can be.

One way to continue growing in your profession is to find someone who will continue to teach you. That's what a mentor does. Books are important, but they're not enough. You simply can't learn some aspects of this business on your own. You need to learn by example.

What Is a Mentor?

We all have mentors whom we look up to in life. We may not recognize them as such, and we may not call them mentors. But they were those folks who were there to show us how to behave, how to get along, and how to cope. It could have been your big brother, a neighbor, a teacher, or a coach. A mentor is someone, other than your parents, who has taught you something about being a person. It is no different in a kitchen.

To become a successful chef, you need to follow someone's lead. Even if you graduated at the top of your culinary class and have been working in the business for 10 years, you still have much to learn. The wealth of culinary information out there is not going to magically jump into your brain. You need to look for it. And it's an easier search if you have someone to help you find it.

I know you won't go up and ask someone to be your mentor. And I am not suggesting that you hold auditions or place an ad. What you should do, however, is pay attention. There are people all around you who can teach you something. Keep your eyes open, and get to know the people you work with. Someone around you is going to inspire you to be your best. Who will it be?

A mentor can take many forms. You may even end up having more than one.

Skills Mentor

A chef can do a zillion things to make the job faster and easier. Most of these skills don't come from books or classes but rather from observation and hands-on experience.

Someone is always going to be faster and more proficient than you. It's usually because she has been around the block a few more times and has learned a trick or two along the way. Watch these people carefully. Are they doing something different, or are they simply faster?

What knives do they use? Are they the same as yours? If not, ask why. People have preferences for a reason. Do they have special tools for certain tasks, or do they use whatever is lying around? How do they care for their tools? How does what they use and do compare to what you use and do?

How does their station look? Is it clean? Is their *mise en place* organized and easily accessible? Are there plenty of back-up ingredients? Are there clean side-towels and wet ones? As they work, do they take a moment to clean as they go? And how is clean-up for them after the rush? Is it overwhelming, or is it a snap? How do they organize their day's work? Is there a method behind the order in which they complete their daily tasks? In all likelihood there is. Do they make lists, or do they keep it all in their head?

Behind You! _____

Keeping lists is a great way to keep yourself organized. One boss I had liked keeping our daily prep list on a large dry-erase board. As a task was begun, it was crossed off, so that everyone could see what was getting done. It was a great motivator, especially when a lot of jobs were crossed off.

What personal habits are in place to help keep focused during the rush? Are they drinking a lot of water? Or is it coffee? Are they sitting down to eat a balanced meal, or are they grazing the pantry station? Do they smoke or drink? How is their working pattern different from what you are doing?

Taste Mentor

If you want to become a superior chef, your goal should be to thoroughly understand food. So start looking for a cook who puts out exceptional product.

People aren't born with a sense of food taste and compatibility. Taste is a personal thing and developing it means tasting and experimenting.

I am not proposing that you set up a laboratory of food compatibility in your kitchen. Nor am I suggesting that you start eating out at a different restaurant each night. Although these are both excellent ways to develop your palate, you probably don't have the time and the resources for them. Instead, seek the guidance of others.

Enthusiastic chefs become all aflutter when something tastes good. These people do not follow trends. They set them. They don't talk about Food TV, the latest cookbook, or the hot new restaurant. They talk about taste. They try new things and are open to new possibilities. When you find one of these chefs, stick close.

I have tried many new things over the years, simply because someone recommended it. Among my favorite foods in the world are dates stuffed with parmesan cheese, pineapple and black pepper ice cream, caramel-vinegar sauce, sweetbreads, head cheese, and steak tartar. I never would have tried any of these foods if someone I admired hadn't suggested them. Now all these flavors are a part of my own taste repertoire. They have rounded me out as a chef.

> **Kitchen Tales** _____
>
> There is an easy method you can use to find a flavor match for a particular food (or even wine). Start with the food you want to pair, and gather other foods covering each of the four flavor basics that your tongue recognizes: salty, sweet, acidic, and bitter. You can use anything you have lying around, like olives, candy, lemons, and old coffee. Take a bite of the salty food, then a bite of the food you want to match. Let them linger together on your tongue for a minute, then clean your palate with water and bland bread or crackers. Repeat the process with the sweet food, then the acidic, and then the bitter. Be sure to clean your palate each time. None of the foods will be a great match, but one of them will taste better than the others. When you discover which one does, repeat the experiment with several different foods from that category. So, for example, if the salty worked best, gather a bunch of salty foods on the plate next, like anchovies, blue cheese, capers, or smoked salmon, and see how each of these foods taste with the food you want to match. Keep trying until you narrow it down to the best match. Then come up with a recipe that uses these two foods together.

Attitude Mentor

Do you know someone who never stresses out, never misses a day of work, or moves gracefully under pressure? Maybe it's a dishwasher who is always smiling or a waiter who earns higher tips than anyone else. What's up with these people?

In the professional kitchen, it's hard to exist stress-free. But there are some who do. If you could bottle that sort of attitude, you'd make millions. These people are prime mentoring candidates.

What are they doing differently? Do you think they never hit a bump in the road? Of course they do. It is how they react to the bump that sets them apart. How is their reaction different from the way you react?

How do they treat the bottom-rung laborers? Is it with as much respect as any other worker? The cooks you want to be associated with know that every job in the kitchen is important. If they haven't been in the dishwasher's shoes, at least they are thankful for the guy in them now.

Do some people at work make you crazy? Is there someone whose presence makes you cringe? Would you rather chew tin foil than hear them speak? Why is that? How does your attitude mentor deal with that person? Getting along with co-workers is an important skill, and it can definitely be learned.

How do people treat each other at your job? Do they laugh about colleagues behind their backs? Do they gossip? If so, they can just as easily be laughing and gossiping about you when you're not around. That's not behavior you want to emulate. It is not behavior that is destined for greatness or even middle management. How does your attitude mentor treat other people?

Business Mentor

Food is a business, after all. But it is easy to forget that when you're in the trenches. Even if you are not in a management position, customer satisfaction should be first and foremost on your mind. Those who keep the customers their top priority throughout the night are the ones to watch. The cooks with this mind-set are the successful ones.

Nothing is more frustrating than a customer complaint. When a dish is returned because it is not to the customer's liking, I just want to scream. But that customer didn't send it back because he wanted to frustrate me. He sent it back because he wasn't happy with it. Whether or not that is a fault of mine, I need to fix it. If I can fix it, the easier it is for everyone involved. Regardless of who is at fault, screaming about it serves no one. I need to just let it ride and fix it. Why? Because there is nothing more important than the repeat business and recommendations of that customer.

Who is out there with those customers? It's the dining room staff. So it only follows that waiters and bussers and hosts should be treated well. The cooks who embrace the wait staff as a vital element to the success of an operation are the winners. But alas, the wait staff is often viewed as the opposing team by the kitchen staff. A waiter who is treated like dirt in the kitchen is going to carry that dirt out into the dining room. There is simply no way to do your job well if you feel undervalued. Treat the dining room staff well, and you will be repaid tenfold. In what? Good karma, of course.

Food cost is another critical aspect of success. Waste is the enemy in a kitchen, but when it's not your money on the line, it's easy to forget this fact. Cooks who help keep the food cost in check are the ones who keep the managers happy and eventually rise into management themselves. More money for the restaurant means more money for you. It's that long-term perspective that is vital for success.

Lifestyle Mentor

What do you do after work or on your day off? Are the activities you choose benefiting your career? How do successful chefs decompress after a tough night? Chances are they don't use drugs or booze. They find outlets that enhance their skills and mental attitude.

Keeping healthy is a key lifestyle trait that can make or break a career (see Chapter 16 for tips on staying healthy). The best chefs I know make exercise an integral part of their daily routine. Whether it's running, yoga, weightlifting, or surfing, these chefs know that exercise is just as important for their mind as their bodies, especially in the high-stress environment of a busy kitchen.

Good chefs know that what they put into their bodies is just as important as how they exercise those bodies. Overindulging in food or drink is common in the food business. But there is only so much abuse a body can take before it stops functioning at the high level a good chef demands. The sooner you come to terms with this fact, the more successful you will be.

> **Kitchen Tales**
>
> One of the best chefs I have worked for came in during lunch, prepped all afternoon with us, then left an hour before dinner to go windsurfing on the San Francisco Bay. She'd get back just in time to expedite the dinner shift and was full of energy until the last table was served.

What Do You Do with a Mentor?

If you identify people whom you admire and want to emulate, get to know them. Ask them questions, and not just questions about their knives and their exercise routines. Ask them what they think about the job you're doing.

Getting this sort of feedback from someone you feel comfortable with will help you better accept the information. In this business you'll get criticized plenty. You might as well welcome it. If it's someone you trust, that person can hold you accountable for your mistakes, watch your progress, and help you stay focused.

You should find someone you are not afraid to let see your weaknesses, someone you can comfortably ask questions. Choose someone you trust, whose example you can follow. Pick someone who makes you want to try new things, behave differently, and strive for perfection.

A mentor should ultimately be like a mirror, showing you your real self, flaws and all, because it's only when you see the flaws that you will be able to fix them.

What if You Can't Find a Mentor?

If the people you work with are not meeting your standards for a good mentor, what are you going to do? You can't hire yourself a mentor.

But wait! Yes, you can! Many professional organizations have mentoring programs you can apply for.

Women Chefs and Restaurateurs (WCR) has an e-mentoring program, in which they pair you with a successful professional in a cyber-relationship. Other organizations pair cooks and bakers with mentors. Look into the organizations that interest you, and see what mentoring programs they have to offer.

If you have trouble finding a person who inspires you, why not go back in time? Why did you get into the business in the first place? Was there someone you liked to watch on television, a cookbook author, or a columnist? Start there. Read or watch all this person has to offer. Until you've got a living mentor in the flesh, this is better than nothing.

What Happens When They Let You Down?

People disappoint. It's part of life. One of the best cooks I ever knew turned out to be less honorable than I had originally thought. He was an excellent cook, and we were friends, but I didn't really want to emulate him. So I got his Caesar salad dressing recipe and cut him loose. You take what you can get.

From everyone you meet and every place you work, you'll learn something useful. Sometimes the thing you learn is how not to run a business, or how a professional should not behave. It's still good knowledge to have. I guess that's called negative mentoring.

Are You a Mentor?

Being a mentor takes time and energy, and not many people are up to the task. In the restaurant business, especially, there is little time for nurturing and hand-holding. The people who can do it are lucky. The rewards are great. Like being a teacher, mentoring not only allows you to shape someone else but helps you shape yourself as well.

The Least You Need to Know

- Everyone you meet could be a potential mentor.
- Mentors can help with the technical, physical, emotional, and business aspects of your career.
- Mentors should help you become a better chef and a better person.
- Although it takes time and energy, mentoring is a rewarding activity.

Chapter 16

Staying Healthy

In This Chapter

◆ Watching the food you eat, exercising regularly, and understanding basic nutrition

◆ Calculating the amount of food and exercise you need to stay healthy

◆ Understanding how alcohol, drugs, and tobacco affect your success

◆ Avoiding injury

Staying healthy and fit is not just a good idea. It is the best way to become successful. Your career simply won't be as strong or last as long if you don't take care of yourself.

All You Can Eat

No one trusts a skinny chef? It's a cute phrase. But it was probably perpetuated to make overweight chefs feel okay about themselves. The first impression you present to people goes a long way in determining your overall success. Right or wrong, overweight people simply don't make that great of a first impression. The skinny ones are the stars and often are taken more seriously, at least initially.

I don't remember when it became okay to be fat, but All-You-Can-Eat America has a serious obesity problem.

The fault can be placed firmly in the hands of the food industry. When did it become acceptable to eat three huge meals every day? When did it become a nightly habit to order cocktails, appetizers, and dessert in addition to dinner? Our waistlines are increasing in direct proportion to the food industry's growing bottom line.

America consumes more food outside of the home than ever before. According to the Nation Restaurant Association, Americans hand over $1,400,000,000 (yes, that is $1.4 *billion*) each *day* to the restaurant industry. The average American spends about $1,000 a year eating out. And dining out is not just for special occasions anymore. We do it because we are too tired, too lazy, or too busy to cook and eat at home. This is excellent news for us as food service employees because it means we have no shortage of jobs. But for the health of our nation, it's bad news indeed.

We eat when it's mealtime, not when we are hungry. We eat to keep our hands busy during movies and while watching television. We feed our kids to keep them quiet.

Classic Cuisine

Breakfast? Brunch? Lunch? Dinner? Supper?

What's in a name? Breakfast is literally breaking the fast from the night before. The word *brunch* is an obvious blend of *breakfast* and *lunch*. Its origins seem to come from the affluent world of England in the late 1800s. Lunch is short for luncheon, which is a formal English meal in the middle of the day. Lunch replaced dinner, which was historically the main meal of the day, taken midday. Dinner has since replaced supper, which always referred to the evening meal, but was usually nothing but a light snack.

Besides eating out more, the portions we consume when we're dining out are much larger than our bodies need. Usually, when people eat at home, they don't start with bread, an appetizer, soup or salad, then partake of an entrée with vegetables and a starch, and top it all off with dessert. But in restaurants we do.

As a restaurant worker, you'll need to exhibit a little self-control because it's just as easy to overeat in the kitchen. When food is all around you, you're hungry, and you're busy, it's easy to snack on a handful of whatever *mise en place* is lying around. It's all there, it's already prepared, and it's free. Lunch can easily turn into an all-day graze with a piece of cheese from the walk-in, a handful of candied nuts from the dessert station, a cup of soup, or an impromptu sandwich. And it's easy to forget that you're really eating because you're not using the traditional method of sitting down at a table with utensils.

In terms of health, food service is a dangerous line of work. But the more you know about nutrition and what it takes to stay healthy, the less this lifestyle will impact your body.

> **Kitchen Tales** _____
>
> When I was 15, I got my very first job at Swenson's Ice Cream Parlor in Mountain View, California. Right next to Tower Records, it was paradise. I was surrounded by buckets and buckets of Sticky Chewy Chocolate, the best flavor in the world. When the manager would go into the back office, I and my fellow employees would grab a plastic spoon, dip out some ice cream, top it with a quick squirt from the hot fudge pump, a small dollop of whipped cream, nuts, a cherry, and voilà! A spoon sundae! After four or five of those a day, we were glad our uniforms had elastic waistbands. Amazingly, the spoon sundaes didn't get me fired. Nor did inhaling nitrous oxide from the empty whipped cream canisters. It was the free cone I gave to my best friend. Oh well. I made enough money to buy my first car, a 1974 olive-green VW Thing.

Nutrition

I know you want to be a chef, not a nutritionist. But it is important for you to have a basic understanding of how the body works with food. Not simply so you will be better informed about the food you eat and serve, but so that you will understand the latest dietary trends. The more you know, the better you can serve your public.

The Pyramid

When I was a kid, we were taught the Basic Four food groups. The graphic for this nutritional curriculum was a square divided into four equal quadrants. In each space was one of the four food groups: meat, bread, fruits and vegetables, and dairy. The problem with this model was, although they gave us the number of servings we should have, it looked like we were supposed to have an equal amount of each.

In 1980 the USDA stumbled upon the pyramid, a shape that revolutionized nutrition. The Food Pyramid and its accompanying curriculum were designed to show Americans the quantity of each food they should consume each day and what foods they should limit. In an attempt to improve the Pyramid, the USDA released the new and improved My Pyramid in 2005. When I use My Pyramid to teach children about healthy eating, I find they have trouble understanding it. The old one had more visual impact. It had easy-to-read sections for the food groups, which varied in size according to how much of the food group you should have per day.

Other than becoming more difficult to decipher, the pyramid has not changed much. Now, the serving sizes are measured in cups and ounces, not servings. Also, there is a new exercise component, which tells you how much you should exercise according to your age, gender, and size. (For adults and teens it's about 60 minutes a day.)

Kitchen Tales

I tell people to use the palm of their hand to estimate a serving size. Not the fingers, just the palm. A piece of meat should be no bigger than the person's palm. A pile of pasta, or rice, should be about that size, too. The piece of fruit they choose should be no bigger than their palm. Children's palms are smaller than an adult's, which means their serving size should be smaller, too. It's actually a very good approximation of a serving size.

The Food Groups

The base of the old pyramid was the biggest section, and even kids could tell it contained the food you're supposed to eat more of. Grains and Cereal is the category that includes rice, pasta, bread, and cereal. This does not mean, however, fried rice, mac 'n' cheese, bagels, and cocoa puffs. It means whole grains. Grains contain carbohydrates that fuel the body. But refined grains, especially white flour, contain little else in terms of nutrition. The energy they provide is used up instantly or stored for later (on your hips). By choosing whole-grain products, like whole-grain breads and brown rice, you incorporate the bran of the grain, which provides essential fiber and makes the body work harder to absorb it.

The recommended amount of grain products on the new pyramid is 3 to 10 ounces per day, depending on your recommended calorie intake. The old pyramid suggested 6 to 11 servings a day. It seems like a lot, but check the package to learn what a serving is. Usually a serving of bread is one slice or less, and for pasta, rice, or cereal, it's 1 cup or less.

The next most important food group is vegetables, with a recommended 1 to 4 cups a day on the new pyramid or 3 to 5 servings on the old one. Fruits, although categorized along with vegetables, contain more sugar, and therefore have smaller recommended servings, 1 to 2½ cups on the new pyramid or 2 to 4 servings on the old one.

Fruits lure you with their vitamins and pretty colors. But they are loaded with a lot more sugar than you need each day. (You should know better. Their luscious sweetness is a tip-off.)

The next food up the pyramid, with 2 to 3 cups or servings a day, is dairy. Dairy refers to any food—except dessert!—that is made from milk. It could be cow's milk or milk from another domesticated mammal, like goat, sheep, water buffalo, yak, or camel. (Open your mind. The world is a vast and mysterious place.) Milk, cheese, yogurt, and all their variations are sources of dairy. The fat content determines the calorie count. More fat, more calories.

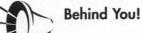 **Behind You!**

Fruit juice is a particularly nasty culprit when it comes to sugar. How many glasses of juice do you have a day, and what size glass do you use? One glass can be enough fruit for the day. Yes, juice has benefits, but not nearly as much as eating an actual apple, especially if the juice has added sugar. A whole piece of fruit is much better for you, with more fiber and less sugar.

Protein refers to meat (four-legged mammals, domesticated), poultry (two legs, feathers), fish (lives in water, with fins, shells, or tentacles), and game (traditionally hunted animals, like deer, boar, squirrels, and possums). Protein also comes from beans (although it's not *complete protein*), which come in the form of legumes (a seed inside a pod) or tofu (bean curd made from soybeans). Eggs are also in this group, even though they live in the dairy aisle. Two to seven ounces or 2 to 3 servings per day are all you need, but most people in America have way more.

def•i•ni•tion

Essential nutrients are those that you must eat, because your body doesn't make them. Amino acids are the building blocks of protein, and of the 20 our bodies need, 9 are essential. All protein that comes from animals are **complete proteins,** that is, they contains all 9 of the essential amino acids. Plants are incomplete, meaning they are missing at least one essential amino acid. They must therefore be combined with other foods that contain the missing amino acid in order to give the body its essential nutrients. Fortunately for us, ancient civilizations figured this out long ago and began combining rice and corn with beans to fill this gap.

The last group of food is junk food. This category includes the cookies, chips, ice cream, and sodas that we all eat every day. The pyramid says to limit these foods, but what they mean is the recommended amount for these foods is zero. The main ingredients in these foods are sugar, fat, and salt. These nutrients are vital for life. We need salt to help balance our electrolytes, sugar for fuel, and fat to insulate and cushion our organs. But we do not need them in the quantity we eat them. In fact, if you follow the pyramid and eat the recommended quantities of the recommended foods, you will get enough fat (in meat and dairy and processed grains) and salt (in meat and dairy and processed grains) and sugar (dairy, fruit, processed grains) naturally.

For the most part, Americans eat the pyramid upside down. The largest food group we consume is junk, followed by protein and diary. We eat more fruit than vegetables, and the grain products we eat are mainly made from refined white flour. In addition, the portions we serve are huge. Not only are we eating the wrong foods, but we are also eating too much of them.

We should be following the pyramid. And our diets should be more varied. It's healthier to eat lots of different choices from the different food groups than it is to eat the same thing day after day.

Calories

So now that you know what to eat, let's figure out how much you should eat every day, and what sort of portions you should be serving your clientele.

Kitchen Tales

It's smart to offer low-calorie options on your menu. Even with dessert, I found that a light, fat-free, or lower-calorie sorbet, fruit plate, or angel food cake provided sales that I would have otherwise missed.

First, we need to cover some basic nutrition biology. Digestion is the process by which food is broken down into its components in the mouth, stomach, and small intestine, with the help of digestive enzymes. Before the body can use the nutrients in food, they must pass through the tissue of the walls of the stomach or intestines. Nutrients are absorbed either into the blood or lymph, two fluids that deliver nutrients to the cells throughout the body and pick up waste. This process is called *absorption*.

Metabolism, the chemical process by which your body uses nutrients, takes place within each cell. As the nutrients are metabolized, they are split into smaller units in a reaction that releases energy. This energy is either converted to heat to maintain body temperature or used to perform work within the cell. Metabolism has two functions, either building up substances (like building muscle) or breaking down substances (like burning fat).

Kitchen Tales _____

This is what food is made of and what it must be broken down into, in order for the body to absorb it:

- Complex proteins (meat, dairy) are built out of amino acids
- Complex sugars/carbohydrates are built from simple sugars, glucose, fructose, and galactose
- Fat is built out of fatty acids

Calories measure energy. They are determined by burning a weighed portion of food and measuring the amount of heat (or calories) it produces. The number of calories you need depends on your Basal Metabolic Rate (BMR), your level of physical activity, and the energy you need to digest, absorb, and metabolize food.

Kitchen Tales _____

You get this number of calories with each type of food you eat:

- Carbohydrates: 4 calories per gram
- Protein: 4 calories per gram
- Fat: 9 calories per gram (notice … over twice as much as carbs and protein)
- Alcohol: 7 calories per gram (no nutrients here, though)

Your BMR is the energy you need for vital body functions when you are awake and at rest, such as your heart pumping blood to all parts of your body. Your BMR will vary with things like gender, muscle mass, age, growth, height, and temperature due to fever or stress.

The following table shows how to determine your BMR.

Determining Your Basal Metabolic Rate (BMR)

BMR of Males = 66 + (6.21 × your weight in pounds) + (12.7 × your height in inches) – (6.8 × your age)

BMR of Females = 655 + (4.37 × your weight in pounds) + (2.32 × your height in inches) – (4.7 × your age)

To determine your daily caloric needs, multiply your BMR by the number that represents your activity level:

- **Sedentary** (little to no exercise): BMR × 1.2

- **Lightly Active** (light exercise 1–3 days a week): BMR × 1.375

- **Moderately Active** (moderate activity 3–5 days a week): BMR × 1.55

- **Very Active** (heavy exercise 6–7 days a week): BMR × 1.725

- **Extra Active** (like a professional athlete): BMR × 1.9

To calculate your ideal weight, first determine your frame size. A medium-framed man has a 7-inch wrist, and a medium-framed woman has a 6-inch wrist. Smaller measurements indicate a small frame, larger measurements indicate a large frame.

- **Females—Medium Frame**

  Give yourself 100 pounds for the first 5 feet of height

  Add 5 pounds for each inch over 5 feet

  Subtract 5 pounds for each inch under 5 feet

- **Males—Medium Frame**

  Give yourself 106 pounds for the first 5 feet of height

  Add 6 pounds for each inch over 5 feet

  Subtract 6 pounds for each inch under 5 feet

If you have a small frame, subtract 10 percent from the ideal weight; if you have a large frame, add 10 percent to the ideal weight

If your actual weight is higher than your ideal weight, your intake of calories must be lower than your daily caloric needs, and you must increase the burn of calories.

If your actual weight is lower than your ideal weight, your intake of calories must be higher than your daily caloric needs.

Just Say No to Drugs and Alcohol

The restaurant scene is a constant party. Festive food and alcoholic beverages are constantly pushed on customers. Drunken patrons are tolerated because they pay, and unless a patron is harmed or a business is sued, the problem is often ignored. When you work in such an atmosphere, it's tempting to join the party.

Classic Cuisine

Escoffier recognized the detrimental effect that alcohol had on kitchen workers. Quick tempers, shoddy skills, and poorly prepared cuisine led him to prohibit drinking in his kitchens. Instead, he made available on a daily basis a nonalcoholic beverage, developed by a doctor, to relieve the discomfort of his cooks. In order to preserve his palate, Escoffier never drank or smoked. He also prohibited vulgar language and beating the lackeys, which was common in the 1800s.

Alcohol, drugs, and even tobacco are all means of coping with the long hours and stress of a high-pressure industry. Employees new to the industry are especially drawn to the glamour of the business, and they often turn to alcohol or drugs as a stress-management tool. Many restaurants encourage this by offering their employees one free drink at the bar after every shift, lovingly referred to as the *shift drink*. Of course, employers know that one free drink will often turn into two or three for which the employee pays.

If you are already working in a restaurant, none of this is news. You know which co-workers hang out at the bar every night. You know which ones are working high and which ones show up to work hung-over. You can see the effect it has in their quick tempers and loss of mental clarity. You see a loss of energy, a sudden drop in morale, or an increase in tardiness or absenteeism.

The effect this has on the industry is catastrophic. It is the root of workplace violence, theft, property damage, fraud, illness, absenteeism, accidents, errors, and low morale. Drug and alcohol abuse creates loss of profit through low productivity, poor customer satisfaction, and high employee turnover, as well as increased insurance and workman's compensation claims.

The solution to this problem is a drug-free workplace. A zero-tolerance policy is common among many corporate-owned operations and is gaining popularity throughout the independent houses as well. The benefit is twofold. First, the policy and practice of drug testing immediately weeds out any job candidates who are users and discourages

Kitchen Tales

Making your restaurant's drug-free policy public knowledge can improve its public image, and the business may receive a reduction in their health insurance benefits as well.

those that may become users. This provides the employer with a labor force of more dedicated professionals. Additionally, the policy increases job safety, efficiency, and productivity. A healthier workforce, both physically and mentally, increases morale, which in turn improves creativity and ultimately customer satisfaction.

Smoking

The restaurant industry is one of the last places where cigarette smoking is not completely shunned. Oh sure, in the dining room it's off limits, but out in the alley by the dumpster, smoke 'em if ya got 'em. Why is it still acceptable to smoke in this business? I could say it's traditional. I could say its European-y. But I think the biggest reason is that it's a five-minute stress reliever, which is about all the time you're going to have free on a busy Saturday night.

The other reason people smoke, of course, is that they think it's cool. Don't let the surgeon general convince you otherwise. Despite what he and your parents said, the cool kids smoked. Sure, they all have cancer now. But let's take a survey. Who's cooler? George Harrison (avid smoker) or Boyz II Men (avid nonsmokers)? I hope you said George. Of course, he died of lung cancer, so the cool factor isn't all its cracked up to be.

The very best argument against smoking for culinary workers is the effect it has on the palate. Smoking actually deadens your taste buds. If there's one part of the body a chef needs, it's the taste buds. Foods that taste good to a smoker don't necessarily taste good to a nonsmoker, and vice versa. The good news is that once a smoker quits and the body has time to heal, the buds start functioning at peak performance again.

Take a Lap

Exercise is the ideal way to cope with the stress of a high-pressure job. But it's difficult to convince people of this fact because we are a sedentary lot. We sit most of the time—in front of our televisions, at our computers, in our cars, in class, and at work. We're even too lazy to get out of our cars for our Happy Meals. What's worse, if you work in the restaurant industry, you are only contributing to the problem. (Unless you work at a health spa.)

Cooks with no regular exercise routine gain weight at work. It's a fact. Even if you're a licensed nutritionist, if you don't exercise, you will become overweight.

> **Classic Cuisine**
>
> Americans love eating, and hate exercising. Sometime after World War II, food stopped being merely sustenance and became entertainment. Around that same time, people stopped working the land for a living and moved into suburbs in record numbers. Pushing a plow burns a lot more calories than pushing a pencil. Kids who grew up with rationing during WWI and WWII didn't want their children to know what it was to be hungry. "Eat your peas! There are kids starving in China!" The wars brought convenience foods into the home, and we combined Swanson's iconic TV dinner with television in 1954. We made couch potato history.

Working in a restaurant can be deceiving. You feel like you're exercising all the time. You're on your feet, and you're exhausted, but you're hardly burning any calories. You need real aerobic exercise every day.

I have found that the key to regular exercise is finding something that you enjoy: a sport, a routine, or a group of friends that will keep you going back, day after day. Regular exercise needs to become something you'll miss if you skip a day. You may have to force yourself at first, but sooner or later, you'll come to enjoy it. It can happen. Trust me.

Avoid Injury

I don't think I ever met a chef who didn't have a standing appointment with a chiropractor. Back injuries have many causes, including sudden lifting and twisting, poor posture, stress, and simply being out of shape.

In a kitchen, you'll be doing a tremendous amount of lifting, so it's important to do it properly. Before you pick anything up, know where you're going to put it. Bend at your knees, and get a firm grip. Place your feet next to whatever it is you're lifting, center your weight above the load, and lift up with your legs. Don't make any sudden twists with your back or waist. Turn with your feet, and make your way slowly to your destination, and put the load down in the same manner in which you lifted it. Bend your knees and slowly lower it without bending over at the waist.

Long hours on your feet demand common sense and good shoes. Even without lifting trauma, your back will get sore from simply standing a lot. Regularly exercising your back will alleviate much of this problem. Sit-ups work for me.

The Least You Need to Know

- ◆ Watch what you eat, and exercise regularly.

- ◆ Follow basic nutrition guidelines.

- ◆ Avoid tobacco, drugs, and excess alcohol.

- ◆ Prevent back injury with good posture, quality shoes, and proper lifting techniques.

Honing Your Skills

In This Chapter

- ◆ Getting a second job
- ◆ Practicing your skills at home
- ◆ Catering on the side
- ◆ Volunteering your way to success

So you have a job, and it's going well. You have the routine down pat, and you are getting really good at peeling a case of apples in less than 15 minutes. You are proud. But, as much as you hate to admit it, you're getting a little bored. No wonder. Peeling apples is boring. (You can't say I didn't warn you.)

This is the point at which many culinary careers derail. The expectation doesn't match the reality. Hang in there. If you can work through this boredom, you'll find the light at the end of the tunnel soon enough.

You may find yourself eyeing someone else's job across the kitchen. Now, watch out! It may seem easy enough, and you could probably do it with no problem. But keep it to yourself! There is no reason you should even try climbing that ladder until you've done what you're doing now for at least three months past your probationary period (preferably six). Your boss is not going to appreciate having to re-hire for your position so soon after hiring you, and he won't care that you're bored. Didn't you tell him during your interview that you would stick it out when the going got tough? That means now. You're bored? So what?

You need to find a way to keep your hands and mind busy when you're not at work. You need to continue to learn and grow. You need to keep up the skills you're not using and develop new ones. Most importantly, you need to stay sane. A number of ways can help you do this.

Get a Second Job

If you have the time, there is no reason why you shouldn't work as much as you can. If you've got the energy, and you really want to be a successful chef, moonlighting is the way to go.

Don't be afraid to work more than one job. When you become a chef in charge of your own staff and menu, you'll be working 14 hours a day anyway. So why not start increasing your stamina now? Did you work during school? Working two jobs will be almost the same, but better, because you won't have homework.

Where to Look

Ask around. Does anyone on the kitchen or dining room staff have a second job? You might be surprised to find out what a common practice it is, especially among the minimum wage earners. (When you make minimum wage, the only way to survive is to make a lot of it.) Find out if they like working a second job. Learn how the other job compares to this one. Do they find that their effort is paying off? If so, ask if they can get you an interview. (By the way, this is an excellent example of why it is important to be nice to everyone you work with.)

Do you have friends at other restaurants? If they are cooking at the same level as you, chances are they are also getting bored. Call them up and ask if they need help in their kitchen. Is their boss hiring? Tell them you have some free time and would like to learn a little more. Perhaps you could help them out in exchange and get them part-time positions at your place of work.

Why Bother?

Working two jobs pays off for several reasons. First is the toughness factor. Never underestimate the value of being tough. You earn respect when you're tough.

But the only way to be tough is by doing, not saying. So get that second job, but shut up about it. Quietly build your stamina, with your nose to the grindstone. Don't mistake bragging for toughness. If you do, you'll build arrogance, not stamina.

Working two jobs will expose you to new ideas, new foods, and new ways of doing things. Every job in the kitchen can be done more than one way. Don't get trapped in a "my way or the highway" frame of mind. If you're not willing to bend a little, getting along with other cooks will be very difficult. You need to go with the flow. No one cares how you were taught to do a particular task. You must keep an open mind and accept suggestions. The best employees are flexible and know how to adjust. It's a skill you will learn by working for multiple employers.

On the other hand, it is entirely conceivable that you could bring some new ideas to the folks at your new job. You not only might have an opportunity to hone your technical skills but your people skills as well. And it's another prime opportunity for you to expand your circle of contacts. Even if you are a part-time employee, you still have an entire staff to meet and impress with your charm and intellect. Never stop building your network.

You may find that you like one job more than the other, but always remember the commitments you make to your bosses. You don't want to burn any bridges. If you play it wrong, you could end up with zero jobs and a bad reputation. If you play it right, you can double your network, your income, and your chances for career advancement.

Behind You!

Always give that second job as much attention as the first. Remember that your goal is to become a successful chef, not to develop a bad reputation. Don't commit if you don't think you can hack it. And don't let the second job cause you to slack off on the first job. Don't be late, and don't use one job as an excuse when you screw up in the other.

Entertaining

In Chapter 7, I encouraged you to hone your skills by cooking at home, and this is something you should continue to do. Now, however, while you are working, you may have less time and energy for it. You're probably eating at work and are not at home much for the traditional meal times. This is when entertaining can help keep you on your culinary toes. Why not throw a party once in a while?

Entertaining is a great way to practice organization and cooking in quantity. It's also a terrific way to flex your creative muscle. If being a chef is your ultimate goal, you'll need to start creating menus sooner or later. Why not start on your own turf, for people you know and like? These endeavors are not career threatening and can be tons of fun.

You could look to any number of books for inspiration. (See my recommendations in Chapter 8 and Appendix A.) I enjoy reading through books to see what people are doing. I rarely follow the recipes, but I do get ideas for presentations, flavor combinations, and themes. Also for inspiration I turn to my menu collection, which consists of menus from nearly every place I have ever eaten. I take what I see other people do, mix it up with what I like, and come up with something of my own.

Kitchen Tales

You could start a culinary club as I did in high school. I called it the Gourmet Din Din Club. We each took turns cooking food with a different theme. We started out pretty generic, with regional cuisines like French and Chinese. But we quickly degraded into goofy themes, like food from the movie *Grease* or food mentioned in songs of the B-52's.

Birthdays, anniversaries, and the holidays are obvious reasons to throw parties. Unfortunately, you'll probably be working on those popular holidays. So why not invite people over to celebrate the more obscure holidays? You could research some regional Italian dishes for Columbus Day. Or have a Presidents Day bash, and serve foods that represent former leaders of the free world, like George Bush Sr.'s *Eat Your Broccoli Gratin*, George Washington's *I cannot tell a Lie Cherry Pie*, or Richard Nixon's *Watergate Spritzers* (served in dribble glasses, so they leak).

Catering

It's entirely possible that you have already been asked to do some catering. If you haven't, stepping out on your own and catering is an easy gig to start on the side. First, tell everyone you know that your services are available. You could make flyers or business cards, but I wouldn't invest too much in advertising. Remember, this is meant to be a part-time job to hone your skills. If more people want to hire you than you can handle, you'll either jeopardize your real job or disappoint catering clients. It's bad either way.

Begin by creating some sample menus. Your clients will probably have an idea of what they want already, but a sample menu shows what you are capable of serving. A typical catering menu should offer a couple of sit-down meal options of 3 to 5 courses (meat, fish, vegetarian), a couple of buffet menus, and a couple of menus of passed hors d'ouevres. If cakes are your specialty, offer several flavors and decorating styles.

Compile a portfolio of your menus, and include photographs of the food you have prepared. If you haven't made these dishes yet, make them and then take some pictures of them.

Don't offer something tricky, like a *croquembouche*, if you haven't made it before. The disaster quotient is high when you try complicated new recipes. Even for the simpler things, be sure the techniques are familiar, the ingredients are readily available, and you have the necessary equipment. Trying something new for a client without testing it would be like getting your hair cut on the day of your prom. If it's bad, it's too late to fix it, and you're just going to look like an idiot.

def•i•ni•tion

The **croquembouche** is a classical French wedding pastry, made by stacking pastry cream-filled pâte a choux puffs (a.k.a. cream puffs) into a pyramid, gluing them together with hot caramelized sugar. The entire pastry is then wrapped in golden spun sugar. It is traditionally served on a pedestal of *croquant*, which is a candy made of molten caramel and sliced almonds, rolled out and shaped quickly, before it hardens.

It's not too hard to find space to work in for occasional catering jobs. Start at work, and ask the owners if they will let you use the space in the off hours. I had a friend once who stayed after the dinner shift ended and used the equipment to produce his gourmet dog biscuits. Many local facilities, including churches, schools, and community centers, are happy to put their space to use, sometimes for a small fee, sometimes for free.

If you aren't ready to start your own sideline, remember that busy caterers always need temporary help. Lending a hand would enable you to meet new people, learn new foods and techniques, and discover new philosophies of food.

Volunteering

Hey, guess what? No matter how raw your skills are, people out there need them. So get out there and help. In every community a number of soup kitchens serve meals to the hungry. (It's not just soup anymore!) Help out a couple of days a week. You'll not only serve your community, boost your skills, and expose yourself to new operating systems, but you'll be adding to your pile of good karma.

One thing about the food business is that there is a lot of waste. That fact really hits home when you find that people in your own town are hungry. One of our local soup kitchens has two guys who make daily rounds to restaurants and grocery stores picking up useable leftovers. It's a great way to get to know everyone in town. Talk about networking!

Look in the phone book or on the Internet under *charitable organizations*, *food banks*, *missions*, or *shelters*. Call them and ask if they need you and your skills. The answer will be yes. Don't wait for the holidays when shelters put out open calls for help. They need help all year long.

You can also find volunteer opportunities through professional culinary organizations. Nearly every professional group has a cause they champion. For example, the American Culinary Federation (ACF) has the Chef & Child Foundation. Their focus is to remind us that childhood hunger and malnutrition exists here in America. The ACF combats this problem, caused both by ignorance and poverty, by entering classrooms and teaching healthy eating and by donating resources to local food banks.

Local school districts often host nutritional programs that are in need of trained chefs. In California, we have the USDA-sponsored Nutrition Network, in which chefs travel from school to school teaching kids about healthy eating. It's a great program and is always in need of assistance. The kids are always surprised to learn that french fries are not a vegetable.

You have no time to work a real shift in a shelter or school? Then bake something and bring it to a food bank, convalescent home, senior center, or children's home. They will be glad to get it, and you can use it as an excuse to try out new recipes. Everyone wins!

Kitchen Tales _____

My local soup kitchen asks everyone they know for help during the holidays. Not just to serve food, but to cook it, too. When I worked at a place with a bunch of ovens, we would cook dozens of their donated frozen turkeys because the shelter kitchen had no capacity to handle such quantities. Nothing is more humbling than delivering Thanksgiving turkeys to an eight-acre park overflowing with hungry people.

The Least You Need to Know

- ◆ A second job can increase your skills, your network, and your income.

- ◆ Cooking for friends is a great way to get creative.

- ◆ Catering not only keeps your skills sharp, but it's also a great way to learn menu development.

- ◆ Volunteering your skills to those who really need it benefits you, those in need, and your community.

Chapter 18

Keeping Up with the Joneses

In This Chapter

- ◆ Reading trends
- ◆ Staying current
- ◆ Using professional organizations
- ◆ Putting yourself in the public eye

With all your responsibilities as a chef, you might not be able to imagine how on earth you can afford to spend time dilly-dallying over books and clubs and eating out. Well, at the risk of sounding hokey, you can't afford *not* to.

If you plan on making a success of this career, you'd better know what's going on around you. You need to get out of that kitchen and see what's happening.

If your employer is smart, he'll finance your foray into the wild. You need to know what the competition is doing in order to stay competitive. Not every owner sees this, though. If he doesn't pay for it, go out anyway. You can deduct it as a professional expense—just remember to keep your receipts.

The Latest Trend

Trying to be the hot new restaurant is a recipe for a short-lived business enterprise. That's not what you should be striving toward. You want staying power. You should try to set the trend, not follow it.

To stay current and popular, make room for new ideas and experiments, but still keep your base happy. You need to provide the comforting options that your regulars return for night after night. If you change your menu too much, they'll stop coming.

Trends in food come and go. Some die out because of health reasons, some because of politics or fashion. Nouvelle cuisine is a good example. This was a food trend that came of age in the 1970s. It was a direct response to the over-the-top, rich and fatty French haute cuisine that was served at high-end restaurants. Tiny portions and exotic ingredients were the hallmarks of nouvelle cuisine, and these miniature presentations became a classic joke. But in response to that, a movement began called cuisine minceur or the cuisine of thinness. The great Michel Guérard created cuisine minceur, taking the best of haute and nouvelle cuisines and turning it into French food that was good and satisfying again. Across the Atlantic, chefs in New York and California were taking note, and up sprang spa and California cuisines, with light, fresh ingredients, sauces made from *reduction* rather than roux, and close attention paid to the regionalism and seasonality of ingredients. As a result of these trends, we, as a country, eat less fried foods, less fatty foods, more vegetables, more salads, and more fish than ever before. The trend disappeared, but its legacy remained.

def•i•ni•tion

Reduction refers to cooking the water out of something, usually a liquid, like sauces, stocks, or soup. But you can reduce the water out of other foods, too, like mushrooms or spinach.

Some trends hit big, and then dwindle, leaving behind something that becomes a part of conventional gastronomy. *Cajun cuisine* is an example of this. In the early 1980s you could find a Cajun restaurant in every city in America. Paul Prudhomme was a superstar chef, and everyone wanted everything blackened. Today, not too many Cajun restaurants remain outside of Louisiana. But from time to time you see blackened something, dirty rice, or jambalaya on a menu. The same goes for *Southwestern cuisine*. At one time every restaurant in town had Indian Fry Bread, tamales, and some version of a dessert taco on its menu. Now, you still see the addition of a habenero chili in a sauce from time to time, but no full-blown trip to Santa Fe.

Kitchen Tales _____

A fellow chef once gave me some good advice regarding menu development. She told me to always have at least one item on my menu just for me. It may not sell, but you'll know it's there. The waiters and staff will know it, try it, like it, and try to sell it. It will keep you trying, stretching, and experimenting. I have had a lot of duds with that philosophy, but I have had a lot of successes, too.

Enjoy Life, Eat Out More Often

The best way to see what the competition is doing is to go there and eat. This seems obvious. But of course, you're working most of the time, especially during the dinner hour. You should make time for it, though. Go out to eat at least once a month, if not two or three times. When you do, be sure to pay attention to everything. Take notes. Is the food good? Why or why not? Is the service good? Why or why not? Can you decipher the flavors, cooking techniques, and ingredients? If not, ask.

When you first venture out into the unknown, pick a restaurant that is similar to yours. Look for similar cuisines or similar themes, similar size and capacity, and similar-size staff.

Make a reservation for a slower night so you can talk to the staff. If you don't know the chef, introduce yourself. Ask to come back into the kitchen and see the operation in action. How does it differ from your place? They may be the competition, but you can all be good sports about it. Who knows? You may even make a new friend!

When you're finished with all the places that are similar to yours, start on the ones that aren't. That new Thai place might spark some ideas. And haven't you been dying to see what all the fuss is about at that taco stand?

Reading

Working full-time doesn't leave you a lot of time for reading. But of course, you need to keep up-to-date with what is happening in your field. One way to stay current is to make a point of cruising the bookstores.

Bookstores make it very easy for you to stay current. The new books are always facing out, in plain view, so you can quickly see what interests you. Not only do bookstores make the books easy for you to find, but they also provide you with super comfy chairs to sit in and read. Lucky for me, most of the big stores serve coffee, too.

But my favorite area of the bookstore is not the chairs. It's the newsstand. (Don't they call it a stand because you can stand and read?) This is where you really see what's current. Most nice bookstores nowadays have an elaborate newsstand, where you can see not only the housewife magazines and foodie favorites, but also the good trade magazines and imports. My two favorites are *Waitrose Food*, a British Import, and *Pastry Art and Design*, which is the upscale cousin of *Chocolatier* magazine. I can hardly wait to go and stand at the stand each month.

And don't forget to check your local paper's food listings. Although they can be a bit predictable in their features, they list local class offerings, farmers' markets, and book signings. And you'll get a good sense of the local flavor.

Professional Organizations

I mentioned professional culinary organizations in Chapter 6, but I want to again encourage you to join one or two if you haven't already. As a student, these groups can help you develop into a professional. When you become a professional, they will keep you up-to-date on industry advancements, help with career moves, and provide opportunities to keep you on your toes.

Joining a professional organization doesn't mean you have to go to meetings or hang out with the tall hats (unless you want to). But they offer benefits that are otherwise hard to come by. Membership typically gets you a monthly or quarterly magazine or newsletter, access and discounts to classes, and discounts to trade shows. Many of them have a headquarters where you can go to study or dine or cook. Most of the websites have *members only* areas, which provide business assistance, industry contacts, and a chance to rub elbows with the elite of the culinary world. They also offer a chance to help others, through educational or mentoring programs and food-related charitable projects. Through these organizations, you can establish yourself on a wider landscape.

Competitions

You've probably seen competitive cooking events as you were flipping past the Food Channel. *Iron Chef* is a game-show version of them.

I love competing. I hardly ever win, but that's not why I do it. I compete to meet people and learn things. I've met an entire network of people through these events, and through them I have made more and more contacts. It's really true. The network works!

You don't have to be a sugar-pulling artist to compete. (Unless, of course, you enter a sugar-pulling competition.) Very many food contests are out there. Practically every company that produces a food product sponsors something. They sponsor these contests to get chefs to use their products, and through them, the customers.

I have entered recipes in contests sponsored by dried fruit and nut companies, the pork council, the egg board, and all sorts of small, privately owned food manufacturers, distilleries, and vineyards. Liquor companies are always sponsoring competitions for recipes using their product, as well as recipes to pair with it.

The competitions can be on paper, in person, or both. You first submit your recipe, and if it makes the final cut, you get to show up and make it. When you get there, not only do you get to see what everyone else has done, but they also see you, your name, and your restaurant. You're in the public eye, among people who appreciate food. These events are a fun way to market yourself and your business. It's a win–win situation, even if you lose!

If you want to go hard-core, there are serious competitions. Culinary teams form through different organizations, including the American Culinary Federation, and competition is fierce.

When I became a certified master baker, I joined the Bread Baker Guild of America (BBGA). Every three years they sponsor and send a team from the United States to the World Cup of Baking (Coupe du Monde de la Boulangerie). One of my former instructors was on the winning team in 1999, and I really wanted to try out the next time around. I talked to a baker from BBGA, and he suggested that I apply for the artistic design category, because few bakers do and my chances of competing would be better. I guess it was a little like playing the tuba. Even if you're not very good, you can probably get a scholarship. I didn't even have to compete in the regional competition because I was the only one to apply. When I got to the finals, I was blown away by my competition. They were so far out of my league, it was embarrassing, especially because my former instructor was there, watching. But I chugged through, and lost, big time. But that didn't matter. I met some great people that I still keep in touch with. They went on to compete in France and brought home second place that year.

Trade Shows

Also trade shows are fun because you get a bunch of free stuff. You don't always have to be a member of the sponsoring organization to go, but usually it's cheaper if you are.

Every company that has anything to do with food has a booth at these shows. Everyone with a product is hawking it and usually giving away samples. You can find the latest in tools, equipment, and gadgetry. There are ingredients and ready-made foods. People are demonstrating and serving the latest trend in food that you just have to put on your menu! You'll find food-related gift items, packaging products, marketing ideas, franchising opportunities, and business assistance.

And talk about networking! Through trade shows I have gotten job offers, literary contacts, equipment deals, and a thousand free plastic scrapers. When you go, wear comfortable shoes, and carry a bottle of water. It's like a marathon.

The Least You Need to Know

- ◆ Eat out more often to see what your competition is up to.

- ◆ Read the latest food publications.

- ◆ Join professional organizations to keep you up-to-date and assist in your career growth.

- ◆ Attend trade shows to compete, network, and keep current.

Culinary Careers

In This Chapter

◆ Finding a culinary career

◆ Classic culinary job descriptions

◆ Alternatives to cooking

Do you know what you want to be when you grow up? After reading this list, you may change your mind. There are traditional cooking jobs, and there are those that are off the beaten path. Although you probably didn't pick up this book to learn what careers are available besides cheffing, I include some options that you might not have considered. Many interesting jobs require culinary knowledge besides cooking. Even if you're not interested in anything but becoming a chef right now, you may change your mind down the road.

The salary figures listed in this chapter are based on a nationwide mean, taken between 2004 and 2006 from surveys of industry professionals, current job listings, and the United States Bureau of Labor Statistics. Actual salaries vary with experience, establishment, and location. Top earning areas in the country are New York City, Los Angeles, San Francisco, and Las Vegas.

Job Descriptions

The names have been changed to protect the innocent—or confuse the masses. I have listed the types of culinary jobs most of you are looking for, and as you will see, many of them go by a variety of names. It all depends on the type of employer. Don't get hung up on the name, because the responsibilities are what matter. You'll find, I'm sure, that even with this comprehensive list, you'll run across a job posting somewhere for *chef* that will require completely different duties. Don't forget that one of the most important skills a chef can have is flexibility.

Corporate Executive Chef, Regional Executive Chef, Executive Chef, Chef de Cuisine, Chef

Average salary: $75,500

Generally thought to be the Big Boss, these high-level chefs may or may not actually work with food. They usually oversee production of a large facility, such as a hotel or hotel chain, restaurant group or chain, cruise line, amusement park, or institutional facility, like a hospital. Responsibilities may include menu development, planning and pricing, food preparation, quality control, purchasing and cost control, supervision, teaching and developing staff, monitoring safety and sanitation standards, and coordination with other departments.

Executive Sous Chef, Senior Sous Chef, Sous Chef, Kitchen Manager

Average salary: $39,000 to $52,000

This position supports and assists the executive chef or general manager in any and all areas, including training, scheduling, motivation, and supervision of staff, conflict management, purchasing, menu development, and menu specifications. This employee will stand in for the executive chef when necessary.

Chef de Partie, Line Cook, Culinary Supervisor, Line Manager, Shift Manager, Cook 1

Average salary: $29,000

This position carries similar responsibilities to the executive sous chef, and in some cases it is the same job. But generally the scope of responsibility will be narrowed to a smaller group of workers, a specific shift, or a department.

General Manager (GM), Food and Beverage (F&B) Director, Food and Beverage Manager

Average salary: $54,000

This person is an overall boss who oversees both the *front of the house (FOH)* and the *back of the house (BOH)*. The GM oversees all operations, including planning, budgeting, ordering, purchasing, receiving, checking inventory, dealing with cost containment, staff hiring, training, motivating, supervising, and scheduling. Some of these tasks may be delegated to lower-level management, such as dining room manager and kitchen manager. You'll find these job titles and organizational systems in larger restaurant groups, where consistency from store to store is vital to the overall success of the operation.

def•i•ni•tion

Front of the house is the dining room, and **back of the house** is the kitchen. Each has its own staff and procedures.

Restaurant Manager, Dining Room Manager, Hospitality Supervisor, Maitre d'hotel

Average salary: $49,000

Dining room managers carry the same responsibilities as chef or kitchen managers, but in the front of the house, where they deal with wait staff, bus staff, and bar staff. Often the job includes purchasing and receiving liquor, as well as supervising the maintenance of furniture, fixtures, and tableware. A dining room manager may also be responsible for the bank, which means balancing the receipts and register at the end of each shift.

Executive Pastry Chef, Pastry Chef, Pâtissier, Baker, Pastry Cook, Dessert Chef

Average salary: $50,000

The title varies, but the general job description is making desserts. The executive pastry chef may oversee several stores. The pastry chef may manage a staff or work solo. The title of baker usually refers to

Kitchen Tales

Women staff over 70 percent of the pastry chef jobs nationwide. The only other area where women's presence is felt more in this industry is in the dining room.

bread maker, but not universally. A pastry cook is typically someone who works under the pastry chef.

Specialty Jobs

A few culinary positions are less common and, because they are so specialized, can demand big bucks.

Banquet Chef, Catering Chef

Average salary: $40,000

This position often mirrors that of the chef or executive chef in terms of managerial duties. A banquet chef is often responsible for hiring, training, motivating, and supervising a large staff as well as menu planning, purchasing, and dealing with inventory and cost control. The main difference is volume. While the chef of a typical restaurant may turn out 25 to 50 plates of each dish on the menu, a banquet or catering chef must produce identical appetizers, entrées, and desserts at an event, with each course being served simultaneously. The volume will vary depending on the operation, but some catered events serve thousands. The logistics of operating procedures, food preparation, and *plating* at that volume are completely different from those of a typical restaurant.

def•i•ni•tion

Plating is the restaurant industry's term for putting food onto plates.

Garde Manger

Average salary: $49,000

This position is typically found in the larger venues, like hotels and cruise lines, that feature large buffet presentations. The garde manger is charged with managing the cold kitchen, which produces salads, hors d'oeuvres, cheese, charcuterie, and crudités platters. The focus is on artistic buffet design. If you really want to make the big bucks as a garde manger chef, learn ice carving.

Butcher

Average salary: $29,000

Butchery is something most chefs do for themselves, unless the operation is huge. In those cases, it is less expensive to buy larger pieces of meat and fabricate them (break them down into specific cuts and portions) in-house. Often, the butcher will also be responsible for some charcuterie, including smoked and cured meats like sausages and salamis.

Sushi Chef

Average salary: $23,000

Sushi is a highly specialized field, but one that has gained popularity in the last decade. Training, while often covered briefly in culinary schools, should ideally come from a sushi master chef. Several schools in the United States offer sushi programs (see Appendix A).

Education

Average salary: $52,000

Not all culinary instructors are disgruntled former chefs. Some actually have the future of the craft in mind as they turn their attention from the restaurant to the classroom.

Culinary schools are booming right now, and they are all in need of qualified, quality teachers. They don't all require teaching credentials, or even culinary credentials, but that helps. You should possess good public speaking skills and an honest desire to perpetuate the craft. It also helps if you are willing to follow someone else's recipes and curriculum.

Kitchen Tales

You can teach in many places besides culinary schools. Many community colleges offer culinary programs. Some require a teaching credential, but for some, a culinary degree of any kind will suffice. High school home economics is becoming a thing of the past, but similar programs here and there still need qualified teachers. As a summer school elective option, school districts often offer cooking, which is usually the first class to fill up.

Community education programs are a great place to begin teaching. Contact your local parks and recreation department and those in neighboring cities. They may be interested in offering cooking classes.

Cookware and specialty food stores frequently offer recreational cooking classes and demonstrations. Appliance and cookware manufacturers, as well as specialty food companies, hire chefs to demonstrate their products in department stores, markets, and at food shows.

You can also market yourself to the party-going crowd. Cooking classes are gaining popularity as a party theme. Kids cooking parties, couples cooking parties, and serious cooking lessons—taught in the comfort of your own home—are all the rage. Also a trend in company team-building uses the kitchen environment to bring a staff together. To break into this market, try marketing yourself with company event planners, at after-school care centers, and at specialty food stores.

Research and Development

Average salary: $65,000

Every packaged food you buy in every store went through the research and development process. Large research and development companies often work for several companies, developing products for outside manufacturing. Also research and development departments work within larger food companies. Large food companies, such as Pillsbury or Kellogg, fast-food chains, ice cream companies, coffee bars, and chain restaurants all employ food research teams to keep themselves on the cutting edge of food trends.

Small-scale research and development companies tend to concentrate on a particular type of food product, like bakery items, condiments, frozen dinners, or health foods. Some have a manufacturing facility on site, and some contract the manufacturing out.

Chefs in these operations spend time researching and perfecting ideas for new products. They travel the globe, attending industry events and food shows, checking out what's new. They play around with ingredients to achieve the right flavor, texture, appearance, and shelf life. The chef is just one cog in the machine that is R&D. There are specialists in science, sanitation, safety, quality assurance, supply, management, buying, marketing, accounting, and customer service, to name just a few. It's an interesting field for food lovers.

Manufacturing

Average salary: $55,000

Food manufacturers pick up where the R&D people leave off. Also known as food technologists, these folks create the products from the raw materials on a massive scale. It's a great field if you are interested in the latest technologies. The focus is on quality and consistency. Jobs in manufacturing run the gamut and include positions such as management of operations, production, development, business, marketing, and sales.

Food Stylist

Average salary: $300 to $800 per day

Food styling has very little to do with eating, a little to do with cooking, and a lot to do with art, design, magic, and patience. The food in pictures you see in print media is rarely edible. That's because it is fingered, manipulated, arranged, and scrutinized for hours under hot lights.

To break into this business, you need to have good-quality photos of your work. Connections don't hurt, either. Once you're in food styling, you'll find that it's the polar opposite of restaurant work. You'll trade in the fast-paced, stressed-out excitement of a kitchen for the hurry-up and wait all day of a photo shoot. If you enjoy sitting around reading magazines while photographers fiddle with your scoop of mashed potato ice cream, then this is the job for you.

> **Kitchen Tales**
>
> Every food stylist has his or her favorite fake ice cream recipe. It usually involves a fatty product and a floury product. This gives the illusion of creaminess, with the crumbly look ice cream gets when it's scooped. My favorite blend is cream cheese and flour. Depending on the product you're shooting, you'll want to play around with quantity, coloring, and mix-ins.

Food Purveyor

Average salary: $53,000

Every product needs a salesman. Companies that sell food products need people to represent them at trade shows, food expos, farmers' markets, and door-to-door. You can work for one product, join a manufacturing company that produces multiple wares, or join up with a large supplier.

These companies typically start their sales employees off with a salary and then gradually ease them into earning commission. If you are selling food products, you will get a lot further with chefs if you understand food and cooking. Plus, food purveyors know all the top chefs and get into all the best restaurants (of course, it's the back door you go through, but still, you're in!)

Specialty Merchandiser

Average salary: $25,000

This position is found in specialty food and grocery stores, health food stores, organic food markets, international markets, and gourmet shops. It involves product purchase, pricing, promotion, and inventory management. It's like any retail merchandising job, except it requires knowledge of food and the ability to gauge food trends. Responsibilities include deciding what foods will and won't sell, what to display and how to display it, what to feature, and what to sample-out. It may also involve, in addition to food products, cookware and appliances.

Nutritionist

Average salary: $44,000

Nutritionists plan food and supervise food programs to facilitate healthy lifestyles. This type of career can take several directions. A large-scale clinical career involves planning food programs for institutions like hospitals, schools, prisons, or elderly care facilities. Often the nutritionists work in conjunction with medical staff, coordinating medication and diet for optimum health.

Food manufacturers often employ nutritionists to analyze the contents of products or recipes. Health-conscious corporations hire nutritionists to plan their company cafeteria menus. Athletes use nutritionists to optimize their performance, and schools hire them to provide healthier options for their children. Home health agencies and public health clinics hire nutritionists to consult with patients. Nutritionists also open private practices, where they offer diet consultations to the general public. This field is experiencing rapid growth due to the aging population and its desire to prevent disease through improved dietary habits.

Most positions require, at the very minimum, a Bachelor's degree in nutrition, dietetics, food service systems, or something related (like culinary arts). Most states require a nutritionist to have some sort of licensing, certification, or registration.

The Least You Need to Know

◆ Job titles vary tremendously.

◆ Salaries vary with location, experience, and the operation itself.

◆ The more education you have, the more money you can demand.

◆ Lots of options are out there if you know where to look.

Part 6

Taking Charge

For many people, success means climbing the ladder into management. But management isn't for everyone. It takes training, understanding, and patience.

Understanding core management principles is a must if you plan on becoming a chef. By definition, the chef is the *chief* of the kitchen, a position of authority. But authority means nothing if the people working for you don't recognize it. As a boss, you need to set up a work environment that is supportive and motivating. Good employees are hard to find but even harder to keep.

Management means looking out for the employees, the product, and the customers. Everyone must be trained to maintain a healthy and safe environment—that means safe food handling as well as safe work habits. A good manager also knows how to prevent disasters and what to do if the prevention efforts fail.

Chapter 20

Moving Up the Ladder

In This Chapter

- ◆ Understanding what it means to be a manager
- ◆ Learning the key functions of a manager
- ◆ Avoiding the traits of a bad manager
- ◆ Motivating your employees

Why are some restaurants successful while others fail? Why do some have high employee turnover, while others have the same staff for 20 years? The answer is management.

Once you prove yourself as a valuable employee and demonstrate a little motivation, you're going to start climbing the ladder. Management means more salary, more responsibility, and more accountability. This chapter will help you decide if management is the direction you want to take.

Is Management Right for You?

To hourly workers, managers are the decision-makers. They determine the three most important parts of an hourly worker's job: schedules, shifts, and salaries.

A manager's job is to use the resources of his business to achieve the goals of that business, which seems pretty cut and dried. The manager needs to get things done by supporting the workers and helping them do the best job they possibly can. But while the basic purpose of the position is the same, a manager in the food service industry has a vastly different job than a typical office manager.

Restaurant management more closely resembles the triage unit of the 4077th MASH than it does the typical business model. During the slow times, a typical restaurant manager is continuously interrupted by salespeople, deliveries, inspectors, and people looking for jobs. During the busy time, everyone has needs, including the kitchen staff, the wait staff, the customers, and the owners. With 500 customers one night and 50 the next, a restaurant manager must be prepared for any circumstance. You must make major decisions in less than 20 seconds and adjust your actions accordingly.

Restaurant management is not like managing an office. It's like managing an office that's constantly on fire.

As you might imagine, management isn't for everyone. But if your goal is to become a chef or run your own restaurant, it is an unavoidable part of the process. Many terrifically talented cooks realize early on that management is harder than it looks and resign themselves to being content as cooks. The pressures of managing are simply too much for many otherwise perfectly capable chefs. Because of these conditions, good restaurant managers are hard to come by.

Managers are typically recruited from within. Promoted from the staff of cooks, they are first put in charge of their particular shift. Because the owners can pay these workers less than they would otherwise pay an experienced manager, they save in advertising, recruiting, and training fees as well.

Behind You!

Quality management requires a different set of skills than being a cook does. Most culinary workers have no management training and no management experience. The quality of their management, unfortunately, reflects this.

Of course, some people have plenty of management experience but just happen to be no good at it. They can't or don't handle the stress or responsibilities well but still insist on being a manager.

You don't want to fall into either of these categories. You need to figure out what management is, what it does, and what you need to know to do it well.

A Manager's Job Description

Just like everything in the hospitality industry, job descriptions vary from place to place. The kitchen manager in one restaurant may be responsible for purchasing, while the same position somewhere else may only require production oversight. You never know until you are there.

Generally, three levels of management exist. At the top is the executive level. This may include the owners, although often owners only have a financial stake and do not participate in actual management. For that, they hire an executive chef. In some places the owners and the executive chef work together, and in some places, the two are the same person.

A manager at the executive level has the ultimate job of ensuring the success of the establishment. Financial accountability, product quality, and employee performance all fall into the lap of the executive. One individual may try to balance it all, or other executive departments or mid-level managers may share this task. For instance, it is entirely possible that a chef of a small restaurant takes care of the payroll himself. He does the scheduling, collects the time cards, and issues the checks. In a larger restaurant an accountant would handle that entire area.

The chef could be completely in charge of food cost, from planning the menus, ordering the food, paying the purveyors, taking inventory, and crunching numbers. Or a steward, sous chef, or line manager could handle these tasks.

Sometimes, however, the chef is middle management. In this case, the chef is probably a working chef, with an executive or corporate executive chef as a boss. A working chef is on the line every night, cooking, expediting, and solving problems. The responsibilities could still include money and product. More often, though, middle management includes positions such as the sous chef, pastry chef, garde manager, and steward, each heading up a department. Usually, these managers have a portion of the responsibility of the executive, such as purchasing for the department, keeping inventory of the product, and scheduling the crew. The job may even entail creative control over part of the menu.

A first-line manager could have the preceding job description if the company's organizational chart is small. First-line managers are by definition working in the trenches, but they have more responsibilities than their co-workers. They may be in charge of product, or they may simply oversee other workers to be sure that work is getting done.

Whatever your particular title and responsibilities are, your general job description will follow these four basic standards of management. How these standards take form will depend on you and your responsibilities.

Planning

Planning is looking ahead and setting goals. This includes daily, weekly, monthly, seasonal and/or annual goals. These goals must consider budget, food cost, employee performance, menu development, marketing, and even your own professional aspirations.

Planning is at the heart of restaurant management. Without it, the job will be even more chaotic and stressful than it already is, without any focus or a clear direction. To make a good plan, you must first understand how your department affects the overall organization. Then you need to determine what your department can do to increase, improve, or maintain the profitability of the business. This could relate to the people doing the work, the organization of the systems being used, and/or the most efficient use of resources (people, food, equipment). If you identify a weak spot, you can put a plan into play.

Organizing

Organizing means taking the plans you've made and figuring out how to combine the money, personnel, equipment, and supplies in the most efficient, productive way possible to achieve these goals. Don't jump straight to organizing without first making a plan. You can't organize successfully without a plan.

> **Behind You!**
>
> Many new managers make the mistake of getting right to work reorganizing. It's understandable. Everyone, especially creative types, wants to put their mark on something. But be very careful that you don't try to re-invent the wheel. The wheel may work fine the way it is.

Leading

Leading requires using good communication skills to interact with employees in order to achieve your planned goals. Leading requires motivating, teaching, and delegating.

You can only be a leader if people are willing to follow you. How much actual authority you have will determine your success in leadership. Authority is the power given to you by the organization. Actual authority is the power the employees let you have.

Like it or not, your success depends on your employees' ability to get the job done. If they don't show up or they slack off, your job is to see that the work gets completed. They have control, and they can decide to cooperate or not. Management by iron fist does not breed caring employees, and "because I said so" doesn't really work with adults. You'll have to develop trust and respect with everyone if you expect them to follow you. They won't do it simply because you have *Chef* embroidered on your jacket.

Coordinating

Coordinating means combining individuals and departments to make your business run efficiently. In a kitchen, this coordinating means working with the dining room, the bar, the scullery, the kitchen staff in the *opposite shift*, and even the valet parkers. It requires nurturing teamwork and a genuine desire to put out a quality product.

> **Behind You!**
>
> Often rivalry exists between kitchen staff and dining room staff. There is also a long-standing tradition of day crew versus night crew. Only management can really address these sorts of problems. Coordinate with the manager of your opposite shift, and be sure that the organization's best interest is the top priority. The last thing you need is your product and equipment being sabotaged by your own team.

Management Styles

Most of us are managed, not managers. Most of our experience comes as a subordinate. But even in this capacity, we learn a lot about management. We know who was good at it and who wasn't. We probably have our own theories as to what made them good or bad. You've probably even uttered to yourself at one time or another, "When I'm a manager, I'm not going to (fill in the blank)." Some classic management blunders, although well-intentioned, never quite get the job done the right way.

Scary Boss

Have you ever had a boss who sent shivers up your spine? In his presence you worked in silence, afraid of saying or doing the slightest thing wrong. Management through fear may seem to work on the surface, but threats do not a happy workplace make. Threats of withholding good shifts, a pay raise, or worse, threats of termination, are coercion and only work if the manager actually has the power and the will to wield these punishments.

Fear can work as a last resort if every attempt to improve productivity has failed. And some people are wired for consequence-based discipline. It could be all they know. But on the average, managing with threats is a bad choice. Being a scary, threatening boss just doesn't pay. Don't encourage rivalry among employees or embarrass or belittle them.

Management is a lot like parenting. All over Disneyland every day parents threaten to take their kids home "right now" unless they stop screaming, crying, whining, or hitting their little brother. But most of these parents have no intention of following through, and the kids know it. That's because Mom and Dad just plunked down 50 bucks a head to get into the place, paid for hotels, rent-a-cars, countless twenty-dollar snacks, plus drove or flew however many miles it took to get there. It's a family vacation at the Happiest Place on Earth, dammit! No way are they leaving. So Jimmy keeps hitting his little brother on the head. Bad management.

> **Kitchen Tales**
>
> You have no doubt seen depictions of crazy chefs yelling and throwing pots. Behavior like that will get you fired these days, but when I was in school, such actions were perfectly acceptable. All of my chefs were brought up in the European apprenticeship system, and that's how they were taught to manage people. We loved them anyway. They had cool accents.

> **Behind You!**
>
> Employees will quickly catch on to empty praise. Good employees would prefer to know how they're actually performing than to hear false praise. Good employees can also tell when a manager has favorites. If you appear to prefer one employee over the others, you will lose the loyalty of the others.

Touchy-Feely Boss

A completely opposite management style is the touchy-feely boss. This boss wants to be your friend and hang out with you. This boss likes everything you do and is a terrible manager. There needs to be a clear line between the supervisor and the employee, or it gets awkward for both parties when the chips fall. "I thought we were friends. How can you do this to me?" See what I mean?

Too many first-time managers worry more about their employees liking them than how they can benefit the business. That is understandable. Being a new boss is a little like running for student body president every day. You need the staff's vote in order to get your job done. But you shouldn't spend your energy campaigning every day. The real issue with an overly social boss is that, although being friendly is good and making your employees happy is admirable, happiness doesn't necessarily breed productive workers. They could be happy, but lazy.

Micromanaging Boss

Some managers are a little too hands-on, watching everything you do over your shoulder and correcting you too often. Some employees can benefit from this, especially at the entry level. But once they've been on the job for a while, employees don't need this kind of supervision. Managers need to know which employees need help and which ones don't. They should lend a hand when needed and back off when necessary.

It's important that your employees know you have the technical skills of the job. Many managers become hands-on as a way of proving they can practice what they preach. This is not a bad idea, as long as you are not in the way, showing off or trying to take over because you can do it better and faster. It is your job as a manager to get everyone up to speed on their own.

Kitchen Tales

If you want to motivate people to peak performance, ask their opinion. Put them in charge of something. Nothing says "you're valued" like responsibility.

Because they posses the skill and know-how of the people they manage, many managers have a narrow view of how specific tasks should be done. It is important to remain open to new ideas and graciously accept input from your employees. They are going to have good and bad opinions about the work, co-workers, and your performance. Employees must feel welcome to bring you their thoughts either way. What's more, you need to investigate these ideas and follow up with the employee afterwards. This is the only way they will know you are listening. Sometimes the input will be a dud; sometimes it will be a gem. The only way to know is to remain open to all suggestions. If you don't, you will miss out on potentially important growth, both professionally and personally.

The M.I.A. Boss

Some bosses are never around, which is usually pretty nice for the employees. There is no pressure, no incentive to perform at peak efficiency, and plenty of time to fill their backpacks with free stuff.

Good employees, however, don't like it when their boss isn't around very much. How can a boss notice the kind of job you are doing if he's not in the building? How will he know who to promote and who to let go? Being invisible is a clear sign that you don't care about the workers.

Bad management is the reason for invisibility. This could be the invisible manager's fault, but it's more likely that a higher level of management piled too much work on the individual. This is common in the restaurant business because many places cannot afford multiple levels of management and the salaries they accrue. So one manager, usually the executive chef, gets to do it all. This is the manager who is buried in the office, handling purchasing, budgeting, food costs, scheduling, hiring, training, and maybe even developing menus. This manager needs to learn how to delegate.

Delegating is a skill in itself, and it's hard for many people to let go of certain tasks even when they have more important things to do. But delegating is necessary, not only for the daily operation of a restaurant but also for the well-being and morale of its employees.

Requests for assistance need to be made carefully and with some forethought. If you just start handing off the unpleasant tasks to your employees, they're going to catch on pretty quickly and start resisting. And don't expect someone who is already swamped with work to take on something you can't get done.

Even if employees have the time and ability to add on some extra tasks, some will want to know what's in it for them. These people may not be your best choices for added responsibility because the responsibility itself, with its implication of increased importance within the company and possible movement up the ladder, may not be enough for them. They want cash. But some employees will welcome and, in fact, long for extra responsibility. Carefully divide your tasks and match them to these individuals. Who knows, some of them may thrive on it.

Motivational Supervision

How do you get people to perform at their top levels? Unfortunately, there is no one magic solution. First, you need to understand all your employees as individuals. Very few of them are working for the same reasons. Some work for money, some for love, some for fun. It's up to you as a manager to figure out who's who.

You don't hand out surveys or hold interviews. You get to know them the same way you get to know everyone else in your life. Watch and listen. Are they good workers? Fast? Slow? Are they friendly, or do they keep to themselves? Do they have hobbies, other jobs, families? What frustrates them? And most importantly, what inspires them? Good managers figure out their employees' individual attributes and what inspires them.

Make sure that your employees know exactly what you expect from them. Don't be vague in any way. If you need to draw a diagram for one guy, do it. If you need to demonstrate it, do it. If you need to get a translator, do it. You must be able to communicate specifically.

Don't demand anything unrealistic from your employees. Know what each employee is capable of, and adjust your needs to their abilities.

Assess their work regularly, and praise them openly and sincerely. If you see improvement, mention it. If you see failure, always deal with it in private, never in the presence of co-workers.

Be sure everyone knows that his work is valued. Especially in jobs that involve repetitive tasks, a person needs to know that this incredibly boring stuff matters to someone.

Behind You!

"Employee of the Month" may seem like a good motivation tool. But in a small kitchen environment, it frequently leads to disgruntled workers. Rather than handing out certificates, make a point to compliment everyone every day.

Foster a team mentality. Everyone wants to belong. Even the rebels need to belong to a rebellion. Keep everyone up-to-date on changes within the organization, and be sure they all know where they stand in terms of job security, promotion, vacation, pay, and scheduling.

When you're wrong, admit your mistake. When you're sorry, say so. Then move on.

Sometimes it doesn't work. Sometimes there is simply no chemistry between people. Do your best, and don't instigate conflict. Try to see things from the employee's perspective, and don't be stubborn. As the manager, you need to take the high road.

Friends vs. the Business

Being promoted from an hourly worker to management is thrilling. It means you are a success. You have lived up to your employer's expectations. But promotion is hard on the friendships you've cultivated with your colleagues. You move from being a confidant to being one of *them*. It's an awkward and challenging situation.

You are going to be torn between maintaining your friendships and doing a good job. You should know, right off the bat, that if you take a management job, you must make the job your priority. Nothing should matter more than the success of the operation. If you care more about your friends than whether or not your owner makes money, you are not management material.

Too often managers lose sight of the big picture because they are stuck in the middle between old cohorts and upper-level management. It is all too easy to fall back into a mind-set of *Us vs. Them*. But if your goal is to be a successful chef, you must never forget that *you are Them*.

There are ways to remain friendly and to foster a climate that is mutually beneficial to old buddies and new superiors. But the days of after-hour partying are over. Especially when alcohol is involved, the tendency is to be too open, too friendly. You need to treat everyone equally now. Being buddies with part of your crew is just going to make the other part feel left out, slighted, and treated unfairly. If you appear to show favoritism, this will drag the morale of the others into the mud. Then you've got problems with employees who think they've got you in their pockets and problems with employees who don't trust you, don't like you, and won't do what you want them to do.

Begin your management career by taking your buddies aside and laying it on the line. Make it clear there will be no special treatment, and explain to them why. Promise that you won't take advantage of them, and ask them to make the same effort. If they really are your friends, they'll understand and be happy for your success. If they appear jealous or they refuse to accept your authority, it's time to treat them like just another employee.

The Least You Need to Know

- Management means making the success of the business your first priority.
- Planning, organizing, leading, and coordinating are the cornerstones of good management.
- Avoid making common management mistakes.
- Learn what motivates each of your employees.

Chapter 21

Becoming the Boss

In This Chapter

◆ Hiring the right person the first time

◆ Understanding the interview process

◆ Orienting, training, and evaluating your new hire

◆ Disciplining your staff

In Chapter 20, I explained the different levels of management. Here, I expand on the executive level because the real power resides there. At this level, your title could be Executive Chef, Corporate Chef, or even Kitchen Manager, but most people will simply call you chef. When you become chef, you no longer have only a few responsibilities. You can't just place your orders and go home. Now, it's your show. The people with the money have trusted you with it. You need to take the ball and run with it.

As a supervisor in middle management, you were a boss. But as the chef, you are the big boss. This is the job all foodies dream of. Why is it so desirable? It's certainly not because of the day-to-day tasks it entails. It's because of the fame and money. But this is the fantasy, brought to you, once again, by the lovely folks that work in Food TV. In reality, there rarely is fame or notoriety, and usually little money, at least compared to the top of other professions. What you do have is creativity, responsibility, and a sense of personal accomplishment.

The creativity is the fun part, although you may still be subject to the whims of owners, partners, or investors. Your goal is probably to run the type of restaurant you want, serving the food you want, in the manner you want, to the clientele you want, and to turn a profit. But to get to that point, you'll have to start by serving the type of food someone else wants. Unless you are the owner, you'll have to do what the owners want. Don't look on this as a lesser assignment than running your own place. It's a great opportunity to perfect what you do. If you can get your feet wet on someone else's dime, more power to you!

The Beauty of Being the Big Boss

The responsibilities of executive chef are the one true constant. These are more intense than they were in middle management because the buck stops with you. There are certain things you can delegate away and certain things you really shouldn't. The following sections delve into those responsibilities and will help you get through them in one piece.

Hiring

Hiring is one of the most important tasks a chef does. Finding the right people can make or break your business, and it's as hard as finding the right job. In fact, it's even harder. If you make a mistake, you can't just walk away, like you can if the job you choose turns out to be a dud. Hiring the wrong person is an expensive mistake because you are responsible for firing, compensating, and rehiring that position. All the while, your staff is trying to get the job done with less help. Worse than that, their morale is damaged because you're firing people and they're worried they could be next.

> **Kitchen Tales**
>
> If you go to work in a large corporation, its human resources department will already have hiring practices and policies in place, including standard forms, tests, and screening. But more often than not, the final decision will come down to you, the chef.

So hiring the right person in the first place is a worthy goal. Here's how you can make it happen more often than not.

Plan

Give yourself as much time as possible to find the right person for the job. Ideally, you should have someone lined up before you fire anyone. You want to do everything you can to avoid not having enough people to cover the shifts.

Figure out exactly what you need, and stick to your plan. This means knowing what position and shift you need to fill. You'd be surprised at how many applicants come to an interview with schedule restrictions. You need to decide what you're willing to accept and what you're not. And what if a wonderful candidate walks in but can only work half the time? What will you do? Offer the job anyway and try to find someone else to make up the time, or keep looking? Any settling you do on your needs, standards, or qualifications will probably come back and bite you in the end.

Know in advance what type of training and skills you want in an applicant. Do you want someone with experience, or do you want to do the training? Although experienced hires are certainly desirable for some jobs, you might prefer to train some positions yourself, especially if you are particular about the way you want certain things done.

> **Behind You!**
>
> If you do find yourself short-staffed, you'll need to ask one or more of your employees to pick up extra shifts. Pay them extra, including overtime if necessary. Make it worth their while. That way, they'll be willing to do it again if you ever need them to.

> **Kitchen Tales**
>
> Training someone from scratch is often better than hiring someone with years of experience, especially if those years were filled with bad habits. No one likes to be retrained, and you probably don't have the time or the energy to convince an experienced cook that your way is better than his or hers.

Recruit

If your restaurant doesn't have a human resources department, *you* are the human resources department. As head of your human resources department, you need to recruit the type of people you want to attract. If you don't care who you hire, write "help wanted" on a napkin and stick it on the bulletin board of the local coffee shop. What you'll get through your door is a string of bored, unemployed people with expensive tastes in coffee.

If you do care about the kind of people you hire, first talk to your current staff. Find out if any of them are interested in stepping up or moving shifts. They are your loyal employees. They come to work for you every day. You owe them that courtesy of making them your first choice. Plus, it's good for morale.

If you cannot hire from within, branch out to other sources. First, go to your friends who work in the food service industry. Actively search for the person you want. Talk to your colleagues. Use your network. It's a hundred times better to find an employee who comes with the thumbs up of someone you know than it is to get someone off the street.

Behind You!

If you advertise in the your local paper's classified section, keep in mind that every Tom, Dick, and Harry who needs a job—any job—reads them. You'll get a lot of applications from people who aren't a good fit for the job but are desperate for work.

If you still can't find the person, then it's time to advertise. Make the job description as detailed and accurate as you can. Be truthful about the job itself. Clearly state what you expect and what you can offer. Then be sure to pick the right publications or websites to advertise in. If you are filling an upper-level position, check out the headhunting services in your area. (See Chapter 11 for more on placement services.) If you're in need of a classically trained applicant that you'll be able to further train, advertise at a culinary school.

Select

An application form is a great way to weed out the geeks and freaks. First of all, half the applicants don't bother to fill the thing out. They simply put "see resumé." Do you really want an employee who can't follow even the most basic of instructions?

Next, check the handwriting, although not to look for cryptic messages or to discover hidden personality traits. You're simply looking for legibility. If an applicant doesn't write neatly on a job application, for cryin' out loud, how are you ever going to read the labels he writes for the food in your freezer?

Compare the application to the resumé. Does it match? Is it complete? Before you sit down with the applicant, read the application very carefully. You can then discuss any discrepancies in fact, gaps in time, or missing information when you are face-to-face.

Interview

A face-to-face interview is the only way to accurately judge a candidate. I have reluctantly hired employees long-distance, over the phone, but that never turned out well. Only when you are able to look the person in the eye will you be able to determine whether he or she is someone you can trust.

But the face-to-face interview has its perils as well. One or two traits you notice on first impression can easily hypnotize you during an interview. For instance, the applicant may look a little like your college boyfriend. You'll probably end up hiring him just so you'll have him around as eye candy. Or the applicant has flaming red hair just like the kid that used to beat you up by the bike racks in sixth grade. You won't hire this one out of spite. This sounds crazy, and you may think I am making it up. But such practices are all too common, and they are one step away from discrimination. Be sure to treat all qualified applicants equally.

The applicant could look great on paper but have trouble articulating his thoughts. You may dismiss this person out of hand, but his problem could be as simple as being nervous. Unless you delve more deeply into the qualifications, you could miss a potential gem.

What if the applicant is like you in many ways? Maybe you attended the same school or share the same hobbies. This doesn't automatically make the applicant as good, trustworthy, or responsible as you.

A good way to avoid these common hiring mistakes is to have a strategy for your interviews. Use standard interview questions, like a script. This will help you get the information you need and keep you from drifting off onto other subjects such as what music you like or the kind of cars you drive. If the conversation expands, that's fine, as long as you hit and explore all the points on the script.

When you interview, be sure to ask broad, open-ended questions that are related to the job. Don't ask yes-or-no questions, or you'll get yes or no for an answer. And ask follow-up questions, like "how?" and "why?"

Some applicants will talk endlessly, even if you do ask yes-or-no questions. If they yak and yak, or veer off the subject, you must get control and put the interview back on track.

Try to make the applicant feel at ease. Don't be scary or rude or arrogant. Remember how it feels to be interviewed. The applicant will probably be nervous. Be nice. And as fascinating as you are and as much as the applicant may ask about you and your many thrilling adventures, you should shut up and listen. The more talking you do, the less listening you do. The goal is for you to judge applicants' qualifications, not give them your bio.

Use some of these examples of good interview questions:

- At your last job, what were your duties and responsibilities?
- What did you enjoy?
- What frustrated you?
- What did you find rewarding?
- What did you spend the most time doing?
- What was your working relationship like with your supervisor?
- Why did you leave?
- Why do you want to work here?
- Why should I hire you?
- How could you best contribute to our operation?
- What are your strengths?
- What are your weaknesses?
- What larger responsibilities are you interested in?
- What are your career goals?
- How do you plan on meeting those goals?

Check References

Failing to check the references and credentials of your short list of applicants is stupid. The checking of references is the easiest way you have to ensure you're hiring the right person, but it is so often overlooked simply because it takes time. Well, too bad! Get on the phone. You need to know if these people are who and what they say they are.

Although most chefs will be as busy as you, they're usually willing to take a minute to tell you about their former employees. They will be especially candid if the person in question was a really good or a really bad employee. It's the in-between ones that will usually get the short answers. "Yeah, she worked for me" is not very helpful. Try to get a little more information out of them by asking more direct questions. You don't have to be on the phone for an hour, but you should try to make the call worth your while. If you call and a chef is not available, don't just leave a message. Ask when someone will be available, and call back. You are more likely to get your questions answered this way.

Here are some good questions to ask applicants' references:

◆ What were the applicant's dates of employment?

◆ What was the applicant's job title and responsibilities?

◆ Did the applicant miss work often?

◆ How did he/she perform the job?

◆ Does the applicant have any particularly weak or strong skills?

◆ Did the applicant get along with the other workers?

◆ Why did the applicant leave?

◆ Did the applicant depart professionally and on good terms?

◆ What was the starting and ending salary?

◆ Would you recommend this person for a job?

Easing New Employees Into the Job

Unless you want to go through the hiring process again in a few weeks, you need to spend some time easing your new hires into their jobs through orientation and training.

Orientation

After you hire a new employee, schedule an orientation session. This orientation is an important first step. It makes the new hire more comfortable on the first real day of work, and it shows that you care.

Give the new hire a tour of the facility, introduce the staff, and explain the chain of command. Describe the various idiosyncrasies of your kitchen. Explain the menus, hours of operation, time cards and procedures for punching in, and the way to light the pilots. Cover the locations of the bathroom, the toilet paper, the walk-in, the freezer, the circuit breaker, and the can opener. (Seriously, nothing is worse than having to ask where the can opener is.) If you write all this information down and have it ready for each new hire, the entire process should take all of 15 minutes.

If you are too busy for an orientation, it's an easy thing to delegate away. Just be sure you have some kind of orientation guidelines to follow and that the person you put in charge of the orientation will actually follow them.

Training

Usually there isn't enough time for a thorough training session. What typically ensues is known affectionately as the *magic apron* training method. In this method the new hire is given an apron and put right to work. Knowledge of the job is transferred (magically) from the apron into the brain of the new guy, who will immediately begin wowing you with skill, speed, and complete knowledge of the job at hand. As you might have guessed, this training method doesn't always work very well.

A great way to train is to have the new hire shadow a trusted employee. The best way to learn anything is to watch and then do. Shadowing takes the training out of your hands, so if you use this method, choose a trusted employee and keep your eyes on them. But in a busy kitchen, shadowing is not always possible. Space is limited, and so is time. If possible, start the new hire during a slow shift. You don't want him to be slammed the first day on the job.

Most corporate operations have extensive training manuals. Most independent restaurants barely have recipes, let alone manuals. Spending some time putting together a training manual is totally worth it. If you have a manual, the procedure is standardized, so everyone does the job the same way. Standardization takes the guesswork out of the job. Everyone knows what to expect and how he is doing.

Employee Upkeep

Once you have your new employee trained, you want to keep that person happy and productive. You don't want to have to go through the entire thing again, at least not for the same position.

Nothing is worse than working hard all day and feeling like no one noticed or cared. So regularly evaluate the performance of all your employees. After the standard probationary period, let each employee know that his performance will be formally evaluated on a regular basis. Be sure to stick to your word, and evaluate them when you say you will. Take them aside and present them with a written assessment of some kind. This is important, as it makes them feel as though you value their work.

At the evaluation, be sure to ask how the employee feels about the job. Is it satisfying? Is there something you could do to make it more interesting? Should you provide additional responsibility or training? If you offer it, be prepared to give it. Is the employee having trouble with any tasks? With other employees? Give your employees a chance to get this stuff off their chest, and really listen to them. Do they have any input to give? Be open to it if they do.

In addition to your formal evaluations, you should give your staff constant feedback on their work. When they perform well, say so in public. When they screw up, remember to point it out in private.

Firing

This is the worst part about being the chef. Firing people is horrible. There is no way to make it easy, either. The people you fire are not ever going to like you again, so accept that fact right now. Actually, they may become your arch-nemesis. Whatever. Your first priority is to the business. Remember that, and you'll be fine.

The easiest way to fire someone is to set up clear regulations and a discipline system before you hire anyone. Then before anybody starts to work, be sure he reads and understands these regulations. If you establish the rules first, it shouldn't come as a shock when someone breaks them.

Think about the things that are going to frustrate you about your employees. Absenteeism, tardiness, quality and quantity of work are some obvious potential problems. But don't forget things like uniform care, grooming, equipment care, eating, smoking, drinking, and drug use. A lot can go wrong.

Put into effect a warning system of some kind. Warn the employee as soon as you see behavior that you don't like.

Discuss any poor performance as it happens. Don't hold on to it until you are ready to cut them loose. Dismissal should never come as a shock.

Make the warning immediate and consistent with everyone. And leave emotion out of it. Don't interpret their behavior as a personal affront.

Discipline systems commonly follow a certain path. Begin with an oral warning, follow with a written warning, and then determine a punishment of some sort, such as suspension for a day or two. Termination should occur only if the behavior continues after all the other disciplinary action has failed.

The Least You Need to Know

◆ Hiring the right person is easier if you target the right labor pool.

◆ Having set interview questions makes the process easier with better results.

◆ Take the extra time to orient and properly train your new hire.

◆ Firing is never easy, but you can minimize the unpleasantness by following a strict disciplinary plan.

Chapter **22**

Sanitation and Safety

In This Chapter

◆ Understanding the potential for food-borne illness

◆ Training and certifying your staff in sanitation and safety

◆ The importance of basic first aid

◆ Preparing for emergencies

The first time you step foot into a professional kitchen you will realize right away that people who cook for a living are disgusting. We eat and serve food that has had the mold scraped off of it. We eat and serve food that has fallen on the floor. If it looks and smells fine, we eat and serve it, regardless of its expiration date. We wear clothing designed to camouflage the goop we smear on ourselves.

Aren't you glad there are health inspectors?

In all fairness, you can't say that food service workers are the only disgusting people. Everyone at one time or another has evoked the three-second rule, in which it is believed food that falls on the floor will not be infected with any germs in the first three seconds. This is not an actual rule, but it is commonly observed in professional kitchens. (For your information, germs attach when food hits the floor, no matter how long it sits there.)

Sanitation

Sanitation generally refers to hygienic and healthful conditions. In the restaurant business sanitation refers to both personal hygiene and safe food handling.

Where I live, in Los Angeles County, many cities have adopted an ordinance which states that any business serving prepared food to the public must post their health department rating clearly in a window. This policy has been in effect for many years, and everyone knows that anything less than an *A* is not as clean as it could be. You can imagine how a *B*, or heaven forbid, a *C* would affect your business. This type of ordinance is catching on, but it's a local initiative. Health departments make establishments' ratings available to the public, either online or by phone. But a letter grade in plain view is the wave of the future.

Why? Because according to the Center for Disease Control and Prevention, 76 million cases of food-borne illness are reported every year. Actually, there are probably more incidents because many cases are mild and go unreported. Of those reported, 5,000 were fatal. With over half of the food consumed by America being prepared or eaten outside the home, people need to know how clean a place really is.

Kitchen Tales

When I was a culinary student, my first class was sanitation. After that, I went into the lab for my first basic cooking lessons. While preparing lamb curry, I dropped the cubed meat on the floor. Being an excellent student, I remembered my sanitation training and threw it all away. My chef charged at me, yelling "Are you stupid? Do you think money grows on trees? Haven't you heard of the three-second rule?" Bravely, I confronted him with cross-contamination facts. He was not impressed and made me wash, cook, and eat the meat in front of him.

Training and Certification

Keeping your restaurant clean and healthy isn't particularly difficult, but it does take planning and time. The most important thing an owner can do to ensure safe food handling is to train the staff. That means the entire staff, front of the house, back of the house, and everyone in between, including office help, security, and even parking attendants. Anyone who has cause to set foot in the kitchen, even just in passing, should know sanitation standards, so he can follow them and watch for infractions.

You can train employees in food sanitation in several ways. Dozens of books, seminars, and courses cover the basics. The National Restaurant Association Educational Foundation even issues certificates of completion for its industry standard Servsafe program. Many jobs require their employees to hold a Servsafe certification, and many counties require that at least one person per shift hold a sanitation certificate.

Remember, too, that all employees need to understand the training. If you have language barriers in your kitchen, you must make the effort to get a translator and provide bilingual signage.

Training should include the proper way to mix sanitizing solution, do dishes, and clean counters, tables, menus, and equipment. Everyone in the house should know how to do things like refill hand soap and paper towels when necessary. Anyone who runs the dishwasher, including the wait staff and

Kitchen Tales

The National Restaurant Association Education Foundation is your one-stop-shop for *ServSafe* training. Find more information at www.nraef.

Behind You!

Certification is all well and good, but if even one person on staff is not trained and monitored, your training is much less effective. It only takes one infraction to lower your Health Department rating. It only takes one infraction to make someone sick. In either case, you've damaged the public's perception of your business and ultimately your profitability.

cooks who may occasionally start it up, must know how to check and refill the dishwashing soap and sanitizing solution, and how to fill the dishwasher with clean water. Anyone who might possibly spill something needs to know the proper way to mop up. And everyone, absolutely everyone, needs to know how to wash his hands properly.

Food-Borne Illness

Food, especially when it's moist, warm, and rich in protein, is super-inviting to bacteria. Although you've probably heard about bacteria like E. coli and salmonella, the two most common causes of food poisoning, there are actually more than 200 known food-borne illnesses out there.

Food-borne illness is spread by cross contamination, which is the spread of bacteria from one surface to another. Most kitchen employees know not to cut vegetables on a board that is covered with raw meat juice. (Many kitchens use color-coded cutting boards to help kitchen staff remember to cut meat on a separate surface.) But few

def•i•ni•tion

The **window** is the shelf above the cook's line where the food is placed to be picked up by the waiters. Often, the window or part of the window is warmed by heat lamps. While they keep the food warm, they do not necessarily keep the food out of the danger zone.

realize how many microorganisms can live and breed in a side-towel. Cross contamination can take place between a work surface, knives, utensils, tableware, and even food itself. And disease often spreads simply because hands go unwashed.

Most cases of food-borne illness start with food that is held improperly. Bacteria thrive in anything warm, moist, and protein rich. When the conditions are right, say on a Denver omelet sitting in the *window* too long, bacteria will multiply. That's because the window is usually in the danger zone.

The danger zone is the temperature range that bacteria love, between 40 and 140 degrees Fahrenheit. Once the temperature drops below 40 degrees, the bacteria freeze and lay dormant until the item is defrosted. If the bacteria reaches 140 degrees or above (as in most cooking), it dies. So your Denver omelet is safe if it's cooked thoroughly and served hot. But if it is allowed to fall into the danger zone, as it does the longer it sits at room temperature, more bacteria are attracted to it, and it becomes contaminated again. Once food has entered the danger zone, it must be re-heated to 165 degrees to be considered safe to eat.

Viral Contamination

Often waiters prepare some dishes, such as salads, soups, or desserts. But even if they have no contact with the food at all, they can still spread disease. A common cause of food-borne illness is viral contamination spread by a sick person. These germs, spread through touch, are another form of cross contamination. While much of the attention regarding sanitation focuses on the kitchen, the dining room staff comes into contact with the public and therefore has more power to prevent the spread of disease. Since we can't control the sanitation habits of the guests, we need to stop the spread of disease from them.

If a sick customer coughs and covers his mouth with his hand, rubs his eyes, or sneezes into his napkin, those germs will end up on every utensil, glass, table linen, menu, piece of furniture, credit card, money, and door handle the customer touches while dining. The staff busses the table, brings everything to the dish station, grabs a towel, wipes down the table, grabs clean linen and clean tableware, and resets the table for the next party. Unless the staff washed their hands between the stop at the dish station and the clean tableware, and unless they used a towel moistened with a sanitizing solution to clean the table, menus, and chairs, that clean table is still covered in microorganisms. Can you see the dangers of an untrained dining room staff?

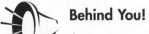

Behind You!

The most important thing you can do as an employer, supervisor, or manager, besides training your entire staff, is to make them feel comfortable enough to speak up when they see that something is being done wrong.

HACCP

The Hazard Analysis Critical Control Point (HACCP) is a food safety program that was designed by NASA and adopted by the Food and Drug Administration (FDA). The program is used by every food manufacturer and health department in the country. It controls the safety and sanitation of food to help prevent problems from occurring. HACCP follows the flow of food through purchase, receiving, storage, and service, identifies potential hazards, and addresses them. It examines the critical control points, where hazards can be controlled or eliminated, and sets the standards for prevention at these points.

The holding and cooking temperature of food is a good example of a critical control point. HACCP procedures include training people on knowing proper cooking and holding temperatures, installation of thermostats and thermometers for gauging temperatures, learning what to do when temperatures are off, and setting up a system of monitoring and regularly documenting temperatures.

Safety

In a work environment filled with sharp blades, sizzling oil, scalding liquid, and open flames, you'd think that safety would be on everyone's mind. But stupid accidents happen all the time because people forget about the dangers in a kitchen.

Accidents hurt the victim as well as the business. When you're hurt on the job, you have to either ignore it and keep working or go get help. If you need to leave for help, the kitchen is suddenly short staffed. You punch out and lose a day's pay. If it's really bad, you have workman's compensation to deal with. And if it's really, really bad, there is disability insurance and several days or weeks of work lost. Someone else will have to be hired to replace you.

> **Kitchen Tales** _____
>
> Chefs are like old soldiers, openly displaying, with pride, their scars. And like salty old sailors, they spin yarns about how they got their scars. One chef tried to convince me the scars on his arm were from the time he slipped and fell into the deep fat fryer. My worst wound involved dropping a pot of boiling water, which splattered up onto my legs. As the scalding water blistered my skin, I ran to the walk-in and took off my pants, which didn't seem to phase the busboys who kept coming in for half-and-half. (Come to think of it, though, they sure needed a lot of half-and-half that night.)

First Aid

A good first-aid kit is an essential part of any kitchen. Make it a complete kit, and restock it on a regular basis. According to the Occupational Safety and Health Administration (OSHA), restaurant management should be prepared to administer first aid for the most common kitchen injuries, which include sprains, muscle strain, cuts, burns, and fractures. An eye-flushing station should also be near any chemicals, such as cleaning supplies.

> **Behind You!** _____
>
> RICE is the acronym to remember in the event of the most common kitchen injury, the sprain. It stands for Rest, Ice, Compression, and Elevation.

If there are no emergency facilities nearby, many insurance companies require that someone certified in first aid be on the premises at all times. Certifying your staff in first aid is a good idea anyway because restaurants are home to other catastrophes, too, like choking and heart attacks. And whenever you have booze and money and public access, there is always potential for violence.

Training

Training on the use of all equipment, basic safety rules, and emergency procedures is the best way to prevent injury. The training should be consistent and taught by a manager or supervisor from a book or manual. It should be mandatory, even for new hires who appear to be experienced, and there should be periodic mandatory reviews. If all this seems inconvenient, just remind yourself that injuries hurt the business as much as the victim.

Equipment safety training should include all large and small appliances. Everyone needs to learn how to start, stop, and clean each appliance safely.

The safety rule reminding employees not to stick their finger in an electrical socket may seem obvious to anyone who's ever watched Wile E. Coyote cartoons. But restaurants are notorious for having a lot of outlets, puddles, and old equipment lying about. Believe it or not, restaurant workers get electrocuted all the time—sometimes fatally.

Behind You!

Machinery has two dangerous spots to watch out for: the point of operation (the blade or the flame, for instance) and the point of power transmission (the gas hookup or the electrical outlet).

All employees should be taught these basic safety tips:

◆ Always say "behind you."

◆ Don't put knives into a sink full of water.

◆ Turn pot handles inward.

◆ Don't scoop ice out of the ice machine with anything made of glass.

◆ Wrap cut can lids and other sharp trash in thicker trash before dropping them into the garbage.

◆ Report all spills.

◆ Always use dry oven mitts, hot pads, or towels for handling hot cookware.

◆ Never put water into hot grease, or vice versa.

◆ Keep loose clothing and hair away from flames.

◆ Turn off the oven and stove when you are done.

◆ Never run, especially around the ice machine.

◆ Don't lift pots that are too heavy.

◆ Don't pick up something hot until *after* you figure out where you are going to put it down.

Disasters

Emergency procedures are often the most overlooked aspect of safety training because we don't like to think about disaster hitting. But it could, so it's best to be prepared. Post emergency numbers, and clearly mark and make emergency exits accessible.

Every employee should know what to do in the case of the most likely disaster in your area. Earthquakes, hurricanes, and tornados hit every year. Just because they haven't hit you yet doesn't mean they won't.

Behind You!

Be prepared. Have an emergency kit somewhere in your restaurant within easy access. It should contain, at the very least, a first-aid kit, a flashlight with extra batteries, a transistor radio with extra batteries, water, energy bars or some other non-perishable food, matches and lighters in a waterproof bag, and paper and pens. Make sure every employee knows where the kit is stored.

Be sure everyone knows the safest route out of the building, and designate a meeting spot outside. In the case of an emergency, you'll need to account for all your employees.

The Least You Need to Know

◆ A well-trained staff can avoid basic cross contamination.

◆ Make all employees aware of basic safety procedures.

◆ Good employers are prepared for all emergencies, from accidents in the kitchen to natural disasters.

Part 7

Your Own Place

Many chefs dream of owning their own restaurant. However, only one third of restaurants make it past their first three years in business. Planning is the key to success.

A business plan is a necessary element of opening your own shop. If you do it right, the plan can carry you through the life of your business. Do an inadequate job, and you may find yourself in the two-thirds majority.

The more time you spend looking into the details of your business, the better. Throughout the process of writing your business plan, you may find that your initial idea isn't really going to fly. So don't be stubborn; come up with something that will succeed.

Don't forget to pay attention to the crummy aspects of business ownership. I guarantee it won't all be glowing reviews and wait-list Saturday nights. It will also be rat traps and grease fires and stolen steaks. If you are well prepared, nothing will take you by surprise.

Chapter 23

Owning Your Own Restaurant

In This Chapter

◆ Owning your own restaurant

◆ Considering your chance of success

◆ Creating a business plan

◆ Finding the money to make it happen

For years I thought I was a jinx. And so did my friends, because every restaurant I worked in went out of business after I left. It got to be funny, in a sad sort of way. But I have since come to realize that I wasn't a jinx at all. I was a good luck charm. After all, they were all in business as long as I worked for them.

The following chapter is a very basic overview of what it takes to run a restaurant. I am simply pointing you in the general direction of ownership. You'll definitely want to consult with professionals, including lawyers and accountants, before you get too far into the process of opening your own place.

Understanding the Risks Involved in Opening a Restaurant

Restaurants come and go on a regular basis. About one third of all new restaurants fold within the first year, and two thirds of those that survive the first year never make it past year three. Generally, it's thought that if an establishment can make it past year three, it's golden.

Everyone knows that the success rate is low. And yet, people continue to open new restaurants all over the place.

> **Behind You!**
>
> If you're thinking about ownership, be sure to visit www.restaurantowner.com. It is a membership-based site with lots of good products for sale, including manuals for business plans, training manuals, marketing, menu development, and a lot more. There are also discussion forums and online seminars.

Knowing how bad your chances are, do you still want to open your own place? Of course you do, because it's your dream. And like a teenager behind the wheel, you feel invincible. You know the chances of success are slim, but that's because no one else has done it like you will.

The fact that owning a restaurant is everybody's dream is partially to blame for the low success rate. All it really takes is money to make that dream come to life. So everyone with money does it. And guess what? Most of them have no business being in the restaurant business in the first place.

But that's not you. You have the background, the training, and the expertise to make it work, right?

You'd better hope so.

Creating a Business Plan

The one thing you know you're going to need is money. Unless you've got a money tree growing in your backyard, you'll need to find a way to raise some. This means convincing someone that your restaurant will be a worthy investment. Enter the business plan.

Your business plan can make or break your chances of running a successful restaurant. If you write it properly, it will remain a blueprint for every aspect of your operation, from the day you open to the day you close, and (hopefully) the 30 years in between.

Zillions of tools are available to help you with your business plan, including business consultants, books, templates, websites, and classes. Look at several models before you start writing one. Obviously, you want to look at business plans that were successful, but there's a lot to be said for learning what not to do. Visit friends and family who own businesses and ask them for advice. People who know and like you are going to be more eager to help, and expect less in return, than those who don't.

The information you gather for your business plan will generally be the same, regardless of the format you use. But some outlines are more thorough than others. The more detail your business plan has, the more useful it will be to you and the better your chances of success in the long run will be. That's because if you think of everything before it happens, you'll be prepared.

The process of developing the business plan is very helpful because as you work through it, you just might discover that your ideas aren't so great after all. That's okay, because it's not too late to completely change your concept into a profitable one.

What Goes Into the Plan

To begin, you need to have a clear idea of your ultimate goal. What's your business all about? The people considering giving you money are going to expect you to know.

Describe in detail your concept, your menu, and the size and decor of the restaurant. Estimate the cost of an average meal.

Describe your location. Are you planning on leasing an existing place, or are you building from the ground up? What kind equipment will you need? Will it be new or used?

Discuss in detail all financial information, including the amount of money you'll need to open (start-up capital) and how much money you'll need to keep the place running until it turns a profit (operating capital).

Forecast your long-term income and expenses. Start by determining the number of plates you'll serve a day. This means determining the meals you'll serve (breakfast, lunch, dinner, etc.), the number of chairs you'll have in your dining room, and the number of *seatings* you'll have for any given meal. When you know the amount

def•i•ni•tion

A **seating** is the number of times the tables in your dining room are turned. They don't all turn at once, but they generally turn the same number of times. Reservations are taken based on estimated seating times.

of the average ticket, you can then compare it to your operating expenses. To do this, decide how many employees you will have and how much you will pay them. Estimate rent, utilities, services (such as laundry, housekeeping, valet parking, and pest control), and insurance, as well as the cost of raw materials.

def•i•ni•tion

Cash flow is the movement of money into and out of your business. Variables that influence cash flow include inventory, accounts receivable and payable, and your credit. If your total unpaid bills are greater than your expected sales, then you've got negative cash flow, which isn't a good thing.

With this information, you can calculate your break-even point, the length of time until you either stop losing money or begin making money. Armed with these specifics, you can project sales (you should prepare both optimistic and pessimistic reports) and prepare a *cash-flow* analysis.

Explain how you plan to market your business and identify the kinds of customers you seek. Your concept will determine the group of people you decide to go after. For instance, if you are planning to open an ice cream parlor, you probably wouldn't paste up posters at a Weight Watchers meeting. Based on who you are targeting, you can determine how to advertise, by using flyers, coupons, print ads, television, or radio. However, by far the best form of marketing is word of mouth. Most people don't dine out at a new place unless a friend has recommended it. Knowing this, you need to see every inch of your business as a potential marketing tool, from the parking lot to the bathroom. Does every inch exude your concept? It should. Read more about developing your concept in Chapter 24.

Next, figure out exactly who your employees will be. You need to name all key personnel, including partners, managers, dining room staff, and kitchen staff. Don't forget support personnel, like scullery, stewards, parking lot attendants, housekeeping, laundry, gardeners, and security. Here is where an organizational chart can be helpful. Then, determine the hours and the schedule. The more detailed this is, the more accurate your operating cost forecast will be.

A detailed plan of daily operations is essential, from who opens up to who locks down, and everything in between. Include how you plan on dealing with potential problems, such as broken equipment, plumbing problems, food shortages, sick and injured employees, and theft, to name a few common occurrences.

Of course you don't want to think about an exit strategy when you are writing your business plan. But you should have a clear idea of what to do in the event that your dream doesn't quite cut it. Spell out on paper who gets what and who pays for what, just in case.

Identify Funding Sources

The amount of money you'll need to start your place will depend on the concept, the size of the operation, and the location. What are you starting with? Are you moving into a space that had a restaurant as a previous tenant? If so, you may be able to use much of what is already there, like equipment, fixtures, and furniture. (Also, investigate the former tenant's business history.
Why are they leaving, and could it happen to you?)

Now, figure out what you already have. What are your personal resources and assets? Take into consideration everything you have of value. Retirement funds, life insurance, savings, real estate equity, credit cards, vehicles, and even collections can be sold or used as loan collateral.

> **Behind You!**
>
> A common problem in restaurants is tying up assets in standing inventory. Try to keep as much of your assets as liquid as possible. Without cash on hand, one busted toilet could shut you down.

If you don't have much, the next step is to go to your friends and family. You have a better shot at getting a loan from someone who knows you and believes in you than you do from a stranger. And you can probably negotiate a better interest rate with your dad than you can with the loan officer at the bank. Nevertheless, you should still treat them professionally, and put everything in writing.

> **Kitchen Tales**
>
> Numerous small business loans are available, both from local, state, and federal agencies as well as numerous private lenders. Start with the Small Business Administration (SBA).
>
> Although a restaurant is viewed as an incredible risk to lenders, your chances are better if you have a thorough business plan. Women, minorities, and veterans should look into specific small business loans available just for them. Visit the SBA at www.sba.gov.

Ownership Types

If you're doing this project on your own, and you plan on keeping all the profit, then what you have will be a sole proprietorship. This means one person owns the business, and that person is responsible for all aspects of the business.

Partnerships

Partnership is similar to sole proprietorship, but extra people share the profits and risks. People partner up for a number of reasons, such as similar concept ideas, similar background or career history, or similar last names. Most partnership horror stories involve one party not living up to the expectations of another. Knowing this, put all the details in writing. The agreement needs to spell out each person's responsibility clearly, including who reports to whom, who makes what decisions, what are everyone's salaries (owners often take none until the business turns a profit), and how the profits will be divided. Disagreements happen, so pick a partner you'll be able to discuss, persuade, and compromise with, because someone's got to win in the end. Don't forget to include an exit strategy as well. One partner usually buys out the other, either in a lump sum or over time. Then, after all is written down, each person's separate lawyer should review the document.

Limited Partnerships

A limited partner is an investor. This person usually has limited liability and is not involved in the day-to-day operations. Again, spell out all stakes in the agreement. Will the partner provide money, time, or both in exchange for owning part of the business? Agree on paper what will be the return on the investment, what percentage of profit the partner will receive, and how it will be paid out (quarterly or annually?).

The beauty of a limited partnership is in the security. If the business folds, the investors lose only the initial investment. They pay out no debt. As with the partnership, you'll need a lawyer to set up a limited partnership.

Corporations

Creating a corporation that owns your business is another choice. One person can be the sole shareholder and own the business completely. Incorporation provides a safety net if the business fails because, unlike a sole proprietorship or partnership, the shareholders hold no liability for the company's debt. Their loss cannot exceed the amount paid in. One of the downsides of incorporating is double taxation, in which profits are taxed as income to the corporation and then as income to the shareholders. Different types of corporations exist, some with more tax burden than others. To set up a corporation, you'll need an accountant and an attorney.

Behind You!

You can avoid the double taxation by filing for S Corporation status with the IRS. By creating an S Corporation, the income is treated as it would be in a sole proprietorship or partnership, skipping the corporation and going straight to the shareholders, who report individually on their personal tax returns. Talk to an accountant and a lawyer to see if this would be right for your situation.

If you are thinking about joining an existing business as a partner, get your hands on all financial statements, and have a neutral third party review them. Both the profit and rent should be about 10 percent of the total sales. If their claim is for more profit or if the rent seems steep, you may want to reconsider.

The Least You Need to Know

◆ Most new restaurants fail within three years of opening.

◆ A good business plan will improve your chances of success.

◆ You can finance your venture with loans, join forces with others, or incorporate.

Chapter 24

Opening Up

In This Chapter

- ◆ Determining your concept
- ◆ Finding your market
- ◆ Designing your restaurant and menu
- ◆ Getting good help

The to-do list for opening a restaurant is seemingly endless. Yet the very first item on that list should be to decide what your concept is, because the concept will dictate every other step you take, from location to marketing to menu.

The Concept

Sometimes goofy restaurants make money, and serious restaurants fold. Your concept can be successful whether it's at either extreme or somewhere in the middle.

Your concept is the image you hope to present to the public. It may be as simple as a hamburger stand or as elaborate as a Hawaiian luau tiki-room bar. Whatever it is, you need to research it.

Every restaurant has a concept, with the focus on a category of some kind. Sometimes it's obvious, other times it's more subtle, but that doesn't matter, as long as you understand the focus and follow it throughout the operation. The typical focus is a regional or ethnic cuisine, such as French, Chinese, Mexican, Pacific Northwestern, or Italian. In these cases, the focus is often narrowed further because many cuisines have even more defined regional differences, such as Provençal, Sicilian, or Cantonese. Although such specialization isn't necessary, it does help define your concept a little better.

> **Kitchen Tales**
>
> How many totally goofy restaurants have you been to? Ever heard of Medieval Times? There you can watch jousting and eat with your hands. Sounds crazy, but this franchise, which began in Spain, has been a success in the United States, opening nine locations since 1983. In a theme restaurant, the cuisine and service take a back seat to the ambiance. The main reason people go to the Hard Rock Cafe is not for the food. It's for the rock theme. It's entertainment, first and foremost. These restaurants are more often located in popular tourist spots because they do not rely on regular customers.
>
> But just because the theme is first and foremost doesn't mean the food and service don't matter. They still have to be good, or even the tourists will stay away.

You can center your concept on a particular ingredient, like garlic, or seafood, or steak. Restaurants like this are often found in tourist destinations and feature ingredients particular to the region.

A specific meal can be the focus of your concept as well. There are terrific places known for their great breakfasts or sandwiches or desserts. When I was at college in Boulder, we frequented a great place, The Aristocrat. They served incredible pancakes the size of your head and an even bigger plate of crispy hash browns. We couldn't get near the place on Sunday morning. I don't even know if they were open the rest of the day, but who cared?

And don't forget your concept can even center on just one dish. In newspapers and magazines across the country you'll find the annual *Best Of* lists, telling you where to go for the best burritos, cinnamon buns, chili, BBQ, margaritas, corn dogs, and so on.

Whatever your concept is, do your homework. First, look around for similar places, and study them. What are they doing right? What are they doing wrong? How does your idea differ from theirs?

Kitchen Tales

My favorite theme restaurants:

◆ **The Bear Pit,** Mission Hills, California

Really great Missouri-style BBQ, sawdust on the floor, and flowing waterfall art.

◆ **Quark's Bar,** Las Vegas, Nevada

Really, only if you are a Star Trek fan are you going to like it here. But boy … will you like it here.

◆ **Casa Bonita,** Lakewood, Colorado

Two words: Cliff divers!

Choose your concept carefully. Don't decide upon an idea without careful consideration because you should be willing to live with it, ideally, for the next 30 years.

Now, take your concept and expand it. Think about the entire operation, being as specific as possible. From the time the customer pulls into the parking lot to the last trip to the restroom, you want the atmosphere you create to be consistent, unique, and memorable. Your goal is to get the customer to talk about the experience at the water cooler the next day.

The Market

Now that you have a concept, you need to find a market for it. To whom is your concept going to appeal? Look around you. Do you see your market? Are you going to attract the ladies-who-lunch crowd? Do you want a family-friendly idea? Is it so upscale that only the wealthiest market will attend? An understanding of *demographics* will help you figure out your market.

For instance, you can make some generalizations about people based on their age. Young people, college age and younger, have less expendable income and tend to spend what they do have on fast food and pizza. Young families will sit down to eat but mainly in family-friendly, high-value

def•i•ni•tion

Demographics refers to the characteristics of a population. It considers things like age, gender, ethnicity, income, education, housing, and mobility. From that information, you can determine a generalization about the people, their spending, and particularly their eating habits.

operations. They prefer casual, value-oriented places, with salad bars and all-you-can-eat specials. Upscale restaurants are reserved for special occasions, when Mom and Dad pick up the tab. The baby boomers (45 to 65 years old) tend to spend more freely than their kids. They are affluent professionals or grandparents who appreciate value. The 50-to-64-year-olds have the most money to spend and mainly focus on the quality of service and food when they dine out. Seniors 65 and older are often on fixed income and appreciate value menus. They tend to eat smaller portions earlier in the evening.

But bear in mind other marketing considerations besides age and income. Are there more apartments or single-family homes in the neighborhood in which you want to open the restaurant? This directly relates to income and class. But it is not necessarily cut and dried. While apartment dwelling can mean a lower income over all, it could also indicate a younger demographic of college-age or young professionals.

Do people have cars, or do they take the subway? If you're in a town where people often use public transportation, a site closer to the stations or stops is preferred. If most people drive to their destination, provide enough parking to accommodate your customers on your busiest nights. Will you need a valet service? Will parking or delivery trucks cause tension in the neighborhood? Always check local ordinances.

Watch the area carefully. Do you think your idea for an English tea room will hit it big here, or is it more of a sports-bar neighborhood? Are you going to appeal more to men or women? You may find that the little old ladies have been hoping for a place they could go for a pint.

Classic Cuisine

Why are there so many Starbucks, and why are they so successful? The sheer number of shops contradicts everything we know about real estate and marketing. The concept is a reaction to long lines of customers. If there is another shop nearby, the wait will be shorter. Stores on the opposite side of the same block address customer's traffic patterns, daily habits (caffeine addiction), and fear of change. And while they all look alike, each store is actually quite different, geared specifically toward the neighborhood and its inhabitants. Brilliant!

Check the demographics in your area to determine what type of market it is and what would go over well. Alternatively, you can take your concept and search out the demographic that you're aiming for. These statistics can be very helpful in finding the right location and developing the right marketing strategy.

The Location

You know that neighborhood restaurant that continuously changes hands? That bad-luck spot? Every town has one. People keep trying to make a go of it. Over and over the restaurants fail. But the problem is not bad luck, it's bad planning. No amount of *feng shui* can save a place whose concept and location don't match.

If you start with a location, study the neighborhood and figure out what concept will work there.

def•i•ni•tion

Feng shui is a Chinese custom of arranging a space to make it peaceful and harmonious.

What were the restaurants that failed in that location? Do some investigating. Why are they gone? This is a very important concern because you don't want to make the same mistake.

If you are starting with your concept, then the process works in reverse. You need to find the perfect spot. For this, think about whom you want to attract.

The clientele you want to entice is the most important consideration when looking for a location. First, you want your restaurant to be the exciting new place, not just another in a long line of the same style restaurants on your local restaurant row. The exciting new concepts make an impact if they are done properly. I mentioned Medieval Times earlier. This place would never play in the suburbs because the demographics are all wrong. Sure, suburbs are full of families, but all the kids have homework. So they plunked one down in Buena Park, near Disneyland, Knott's Berry Farm, and a hundred hotels, where it fits perfectly.

Location doesn't refer simply to the neighborhood but includes traffic, visibility, and accessibility. Is there a lot of foot traffic or a busy street? Ten thousand people may be walking by each day, but if they're all on their way to the bus stop after work, the location may be wrong. A busy street is no guarantee for success if there is no place to park. After all, freeways are very busy, but you can't dine unless there's an off-ramp. A classic example of this is a city with a million one-way streets. I will only circle around so many times before I get frustrated and go home.

Is it hot where you are? Will you need outdoor seating? Air conditioning? Is it cold? Will you want a fireplace?

If you can narrow your concept and find a spot, then investigate the rent. Can you afford the lease? If it exceeds 10 percent of your projected sales, you need to reevaluate the concept or look for a new location. No spot is so good that it's worth opening up a losing venture.

The Menu

If you're a chef, writing the menu will be the best part. I bet you have already planned this, at least a little. Now really take your ideas and work them out in detail. From this initial menu, determine your needs in the dining room (flatware, dishware, glassware), in the kitchen (large and small appliances, tools, storage), for pricing and initial product expenses, as well as staff needs.

First, write the complete menu. Include everything on each plate, the portion sizes, garnishes, and even condiments. Then write out all the recipes, and determine how much of what ingredients you will need to order. You'll want to have some staple ingredients on hand all the time, so include those, as well as cleaning and storage supplies, like brooms and plastic wrap.

> **Kitchen Tales**
>
> You'll need to decide about liquor now. If you are going to serve it, you'll need a license, which is regulated on a state or local level. Beer and wine are typically licensed separately from hard liquor. A limited number of liquor licenses are allowed in any particular area, so you may need to buy the license from an existing holder if your area has no new licenses available. Liquor licenses can be renewed, usually on an annual basis, provided no offenses were committed, such as selling to minors.

Then it's time to test recipes. Be sure you can make the food easily in a consistent and expedient manner. You want it to be as easy to make 50 orders as it is to make 5. Oh, and you should be sure it tastes good. Play around with presentation. Elaborate displays can take a long time. Too many garnishes and sauces can end up looking like a mess on a busy Saturday night. Take some time to think about light here, too. Your plates may look gorgeous under a florescent light, but how does the look change by candlelight? While most women look better that way, most food doesn't.

All along, keep your idea of concept in the front of your brain. Once you have all these items worked out, you can realistically determine pricing and compare it to your salary needs.

The Layout

The look of your restaurant will depend on your concept. But as you are making your plans, remember to pay careful attention to the functionality of the space.

The comfort of your patrons should be the first consideration when you are determining the layout of the dining room. On the other hand, safety should be the first consideration when you design the layout of your kitchen.

In the dining room, you need to maintain comfort, traffic flow, and ambiance, while still accommodating as many seats as you can. Each seat and each table should be comfortable and pleasant. Think about light (both natural and artificial), and sound (from the street, from the kitchen, and from within the dining room). Don't forget customer service areas, including a host station, public restrooms, public phones (if there is such a thing anymore), and a comfortable waiting area. Take into consideration, too, any waiting area that may extend outside.

Every bit of movement during a busy shift needs to be as efficient as possible. Also, remember to allocate space for storage, dishwashing, and administrative areas. An employee restroom is an important consideration, so they don't have to share with the customers.

In the kitchen, think about the flow of traffic in and out and the flow within the kitchen. Are the doors big enough for two-way traffic? Do you need double doors or two separate doors, one in and one out? Are there blind corners? Some kitchens have mirrors installed so that you can see if someone is about to clock you as they come around a curve. Some places simply instruct their staff to yell "corner!" as they make the turn.

Ambiance

Ambiance refers to the overall mood evoked by a particular surrounding. A good restaurant should be a pleasant place to be. There are a lot of things that contribute to that overall pleasant mood. The quality of the food and service are, of course, paramount. But other, more subtle, factors affect a restaurant's ambiance as well.

The style of your food and the location of your restaurant will help to determine the ambiance, but you can do several things to enhance the dining experience. Décor is very important. Many restaurateurs spend big bucks on high-profile designers to entice customers. You may find this approach a good fit. Or you may believe that the food should speak for itself. Regardless of your views, your décor will create an atmosphere, whether you want it to or not. Spend time considering things like patterns (on the floor, the upholstery, the linen, the tableware, and even the wait staff). Color is important, too. Colors in warm tones make a room feel cozy, while bright colors make rooms appear larger. Certain colors have special meanings to certain cultures. If your restaurant specializes in a cuisine from a certain part of the world, it's a good idea to do some research on the cultural significance of color to that region.

Another huge mood enhancer (or killer) is music. Have you ever noticed that fast music in a restaurant causes you to chew faster? This is fine if your intention is to turn tables quickly. But that may not be the kind of ambiance you want.

If you want to play recorded music from your own music collection anywhere in your restaurant, you'll need a license. This includes not only the dining room and the bar, but also the bathrooms and on the answering machine, too. You are required to purchase a license from one of the performance rights societies, which include Broadcast Music Inc. (BMI) and The American Society of Composers, Authors and Publishers (ASCAP). These societies collect money and distribute a portion of it to the artists.

> **Behind You!**
>
> Infringement of copyright law carries steep penalties of up to $100,000 if the infringement is thought to be willful.

If you don't want to pay the fee, you can purchase what is commonly called *canned* or *elevator* music, from a company such as Muzak. You could also install a coin-operated jukebox in your restaurant, but keep in mind that these also require a license—a jukebox operating license.

> **Behind You!**
>
> The National Restaurant Association has put together a great pamphlet on the subject of music licensing titled *Music Licensing and You*. You can find it online at www.restaurant.org. Type *music licensing* in the *search* box, and it will direct you to a PDF file full of good info.

Until recently, U.S. copyright law required any business using radio or TV broadcasts in a public place to have permission by the owner of copyright. But in 1999 a new bill was signed into law, The Sonny Bono Copyright Term Extension and the Fairness in Music Licensing Amendment. This law exempts certain businesses from paying copyright fees. This means that you can play the radio or television for free if your restaurant or bar is smaller than 3,750 square feet, does not charge an entrance fee, and does not retransmit the broadcasts. It's good news for you, bad news for the artists.

The Staff

Never underestimate the importance of a strong staff. So far, I have talked a lot about the management and supervision of kitchen staff but relatively little about dining room and administrative positions. If you are opening up your own place, consider these positions just as carefully as you do your sous chef.

The dining room should have its own boss, whether you call that position dining room manager, maitre d', or host/hostess. The job description includes responsibility for hiring, scheduling, and supervising the wait staff, bussers, bartenders and hosts; ordering dining room supplies and managing the inventory of those supplies; running *the bank*; and balancing the receipts each night.

def•i•ni•tion

The bank is the till or the register. The employee who runs the bank is responsible for all the money earned that night, making change, processing credit cards, and making the nightly deposits.

The number of administrative positions you need depends on the size of your operation. But regardless of size, get yourself an accountant. He can help with accounting and payroll systems, managing insurance benefits, taxes, investments, and even business forecasts. Treat the hiring of a CPA as you would any other employee, and check his references.

When It's Time to Expand

When your business is a success, it is quite natural to want to capitalize on it and expand. A second and third location is tempting. But be sure to do as much research and pre-planning at your second site as you did in the first.

Locations and demographics are by no means constant. What works in one busy downtown may not work in another. The failure of the second location is a common cause of overall business failure. So investigate the new location carefully. Look at existing competition. Is it stronger than the competition at your first location? How about traffic? Are there similar businesses providing traffic for you?

Behind You!

Don't rely on your existing location to fund the second. Treat the new place as a completely separate entity. One of the biggest reasons that a second venture fails is that the owners were not prepared for it financially. Save plenty of money so that if your second store isn't as successful as the first, you have something to live on.

Most importantly, examine your presence in the operation. Are you indispensable, or have you trained others in the daily operation? Are you always there, or does it run well without you? If you feel that your absence would be detrimental to either store, then forget a second venture. You can't be at two places at once.

Franchise

If your business is successful, you might consider selling franchises. But before you jump into it, be sure your shop is a good candidate. First, it should be unique. The product, service, theme, or ambiance needs to be different enough from your competitors to make it interesting. Your operating systems should be thorough, successful, and easy to reproduce. Also be sure that the potential for earning is enough to both make a profit and pay a royalty.

Other Ways to Grow

Some ways to grow don't require a new location. Consider expanding the services at your current location. You could open up for a meal that you don't currently serve. Breakfast, brunch, lunch, tea, or late-night seatings can generate a new customer base. Create a take-out menu to tap into the busy working family market. Catering is another classic means of generating additional income, either on or off premises. Your regular customers may jump at the chance to have you cater their parties.

You can also expand on the Internet. Offer to ship products, such as specialty foods, cookware, or cookbooks, nationally or internationally. A website can circulate your name and generate profit through your products, as well as interest in the restaurant itself.

Media coverage is good, too. Get out and do things media-worthy. Participate in local charity events, farmers' markets, food shows, and competitions.

The Least You Need to Know

- ◆ Figure out your concept first.
- ◆ Your concept will determine location, market, and design.
- ◆ Spend time selecting a quality staff for all positions, not just the ones in the kitchen.

Chapter 5

Things You Don't Want to Think About

In This Chapter

- ◆ Training your staff for emergencies
- ◆ Handling pests
- ◆ Understanding insurance coverage
- ◆ Dealing with thcft

I am a California girl and have lived through my share of earthquakes. Luckily, the places I worked incurred minimal damage. But many places never recover from these disasters. Businesses suffer financial loss from damage to the property as well as from loss of business due to extended closure.

Even disasters that take place far away can impact business. After the terrorist attacks of September 11, 2001, restaurant workers across the country lost their jobs because people simply didn't feel like going out to eat as much. Times change. Businesses go through bad times and good times, and not everyone survives when America decides not to eat out.

But it is possible to plan ahead. Train your staff for likely emergencies. Insure yourself adequately. Treat your employees well, even if you have to let them go. After a disaster, when things return to normal, you might want them to return to work for you.

Stumbling Blocks

Disasters happen. No matter how hard you try, you can't be prepared for everything. You can do nothing more as a business owner than insure yourself, train your staff, and stockpile good karma.

Fire

Fire is obviously the most significant danger in a professional kitchen. I have never worked in a restaurant that burned down, but I have seen many things, as well as a few people, catch on fire.

One student got his head too close to a propane torch and caught his floppy chef hat on fire. Luckily, we put it out before it got to his hair. When he wore the burnt hat to school the next day, he earned the nickname *Cappy*. I guess he didn't have an extra.

I saw another cook light his sleeve on fire after a particularly hearty flambé. The next day he tried to start a new trend in chef-wear with a fabulous short sleeve design, courtesy of his tailor (a.k.a. his mom).

It's only funny when it doesn't happen to you.

All employees must be instructed in preventing and extinguishing fires. Teach them how to avoid fires in the first place, and how to put out various types of fires. Most importantly, give them an evacuation plan.

The following table outlines the most common types of fire that occur in a kitchen.

Fire Classification

Class	What's on Fire	How to Put It Out
Class A (Remember it as A for *Ash*)	Ordinary combustibles like paper, wood, cardboard, and plastic	Extinguish by water and the removal of oxygen (smothering)

Class	What's on Fire	How to Put It Out
Class B (Remember it as B for *Butane*)	Flammable liquids including gasoline, kerosene, propane, butane, grease, and oil	Use baking soda or a large pot or pan to cut off the supply of oxygen to the flame, or use a class B fire extinguisher. Water will only spread this fire, making it bigger
Class C (Remember it as C for *Circuits*)	Appliances, wiring, outlets, and circuit breakers	Trying to put this type of fire out with water will cause electrical shock. Use baking soda or a large pot or pan to cut off the supply of oxygen to the flame, or use a class C fire extinguisher.

Regular fire inspections are important, both by your local fire department and by the company that provides your extinguishers. Inspection ensures that the suppression systems are operational at all times and easy to access.

Fire extinguishers should be the last line of defense in an emergency, because, although they work the best, they contaminate everything they come in contact with. A little fire that is extinguished by chemicals, when it could simply be covered with a lid, can turn a minor inconvenience into a money-sucking closure for, at the very least, the rest of the night.

Hood-mounted fire suppression systems are usually required by insurance companies and local fire codes. Heat or smoke can activate them. Be sure that your staff knows how yours operates and how they can avoid setting it off accidentally. When the hood system goes off, cleanup from a chemically extinguished fire can mean several nights out of business and certainly a loss of repeat business from everyone whose meals were contaminated.

Smoke-activated hood systems run the biggest risk of prematurely going off. At my house, even steam from the shower can set off our smoke alarm, not to mention the fumes I generate when I grill a particularly well-marinated piece of meat. Imagine what happens when you burn a hotel pan full of beef bones. Your staff needs easy access to a well-ventilated area away from the customers, preferably out a back door and into an alley. When food starts smoking, the item can be rushed out and allowed to cool where it won't set anything off.

Make everyone aware of an emergency evacuation plan. Everyone needs to know how to exit and where to go in the event of an emergency. (For information on training your staff in safety procedures, see Chapter 22.)

Pests

Everyone has a different standard when it comes to clean. I am always amazed at what passes for clean in the food service business. Built-up, caked-on grease covers everything in a professional kitchen. Pots and pans, the legs and the underside of work tables and bins, the floor, the drains, and the appliances can easily accumulate food and grease. What looks clean to the untrained eye usually isn't. The rodents and bugs know where the grease is. They know where the bins of sugar, nuts, and flour are, too. They can make a good life for themselves in a restaurant.

Insects particularly enjoy the bar, where hidden sugary soda nozzles, cut fruit, and sticky floors provide a banquet.

You can hire services to come in periodically to bait and spray for pests. It's a good idea because you are going to have little visitors in your place, no matter how clean you are (or think you are).

Kitchen Tales _____

I once had a job that required me to open the restaurant every morning. Upon entering the back door, I had to cross the kitchen to get to the alarm shutoff and the light switch. This particular restaurant had quite a little mouse problem. To combat it, the night crew laid sticky traps on the floor as they left. So each morning my goal was to make it to the alarm and light without stepping on any dead mice. And I didn't always make it. What a way to start the day!

Animals will also find their way to your dumpster. Wandering packs of hungry animals know where to find the best scraps. A clean dumpster is not an oxymoron. All garbage should be bagged, and the dumpster should always be closed. Tightly close the grease barrels as well.

Insurance

Plan ahead. Be prepared. Think about circumstances you don't want to think about. Or let an insurance agent do it for you. Insuring your business against fire, theft, and a lawsuit is one of the few shields you have against disaster. A wide range of coverage is available with lots of help in deciphering the details (see *Additional Resources*, Appendix A).

Required Coverage

The following types of insurance are required for any restaurant:

- **Workman's Compensation Insurance** is for workers who are injured on the job. Workers are entitled to these benefits whether the fault is their own or the employer's.

- **Disabilities Benefit Insurance** is for workers who are disabled outside of the workplace.

- **Unemployment Insurance** is paid into a fund by the employer in the event that a worker is laid off.

- **General Liability Insurance** covers customers and other nonworkers who are injured on the premises.

- **Product Liability Insurance** protects you in case someone becomes ill from eating your food.

- **Liquor Liability Insurance** is necessary in states that hold the server of alcohol responsible for injuries or damage that occurs due to intoxication.

- **Auto Liability** is necessary if you have a company vehicle, such as a delivery van.

Recommended Coverage

In addition to the required insurance policies, you should consider taking out a few additional policies. You'll be glad you did if you ever need them:

- **Fire and Extended Coverage** protects in the case of fire and related disasters, as well as vandalism.

- **Business Interruption Insurance** covers fixed costs and expenses if your business is shut down by fire damage.

- **Mortgage Insurance** covers your mortgage during a disaster.

- **Business Life Insurance** protects creditors and partners from financial loss if death occurs.

◆ **Federal Crime Insurance** protects against robbery and burglary.

◆ **Health Insurance** provides medical coverage for employees. It is often too expensive for small business owners. Some businesses elect to pay a portion of the insurance, while the employees pay the rest.

Theft

Theft is a huge problem in the food service industry. Actually, it's a problem in every industry, but preventing people from stealing food is a lot harder than preventing them from stealing office supplies. Not only do you need to watch what walks out the back door, but you also need to watch what gets consumed on the premises.

Kitchen employees have difficulty differentiating between their kitchen at home, where they own the contents of their cupboards, and the kitchen at work, where someone else owns everything.

An employer can take several preventative measures to help minimize theft. First, feed your staff. I have been in jobs where there was a mandatory dinner or lunch break, and we had to sit at the family table and eat. This is smart because not everyone has good eating habits. Workers will snack less if they are not hungry. Educating them in basic nutrition is helpful, too, making them aware of the risks of a bad diet.

Behind You!

Pilfering takes many forms. It's not just food and booze that walks out the door. You'll want to keep your eye on all your cookware, nonperishables like parchment paper and first-aid supplies, and even your furniture. No kidding! If your staff has keys, and access to the place when you're not around, you never know what can end up decorating their homes.

Take inventory often. If you make each supervisor responsible for monitoring the product during his shift, you'll have more people with their eyes on the goods. Inventory is not just keeping an eye on the storeroom, but is also monitoring the flow of product each day. You need to know how much of what is used when, and how much was sold, burnt, or thrown out at the end of the night. I've had supervisors check garbage cans at regular intervals throughout the day, to be sure product isn't ending up there. You may even go so far as to offer an incentive to supervisors whose inventory stays on the mark each night.

In addition to the obvious products like meat, dairy, and vegetables, keep an eye on spices, oils, and booze. Expensive items, like saffron and vanilla beans, fit easily into a pocket, and I have come across more than one person enjoying the wine reserved for cooking out of an empty cola can. This is not only an expensive problem, but a dangerous one. Drunken cooks, fire, and knives are a bad combination. (See Chapter 16 for more on drinking on the job.)

You can prevent petty theft a couple of ways. Providing a locker room for staff to store their belongings keeps the bags and backpacks out of the kitchen, where the white truffles could *accidentally* fall in. You could also post a security guard at the employee exit, who would check backpacks, knife rolls, and pockets. The only place I worked that went to that extreme is the only one that is still in business, 15 years later. It was a little disheartening at first, feeling like I wasn't trusted. Then again, it was comforting to know that if my wallet ever went missing, it would likely be found.

The most important thing you can do to deter theft is to be a good boss. People are less likely to steal from someone they respect and admire, and who takes care of them. If you are a crummy boss, some employees will feel entitled to whatever they can steal.

The Least You Need to Know

- Train your staff for all likely emergencies.
- Control pests by careful cleaning.
- Several types of insurance coverage are mandatory, and some are just a good idea.
- Manage theft by careful observation, strict standards of inventory control, and focus on quality management.

Additional Resources

Life as a chef is more than cooking and reading cookbooks. I have included a short list of extracurricular activities that I know you'll enjoy. A whole wide world is out there for you to explore.

For Fun Culinary Websites

The Tweezer Times
www.tweezertimes.com

This site promotes food styling and photography and provides advice and assistance to small business owners and freelancers.

Shameless Restaurants
www.shamelessrestaurants.com

Restaurant reviews from the inside. This site is a veritable fount of complaints from industry workers, sorted by region. It is a good place to go if you're wondering what it's like to work in a particular establishment.

Tallyrand's Culinary Fare
www.geocities.com/NapaValley/6454/index

This is an all-you-can-eat culinary history buffet. You'll find biographies, a history of cuisine, history of all sorts of foods and recipes, as well as recipes and technical help.

Great Food Movies

Babette's Feast, 1988

A movie about a French refugee in nineteenth-century Denmark doesn't sound that fun, but wait until she starts cooking!

Big Night, 1996

Two brothers emigrate from Italy and open a restaurant in New Jersey.

Chocolat, 2001

A mother and daughter open a chocolate shop in a small French village.

Eat, Drink, Man, Woman, 1994

A master chef and his daughters share life around the Sunday night table.

Like Water for Chocolate, 1993

You'll find mystical, surreal, forbidden love in early twentieth-century Mexico. Yeah. There's food in it, too.

Tampopo, 1987

In a fast-food noodle restaurant, they search for the perfect ramen.

Who Is Killing the Great Chefs of Europe?, 1978

The great chefs of Europe are being killed in the manner of their specialty.

Magazines

Art Culinaire

This is a beautiful hard-cover quarterly publication. It has terrific information on specific ingredients, such as sea urchins, or nutmeg, or beer. Then it presents recipes by today's top chefs featuring those ingredients. Visit the magazine online at getartc.com.

Cooks Illustrated

This magazine gives you the *best of* everything, from the best way to roast a chicken, to the best lemon bars, to the best gadgets, products, and methods. It's serious, reliable stuff.

Pastry Art and Design

This is how pastry chefs stay on top of the industry, see what their competition is up to, and get ideas. It's all a bit frou-frou, but you occasionally will find some practical information. If nothing else, it's a grand source for mockery.

Restaurant Startup and Growth

The name says it all. This periodical covers everything from training to equipment purchase.

Saveur

I've learned more from this magazine about international food than any other resource. The writers go everywhere and try everything. I'm getting hungry just thinking about it.

The Art of Eating

This well-written, serious quarterly publication on food and wine from around the world includes regional cuisine, ingredients, traditions, recipes, reviews, and resources.

More of My Favorite Books

Vegetables (1996), *Seafood* (1997), *Desserts* (1998), and *Meat and Game* (2001), by Charlie Trotter (Ten Speed Press)

Here is fabulous inspiration from a truly innovative chef.

Ladyfingers and Nun's Tummies, by Martha Barnette (Vintage Books)

This gives historical reference for goofy foods.

Rare Bits, by Patricia Bunning Stevens (Ohio University Press)

Learn interesting recipe origins.

Simple Cooking (1996), *Serious Pig* (2000), *Pot on the Fire* (2001), by John Thorn (Harper Collins)

Enjoy good laughs, good recipes, and best mac 'n' cheese ever.

The International Dictionary of Desserts, Pastries and Confections, by Carole Bloom (Hearst Books)

This is a must-have resource for pastry history.

Garde Manger: The Art and Craft of the Cold Kitchen (Culinary Institute of America)

Beautiful, inspirational photographs picture classic recipes.

The Professional Garde Manger, by David Paul Larousse (John Wiley and Sons)

Discover classic recipes that work.

The Meat Buyer's Guide (North American Meat Processors Association)

This is an invaluable guide to buying meat for the professional chef.

The Commercial Guide to Fish and Shellfish (Urner Barry Publications)

This publication lists hundreds of fish and shellfish varieties, with essential information about buying, selling, and eating.

Parisian Home Cooking, by Michael Roberts (William Morrow and Company)

Discover the way the real Parisians eat.

The Beautiful Cookbook Series (Merehurst Press)

These are beautiful books, but not just for the coffee table. They have accurate, authentic recipes, too.

Letters to a Young Chef, Daniel Boulud (Perseus Books Group)

This short read reinforces everything I told you in this book. (You may find it comforting to hear it from a famous guy.)

Professional Organizations

American Culinary Federation
www.acfchefs.org

This is the mother of all culinary organizations.

Bread Bakers Guild of America
www.bbga.org

Artisan baking at its best.

James Beard Foundation
www.jamesbeard.org

The who's who of food is here.

International Association of Culinary Professionals

www.iacp.com

You'll find a great resource for networking, charitable programs, and scholarships.

Les Dames d'Escoffier

www.ldei.org

This is a well-regarded leadership organization for women in culinary arts.

National Restaurant Association

www.restaurant.org

The best food business resource in America is here.

Retail Bakers of America

www.rbanet.com

This nationwide organization is dedicated to the professional baker.

Women Chefs and Restaurateurs

www.womenchefs.org

Advocates improving the restaurant industry by promoting culinary education and advancement of women.

Women's Foodservice Forum

www.womensfoodserviceforum.com

Champions the advancement of women in food service through highly successful leadership development and mentor programs.

Culinary School Directory

This appendix lists some excellent websites that contain much more information than I could ever list in this book. Many of them will link you directly to the schools you're interested in, and help determine which school is right for you. Following these sites is my own list of schools. It is by no means a complete list. I have only listed schools in the United States, and I have only listed one per state.

Let me explain.

First, I have not included the Mother of all Schools, the Culinary Institute of America (CIA). Why? Because you probably already know it, or know of it, and you can easily find information on it in the resources I have provided in this appendix. Second, I did not include two other wonderful and very large schools, The Art Institutes (AI) and Johnson and Wales (J&W). They are great schools, and you can look them up, too, on your own. These schools have many, many campuses all over the country. I did list the main campus of J&W under *Rhode Island*, simply because it is the only game in town.

I searched for schools that offer the highest degree in culinary art. Numerous schools offer a diploma or certificate, but few give an Associate's degree, and even fewer offer a Bachelor's degree. Many schools offer degrees in hospitality management of one kind or another. But I have an idea that most of you are looking to become chefs, not necessarily food and beverage managers, so I tried to look for degrees specifically in culinary art. If a school also offers a degree in baking or pastry, it won my affection over other schools in that state. Other criteria I used included faculty credentials, the size of the facility, and the accrediting body. Because I used to work for the Accrediting Council of Independent Colleges and Schools (ACICS), I know what it takes to become accredited, and I know how serious a commitment it is when a school decides to offer a degree. A school that offers a degree is simply more on top of its game than one that doesn't.

That being said, schools that offer no degree, like the French Culinary Institute in New York City, are still worth something in name recognition. Of course, in most cases, you will pay more to be trained by a famous chef than you would to get an actual degree. Is it worth it? Not for me. If you're really searching for a lifelong career, a degree will get you farther. But only you know for sure what's right for you.

You will find a few listings that do not fit the criteria I just mentioned; I chose them simply because they were the best option statewide.

Culinary School Guides

Chef 2 Chef Culinary Portal
chef2chef.net

This site has everything. They list the Top 100 everything, including chefs, schools, teachers, books, restaurants, and websites. They list forums to join for professionals and amateurs. There a zillion recipes and job postings. There are supplies, books, magazines, business resources, and more, much more, so much more I can't type it all out. Just go there.

Cooking Schools.com
www.cookingschools.com

Well over a thousand culinary schools are listed by state, with direct links to the schools websites given.

Culinary Ed
www.culinaryed.com

Culinary schools are listed by state, as well as related links, including recipe banks, supplies, and funky specialized products like cedar planks and garlic juice.

Culinary School Finder
www.culinary-school-finder.com

Here you can search for schools by city, state, career, or specialty. It also features some interesting articles and biographies.

Shaw Guides
www.cookingcareer.shawguides.com

It's easy to get lost in the Shaw Guides, because it's a guide for everything, not just cooking schools. But in terms of cooking, it includes all the big names, as well as schools geared toward wines and recreational cooking.

United States Department of Education
www.ed.gov

This is an overwhelming site, but it has all the information you need to pick a worthy school. From the home page, go to *quick click* and select *accreditation*. From there you can learn all about accreditation, access data bases on accrediting bodies, search by region or specialty, and then link to the accrediting body website to find listings of the schools they sponsor.

Office of Post Secondary Education
www.ope.ed.gov/accreditation

This very user-friendly site lists programs accredited by accrediting agencies and state approved agencies recognized by the U.S. Secretary of Education.

Culinary Schools by State

Alabama

Culinard
65 Bagby Drive
Birmingham, AL 35209
1-877-429-CHEF (2433)
www.culinard.com

Accredited by the Accrediting Council for Independent Colleges and Schools

Program offerings:

50 week diploma in pastry

18 month diploma in culinary art

21 month occupational Associate's degree in culinary art

24 month occupational Associate's degree in pastry

4 year Bachelor's degree in culinary arts management

Alaska

University of Alaska, Anchorage
Division of Arts and Hospitality
3211 Providence Drive
Cuddy Hall
Anchorage, AK 99508
907-786-1800
www.uaa.alaska.edu

Accredited by the Northwest Association of Schools and Colleges

Program offerings:

1 year certificate in culinary art

2 semester certificate in dietary management

2 year Associate's degree in culinary art

4 year Bachelor's degree in hospitality and restaurant management

Arizona

Cochise College
901 North Colombo Avenue
Sierra Vista, AZ 85635-2317
520-515-0500
www.cochise.org

Accredited by the North Central Association of Colleges and Schools

Program offerings:

6 month certificate in garde manger

6 month certificate in chef de cuisine/food preparation

6 month certificate in chef pâtissier

1 year certificate in sous chef

2 year Associate's degree in culinary art

Arkansas

Arkansas Tech University
Hospitality Administration
Williamson Hall
Russelville, AR 72801
1-800-582-6953
www.atu.edu

Accredited by the North Central Association of Colleges and Schools

Program offering:

4 year Bachelor's degree in hospitality administration

California

Los Angeles Trade Tech
400 West Washington Boulevard
Los Angeles, CA 90015
213-763-7331
www.lattc.edu

Accredited by the Western Association of Schools and Colleges

Program offerings:

2 year Associate's degree in culinary art

2 year Associate's degree in professional baking

California Sushi Academy
4509 Centinella Avenue
Los Angeles, CA 90066
310-301-1866
www.sushi.academy.com

Certified by the State of California Bureau for Private Postsecondary and Vocational Education

Program offerings:

12 week intensive sushi chef course

5 day intensive sushi chef course

1 day basic sushi chef course

1 day advanced sushi chef course

Colorado

Colorado Culinary Academy
At Mesa State College
Bishop Campus
2508 Blichmann Avenue
Grand Junction, CO 81505
970-255-2600
www.mesastate.edu

Accredited by the North Central Association of Colleges and Schools

Program offerings:

1 year certificate in culinary art

2 year Associate's degree in culinary art

Connecticut

Connecticut Culinary Institute
230 Farmington Avenue
Farmington, CT 06032
1-800-762-4337
www.ctculinary.edu

Accredited by the Commission of Career Schools and Colleges of Technology

Program offerings:

15 month diploma in advanced culinary art

35 week diploma in pastry art

Delaware

Delaware Technical and Community College
400 Stanton-Christiana Road
Newark, DE 19713
302-454-3900
www.dtcc.edu

Accredited by the Middle States Association of Colleges and Schools

Program offerings:

1 year diploma in food service management

2 year Associate's degree in culinary art

2 year Associate's degree in food service management

Florida

Florida Culinary Institute
2410 Metrocenter Boulevard
West Palm Beach, FL 33407
1-877-523-7549
www.floridaculinary.com

Accredited by the Accrediting Council for Independent Colleges and Schools

Program offerings:

12 month diploma in food and beverage management

12 month diploma in culinary nutrition

12 month diploma in culinary essentials

18 month Associate's degree in food and beverage management

18 month Associate's degree in international baking and pastry

18 month Associate's degree in culinary art

24 month Associate's degree in baking with food and beverage management

24 month Associate's degree in culinary art with food and beverage management

36 month Bachelor's degree in culinary management

Georgia

North Georgia Technical College
434 Meeks Avenue
Blairsville, GA 30512
706-439-6300
www.ngtcollege.org

Accredited by the Council on Occupational Education

Program offerings:

3 quarter technical certificate in restaurant baking

3 quarter technical certificate in culinary art fundamentals

3 quarter technical certificate in hospitality industry fundamentals

5 quarter diploma in hotel/restaurant/tourism management

5 quarter diploma in culinary art

7 quarter Associate's degree in culinary art

Hawaii

Culinary Institute of the Pacific
University of Hawaii–Kapiolani
4303 Diamond Head Road
Honolulu, HI 96816
808-734-9000
www.kcc.hawaii.edu

Accredited by the Western Association of Schools and Colleges

Program offerings:

4 month certificate in pâtisserie

4 month certificate in culinary art

18 month certificate in culinary art

2 year Associate's degree in culinary art

2 year Associate's degree in pâtisserie

Idaho

Selland College
Boise State University
1910 University Drive
Boise, ID 83725-0399
1-800-824-7017
www.selland.boisestate.edu

Accredited by the Northwest Association of Schools and Colleges

Program offerings:

12 month certificate in culinary art

18 month certificate in art

2 year Associate's degree in culinary art

6 month certificate in culinary art

Illinois

Kendall College
Schools of Culinary Arts and Hotel Management
900 North Branch Street
Chicago, IL 60622
1-866-677-3344
www.kendall.edu

Accredited by the North Central Association of Colleges and Schools

Program offerings:

4 quarter certificate in catering

4 quarter certificate in personal chef

4 quarter certificate in baking and pastry art

4 quarter certificate in culinary art/professional cookery

6 quarter Associate's degree in baking and pastry art

6 quarter Associate's degree in culinary art

12 quarter Bachelor's degree in culinary art

15 quarter Bachelor's degree in hospitality management

Indiana

Ivy Tech State College—Central Indiana
50 West Fall Creek Parkway North Drive
Indianapolis, IN 46208-5752
1-888-IVY-LINE (489-5463)
www.ivytech.edu/indianapolis

Accredited by North Central Association of Colleges and Schools

Program offerings:

2 year Associate's degree in hotel management

2 year Associate's degree in event management

2 year Associate's degree in hospitality administration

2 year Associate's degree in baking and pastry art

2 year Associate's degree in culinary art

3 year Associate's degree in culinary art

Iowa

Kirkwood Community College
Business and Information Technology Department
6301 Kirkwood Boulevard, Southwest
Cedar Rapids, IA 52403
319-398-4981
www.kirkwood.edu

Accredited by the North Central Association of Colleges and Schools

Program offerings:

1 year certificate in baking

1 year diploma in food service training

2 year Associate's degree in lodging management

2 year Associate's degree in restaurant management

2 year Associate's degree in culinary art

Kansas

Johnson County Community College
12345 College Boulevard
Overland Park, KS 66210
913-469-8500
www.johnco.cc.ks

Accredited by the North Central Association of Colleges and Schools

Program offerings:

2 year Associate's degree in hotel and lodging management

2 year Associate's degree in food and beverage management

3 year Associate's degree in chef apprenticeship

Kentucky

Sullivan University
Lexington Campus
2355 Harrodsburg Road
Lexington, KY 40504
1-800-467-6281
www.sullivan.edu

Accredited by the Southern Association of Colleges and Schools

Program offerings:

9 month diploma in travel/tourism

9 month diploma in professional baking

12 month diploma in professional cooking

18 month Associate's degree in travel/tourism and event management

18 month Associate's degree in professional catering

18 month Associate's degree in hotel and restaurant management

18 month Associate's degree in baking and pastry art

18 month Associate's degree in culinary art

36 month Bachelor's degree in hospitality management

Louisiana

Nicholls State University
Chef John Folse Culinary Institute
107 Gouaux Hall
PO Box 2099
Thibodaux, LA 70310
985-449-7100
www.nicholls.edu/jfolse

Accredited by the Southern Association of Colleges and Schools

Program offerings:

2 year Associate's degree in culinary art

4 year Bachelor's degree in culinary art

4 year Bachelor's degree in dietetics with culinary nutrition concentration

Maine

Southern Maine Community College
2 Fort Road
South Portland, ME 04106
1-877-282-2182
www.smccme.edu

Accredited by the New England Association of Schools and Colleges

Program offerings:

2 year Associate's degree in culinary art/applied science

York County Community College
112 College Drive
Wells, ME 04090
207-646-9282
www.yccc.edu

Accredited by the Southern Association of Colleges and Schools

Program offerings:

1 year certificate in food service specialist

1 year certificate in lodging operations

1 year certificate in food and beverage operations

2 year Associate's degree in hotel/restaurant operations

2 year Associate's degree in culinary art

Maryland

Baltimore International College
17 Commerce Street
Baltimore, MD 21202-3230
1-800-624-9926
www.bic.edu

Accredited by the Middle States Association of Colleges and Schools

Program offerings:

12 month certificate in professional cooking and baking

12 month certificate in professional baking and pastries

12 month certificate in professional cooking

22 month certificate in culinary art

2 year Associate's degree in professional cooking and baking

2 year Associate's degree in professional baking and pastry

2 year Associate's degree in hotel/motel/inn keeping management

4 year Bachelor's degree in hospitality/business management

4 year Bachelor's degree in hospitality/business management with marketing concentration

4 year Bachelor's degree in culinary management

30 credit hour Master's degree in hospitality management

Massachusetts

Newbury College
129 Fisher Avenue
Brookline, MA 02445-5796
617-730-7007
www.newbury.edu

Accredited by the New England Association of Schools and Colleges

Program offerings:

11 month certificate in hotel and resort management

11 month certificate in pastry art

11 month certificate in buffet catering

11 month certificate in food service and restaurant management

11 month certificate in meeting management

2 year Associate's degree in food service and restaurant management

2 year Associate's degree in hotel and resort management

2 year Associate's degree in culinary art

4 year Bachelor's degree in culinary management

4 year Bachelor's degree in hotel administration

Michigan

Schoolcraft College
18600 Haggerty Road
Livonia, MI 48152-4400
734-462-4426
www.schoolcraft.edu

Accredited by the North Central Association of Colleges and Schools

Program offerings:

1 year post graduate certificate in culinary art-brigade program

1 year certificate in baking and pastry culinary art

1 year certificate in culinary art

2 year Associate's degree in culinary art

Minnesota

Hennepin Technical College
9000 Brooklyn Boulevard
Brooklyn Park, MN 55445
1-800-345-4655
www.hennepintech.edu

Accredited by the North Central Association of Colleges and Schools

Program offerings:

15 month certificate in culinary art

16 month diploma in culinary art

2 year Associate's degree in culinary art

Mississippi

Mississippi University for Women
Culinary Arts Institute
W-Box 1639
Columbus, MS 39701
662-241-7472
www.muw.edu/interdisc

Accredited by the Southern Association of Colleges and Schools

Program offerings:

1 year certificate in culinary art

4 year Bachelor's degree in culinary art

Missouri

Ozarks Technical Community College
1001 East Chestnut Expressway
Springfield, MO 65802
417-447-7500
www.otc.edu

Accredited by the North Central Association of Colleges and Schools

Program offerings:

2 year Associate's degree in hospitality management

2 year Associate's degree in culinary art

Montana

The University of Montana, Missoula
909 South Avenue West
Missoula, MT 59801
1-800-542-6882
www.umt.edu

Accredited by the Northwest Association of Schools and Colleges

Program offerings:

1 year certificate in culinary art

2 year Associate's degree in food service management

Nebraska

Metropolitan Community College
PO Box 3777
Omaha, NE 68103-0777
1-800-228-9553
www.mccneb.edu

Accredited by the North Central Association of Colleges and Schools

Program offerings:

2 year Associate's degree in culinary art and management

2 year Associate's degree in bakery art

2 year Associate's degree in Culinology™ (culinary research)

2 year Associate's degree in culinary art

2 year Associate's degree in food service management

3 year Associate's degree in chef apprentice

Nevada

University of Nevada, Las Vegas
William F. Harrah College of Hotel Administration
4505 Maryland Parkway
PO Box 456013
Las Vegas, NV 89154-6013
702-895-3161
www.unlv.edu

Accredited by the Northwest Association of Schools and Colleges

Program offerings:

4 year Bachelor's degree in culinary art management

New Hampshire

Southern New Hampshire University
2500 North River Road
Manchester, NH 03106
1-800-668-1249
www.snhu.edu

Accredited by the New England Association of Schools and Colleges

Program offerings:

9 month certificate in culinary art

9 month certificate in baking and pastry art

2 year Associate's degree in baking and pastry art

2 year Associate's degree in culinary art

2 year Master's degree in hospitality

4 year Bachelor's degree in food and beverage management

4 year Bachelor's degree in hospitality administration

New Jersey

Atlantic Cape Community College
5100 Black Horse Pike
Mays Landing, NJ 08330-2699
609-343-4944
www.atlantic.edu/aca

Accredited by the Middle States Association of Colleges and Schools

Program offerings:

1 year certificate in catering

1 year certificate in food service management

1 year certificate in hot food

1 year certificate in pastry/baking

2 year Associate's degree in food service management

2 year Associate's degree in culinary art

2 year Associate's degree in pastry/baking

New Mexico

Albuquerque Technical Vocational Institute Community College
525 Buena Vista Southeast
Albuquerque, NM 87106
505-224-3000
www.tvi.cc.nm.us

Accredited by the North Central Association of Colleges and Schools

Program offerings:

1 trimester certificate in food service management

2 trimester certificate in professional cooking

2 trimester certificate in baking

2 year Associate's degree in culinary art

New York

Paul Smith's College of Arts and Sciences
Route 86 and 30
PO Box 265
Paul Smiths, NY 12970-0265
1-800-421-2605
www.paulsmiths.edu

Accredited by the Middle States Association of Colleges and Schools

Program offerings:

1 year certificate in baking and pastry art

2 year Associate's degree in hotel and restaurant management

2 year Associate's degree in culinary art

2 year Associate's degree in culinary art/baking track

4 year Bachelor's degree in hotel, resort, and tourism management

4 year Bachelor's degree in culinary art and service management

North Carolina

Asheville-Buncombe Technical Community College
340 Victoria Road
Asheville, NC 28801
828-254-1921
www.abtech.edu

Accredited by the Southern Association of Colleges and Schools

Program offerings:

2 year Associate's degree in baking and pastry art

2 year Associate's degree in culinary technology

2 year Associate's degree in hotel and restaurant management

North Dakota

North Dakota State College of Science
800 Sixth Street North
Wahpeton, ND 58076-0002
1-800-342-4325
www.ndscs.nodak.edu/instruct/cul_arts

Accredited by the North Central Association of Colleges and Schools

Program offerings:

2 year diploma in chef training and management technology

2 year Associate's degree in restaurant management

2 year Associate's degree in chef training and management technology

Ohio

Zane State College
1555 Newark Road
Zanesville, OH 43701
1-800-686-8324
www.zanestate.edu

Accredited by the North Central Association of Colleges and Schools

Program offerings:

1 quarter certificate in safety and sanitation

2 year Associate's degree in culinary art

Oklahoma

Oklahoma State University, Okmulgee
1801 East Fourth Street
Okmulgee, OK 74447
910-293-4678
www.osu-okmulgee.edu

Accredited by the North Central Association of Colleges and Schools

Program offerings:

79 hour Associate's degree in dietetic technology

90 hour Associate's degree in culinary art

Oregon

Oregon Coast Culinary Institute at Southwestern Oregon Community College
1988 Newmark Avenue
Coos Bay, OR 97420
1-877-895-CHEF
www.occi.net

Accredited by the Northwest Association of Schools and Colleges

Program offerings:

15 month Associate's degree in pastry and baking

15 month Associate's degree in culinary art management

Pennsylvania

The Restaurant School at Walnut Hill College
4207 Walnut Street
Philadelphia, PA 19104-3518
215-222-4200
www.walnuthillcollege.edu

Accredited by the Accrediting Commission of Career Schools and Colleges of Technology

Program offerings:

18 month Associate's degree in hotel management

18 month Associate's degree in restaurant management

18 month Associate's degree in pastry art

18 month Associate's degree in culinary art

36 month Bachelor's degree in hotel management

36 month Bachelor's degree in restaurant management

36 month Bachelor's degree in pastry art

36 month Bachelor's degree in culinary art

Rhode Island

Johnson and Wales University
8 Abbot Park Place
Providence, RI 02903-3703
1-800-342-5598
www.jwu.edu

Accredited by the New England Association of Schools and Colleges

Program offerings:

2 year Associate's degree in baking and pastry art

2 year Associate's degree in culinary art

4 year Bachelor's degree in food service management

4 year Bachelor's degree in food marketing

4 year Bachelor's degree in culinary nutrition

4 year Bachelor's degree in culinary art

4 year Bachelor's degree in baking and pastry art

South Carolina

Culinary Institute of Charleston
At Trident Technical College
7000 Rivers Avenue
Charleston, SC 29423
843-820-5090
www.culinaryinstituteofcharlston.com

Accredited by the Southern Association of Colleges and Schools

Program offerings:

1 year certificate in catering

1 year certificate in hospitality industry service

1 year certificate in baking and pastry

1 year diploma in culinary art

2 year Associate's degree in culinary art

2 year Associate's degree in hospitality and tourism management

South Dakota

Culinary Academy of South Dakota
A Division of Mitchell Technical Institute
821 North Capital
Mitchell, SD 57301
1-800-952-0042
www.mti.tec.sd.us

Accredited by the North Central Association of Colleges and Schools

Program offerings:

24 month diploma in culinary art

Tennessee

Walters State
Sevierville Campus
1720 Old Newport Highway
Sevierville, TN 37876
865-774-5816
www.ws.edu

Accredited by the Southern Association of Colleges and Schools

Program offerings:

1 year certificate in culinary art

2 year Associate's degree in hotel/restaurant management

2 year Associate's degree in culinary art

Texas

St. Philip's College
1801 Martin Luther King Drive
San Antonio, TX 78203
210-531-3200
www.accd.edu/spc

Accredited by the Southern Association of Colleges and Schools

Program offerings:

1 year certificate in baking principles

1 year certificate in culinary studies

2 year Associate's degree in restaurant management

2 year Associate's degree in culinary art

Utah

Utah Valley State College
800 West University Parkway
Orem, UT 84058
801-863-INFO (4636)
www.uvsc.edu

Accredited by the Northwest Association of Schools and Colleges

Program offerings:

24 month Associate's degree in culinary art

Vermont

New England Culinary Institute
250 Main Street
Montpelier, VT 05602-9720
1-877-223-6324
www.neci.edu

Accredited by the Accrediting Commission of Career Schools and Colleges of
Technology

Program offerings:

10 month certificate in pastry art

10 month certificate in baking

10 month certificate in basic cooking

15 month Associate's degree in hospitality and restaurant management

18 month Bachelor's degree in hospitality and restaurant management

2 year Associate's degree in baking and pastry art

2 year Associate's degree in culinary art

Virginia

Virginia Intermont College
1013 Moore Street
Bristol, VA 24201
1-800-451-1VIC (1842)
www.vic.edu

Accredited by the Southern Association of Colleges and Schools

Program offerings:

2 year Associate's degree in baking and pastry art

2 year Associate's degree in culinary art

4 year Bachelor's degree in pastry art

4 year Bachelor's degree in culinary management

Washington

South Seattle Community College
6000 16th Avenue, Southwest
Seattle, WA 98106-1499
206-764-5344
www.chefschool.com

Accredited by the Northwest Association of Schools and Colleges

Program offerings:

15 month certificate in catering and banquet operations

18 month certificate in pastry and specialty baking

2 year Associate's degree in restaurant and food service production

2 year Associate's degree in catering and banquet operations

2 year Associate's degree in pastry and specialty baking

West Virginia

Mountain State University
PO Box 9003
Beckley, WV 25802
1-866-FOR-MSU1 (367-6781)
www.mountainstate.edu

Accredited by the North Central Association of Colleges and Schools

Program offerings:

2 year Associate's degree in culinary art

4 year Bachelor's degree in culinary art

Wisconsin

Blackhawk Technical College
6004 Prairie Road
PO Box 5009
Janesville, WI 53547
608-757-7670
www.blackhawk.edu/eo/associate/culinary.htm

Accredited by the North Central Association of Colleges and Schools

Program offerings:

4 month certificate in quantity production

4 month certificate in baking

2 year Associate's degree in culinary art

Wyoming

Sheridan College
3059 Coffeen Avenue
Sheridan, WY 82801
1-800-913-9139
www.sheridan.edu

Accredited by the North Central Association of Colleges and Schools

Program offerings:

1 year certificate in culinary arts

1 year certificate in hospitality management

2 year Associate's degree in hospitality management

Glossary

accreditation   The official certification of an education program, by any number of recognized organizations, providing assurance to the public that the program is good and the education is of acceptable quality.

apprenticeship   A traditional method of entering a chosen field. In today's culinary world, a governing body periodically assesses the progress of the apprenticeship, which typically must consist of 6,000 hours, or three years, supplemented by additional education.

bain marie   A water bath, literally *Mary's bath*, named for ancient alchemist Mary the Jewess. It's essentially a double boiler, with food suspended in a pan or bowl over another pan of simmering water. Bain marie cooking promotes even, gentle heating. It can also refer to an oven water bath, in which foods (usually custards) are baked in a larger pan of water, to promote slow, even heating.

béchamel   One of the five *mother sauces*, often called a white cream sauce.

beggar's purse   Any little bundle of food wrapped in a thin sheet of dough, crepe, noodle, won ton, or leaf, with the edges gathered up at the top.

biscotti   An Italian cookie, baked once in a short loaf, then sliced and toasted.

blackened   Food, classically fish, coated with a Cajun spice mix and seared in an extremely hot skillet.

BMR   Basal metabolic rate; the amount of energy you use when you are awake, but at rest.

brigade   A system of kitchen hierarchy, based on a military model, developed by Auguste Escoffier.

buffalo mozzarella   A fresh, un-aged, mild cheese traditionally made from the milk of the water buffalo.

burr mixer   An immersion blender, which is basically a blender on a stick that can be inserted into a liquid to create a purée.

busser   One whose job it is to clear, or *bus*, a table of its dirty plates.

Caesar salad   A classic recipe from the 1920s, created by Caesar Cardini, a hotel owner in Tijuana, Mexico. It became popular with the Hollywood elite who traveled south of the border during prohibition. It is made with romaine lettuce and a dressing that consists of egg yolk, olive oil, garlic, Parmesan cheese, and anchovies.

cajun   An ethnic group now settled in Louisiana, descended from the Acadians of Nova Scotia. Cajun cuisine is the hallmark of Louisiana cooking, and includes such famous dishes as Jambalaya and Gumbo.

California cuisine   Beautifully prepared dishes made with regional, seasonal ingredients, using a combination of classic preparation styles.

calories   A measure of heat energy, determined by burning a weighed portion of food and measuring the amount of heat it produces.

canapé   A bite-size appetizer, hot or cold, consisting of a small piece of bread, cracker, vegetable, or other vessel that holds a filling. The word is French for *couch*.

caper   A small berry from an evergreen shrub, which is pickled and used as a salty flavoring or condiment.

Caprese salad   Fresh tomatoes sliced and layered with basil leaves, sliced buffalo mozzarella, and olive oil. The word *Caprese* is Italian for "in the style of Capri."

capsaicin   The compound that produces the biting heat of a chili, measured in Scoville Heat Units (SHU) in increments of 100, with sweet bell peppers at 0 and the habenero chili at 100,000.

carb-free   A diet or food devoid of carbohydrates.

Caréme   Anton Caréme (1784–1833) was the founder of French *haute*, or high, *cuisine*, which is characterized by complex preparations and a heavy use of rich sauces.

carnitas   *Little meats*, mainly shredded pork, cooked until tender, then browned until crispy.

Catherine de Medici   Heiress of the famous Florentine family, wife of King Henri II of France, credited with raising France out of the dark, medieval culinary age into a new era of gastronomic enlightenment.

charcuterie   A station of the kitchen dedicated to cooked meats, pâtés, terrines, and sausages.

checks   A slang term for the black and white pants worn by most professional cooks.

cheesecloth   A thin, gauze material used to strain the whey from the curds of cheese. It has many uses in cooking, including extra-fine straining.

complete protein   Protein from an animal source that contains all 9 of the essential amino acids.

concassé   Peeled, seeded, and chopped tomato.

cover   A customer served. If the restaurant did 200 covers, that means 200 people were served.

crème chantilly   Sweetened vanilla whipped cream.

crème chiboust   Pastry cream and Italian meringue folded together, named for a French pastry chef.

creole   Anyone or anything of mixed race decent. Creole cuisine is Louisiana-based and fuses the traditions of African, French, and Spanish culinary techniques and ingredients.

croissants   A French pastry made of yeasted laminated dough, formed in the shape of a crescent. The shape is said to be taken from the Turkish flag, to honor the bakers who warned Vienna of their impending early morning attack.

croquembouche   A pyramid of pastry cream filled pâte a choux puffs (a.k.a. cream puffs), glued together with hot caramelized sugar. A traditional French wedding pastry.

croquant   Caramelized sugar mixed with sliced almonds and formed into decorative shapes.

cross contamination   The transfer of bacteria, toxins, parasites, or viruses by touch.

crudités   Decoratively cut and presented raw vegetables, served with a dip or sauce.

cuisine minceur *The cuisine of thinness*, created by French chef Michel Guérard, which replaced heavy presentations of classic French cuisine with lighter, healthier options.

dirty rice A Cajun rice dish which may contain any number of ingredients, including sausages, chicken, crayfish, chicken livers, gizzards, vegetables, garlic, and spices.

duxelle Mushrooms chopped fine and sautéed with shallots in butter until completely dry.

enology The study of wine and wine making.

escargot A French dish of snails, sautéed in butter garlic and herbs.

Escoffier, Auguste (1846–1935) The father of modern French cuisine, the brigade system of kitchen hierarchy, à la carte service, and author of *Le Guide Culinaire*, first published in 1903 and still used as a standard reference by chefs worldwide.

expediter The person who calls out orders to the line. The expediter controls when to fire a dish, when to bring it up, and when to take it out to the dining room.

externship A required component of most culinary school programs. This job placement lasts several months and may or may not include salary.

feng shui A Chinese custom of arranging a space to make it peaceful and harmonious. Traditionally it was not meant to bring luck and prosperity as is often touted today.

finger cot A rubber finger covering used to protect open sores.

fire Not just a flame. When the expediter shouts "fire," it means to begin cooking a dish.

flambé The ignition of food in a pan by dousing it with alcohol and lighting it with a flame. The process burns off much of the harsh alcohol flavor, but not, as is often thought, all the alcohol.

fois gras An enlarged goose or duck liver, considered a delicacy, and commanding a hefty price. The ducks and geese are force-fed fatty foods and kept from exercising. The literal translation from French is *fat liver*.

food-borne illness Food poisoning or any illness contracted through the food you eat.

franchise The ability to purchase a brand, trademark, idea, or operating system from an existing business.

Gateaux Saint Honoré   A tart-shaped pastry consisting of *puff pastry*, *pâte a choux*, *crème chiboust*, and *crème chantilly*. Cream puffs filled with pastry cream are dipped in caramelized sugar and glued around the rim.

giradon   A cart on wheels, used for classic table-side service.

habenero   One of the hottest chilies known to man.

HACCP   Acronym standing for Hazard Analysis and Critical Control Point; a method of monitoring food safety first developed by NASA.

hors d'oeuvres   Small appetizers or bites served before the main meal, meant to whet the appetite.

ice carving   Statues carved from giant blocks of ice, traditionally with a hammer and chisel. Today a chainsaw is the tool of choice.

incomplete protein   Protein from a plant source that's missing at least one of the essential amino acids.

Indian fry bread   A savory fried disc of soda-leavened bread, served throughout the Southwest, both as a sweet bread, with jam or honey, or as a savory bread alongside meat dishes.

internship   A full-time, temporary job placement that lasts anywhere from several months to a couple of years.

jambalaya   A Creole tomato-based rice dish that may contain any number of meats and fish.

julienne   A thin, matchstick-shaped cut.

Kitchen Aid   A brand of kitchen appliances, most notably a tabletop standing electric mixer.

laminate   To layer. In cooking it refers mainly to dough, which is stacked with butter, folded, and rolled repeatedly until there are hundreds of layers of dough and butter. The moisture in the butter becomes steam in the oven, causing the dough to puff.

lefse   A Norwegian flat bread, similar to a Mexican tortilla, but made with potato.

Lexan   The brand name of a large, rectangular lidded plastic tub that can hold several gallons of hot or cold food. Also known as a Cambro, which is the same product made by a different company.

maitre d'hôtel   The head waiter or head of the dining room.

marzipan   An edible paste made from ground almonds and sugar, used as a cake layer or molded into shapes like fruit, flowers, and animals.

masa harina   Flour made from dried hominy, which is corn soaked in calcium oxide. It is used to make corn tortillas and tamales and to thicken soups, sauces, and stews.

mirepoix   A basic ingredient of French sauces, stocks, soups, and stews. It combines three aromatic vegetables—carrots, onions, and celery—in a ratio of one part carrot to two parts onion and celery. Sometimes herbs are included as well. The mirepoix is usually sautéed in fat at the beginning of a recipe.

mise en place   A French term meaning literally "installation" or "put in some places." Chefs refer to it as all the ingredients for a dish ready before the cooking starts.

mother sauce   Béchamel, espagnole, hollandaise, mayonnaise, velouté, and tomato sauce. Designated by Escoffier, these six sauces (sometimes it's five, with mayo left off) are the head of their sauce families. To them, any number of variations can be made to create *daughter* or derivative sauces.

neckerchief   A bandana-size cloth, usually white, tied around the neck of a chef to absorb perspiration.

offal   Organ meats or variety meats, used in cooking, including heart, liver, glands, brains, kidneys, tongue, feet, and joints.

OSHA   Acronym for Occupational Safety and Health Administration; a government agency dedicated to workplace safety and health.

pantry   A cold ingredient station of the kitchen, which prepares dishes including salads, sandwiches, and cold appetizers.

pâte a choux   A pastry batter used to make cream puffs, éclairs, and other classic confections.

pâtissier   The French term for pastry chef.

petit fours   Bite-size cakes and pastries.

prep   A station of the kitchen that prepares or readies all the ingredients for the night's dishes.

puff pastry   A laminated dough used in both sweet and savory baking.

ratatouille   A vegetable dish from Provençe, made from cubed zucchini, eggplant, tomatoes, onions, and bell peppers, sautéed in olive oil, garlic, and herbs.

rancidity The disagreeable taste and odor that arises when fats and oils have been exposed to oxygen, light, and heat for too long.

reach-in A refrigerator that you reach into, unlike a walk-in, which you must walk into.

reduction Cooking the water out of something, which thickens it naturally without the addition of a starch or fat-based food.

Robo-Coup The brand name of a food processor.

rolling-rack A large rack with wheels, used to store, cool, or bake multiple sheet pans full of food.

roux A thickener, made from equal parts of melted butter and flour. It can be classified as blonde, brown, or black depending on the length of cooking time and the resulting color. Darker roux has more flavor but less thickening power.

saffron The pistil of a low-growing crocus, highly prized as a spice. The method of harvest is particularly arduous, and therefore, the spice commands high prices. Its bright yellow color was used for centuries as a fabric dye.

sauteuse A frying pan with straight sides and a tight-fitting lid.

scullery The dishwashing crew and station.

sheet pan A professional baking sheet.

side-towel A small towel, cotton or terry-cloth, provided by a restaurant for use by its cooks.

Sheila Shine A stainless-steel cleaner and polish used in many professional kitchens.

Southwestern cuisine A fusion of ingredients and techniques from all over the Western United States and Mexico.

spa cuisine Healthy, upscale cuisine, first served at health spas for patrons trying to lose weight.

steward The head of a staff in charge of inventory and product storage.

stock A flavorful broth made from meat bones and aromatic vegetables, used in the preparation of many dishes, including soups, sauces, braises, and stews.

sugar pulling The art of creating decorative objects out of molten sugar.

sushi A Japanese food made with sticky rice and a variety of foods, including fish (often raw) and vegetables. There are a number of varieties, including those wrapped in seaweed sheets (nori).

sweetbreads   The delicious thymus gland of veal (1- to 3-month-old calf, not yet weaned) or baby beef (6- to 12-month-old calf), which can be poached, sautéed, braised, or used in charcuterie.

Tabasco   A brand of hot pepper sauce, made in Louisiana.

tamales   A Mexican dish of meat, vegetables, or fruit, covered in masa dough, and wrapped in a corn husk or other leaf before being steamed.

tripe   The honeycomb-shaped lining of a cow's stomach, commonly found in *menudo*, a soup favored in Central and South America.

truffles   Exorbitantly priced, dirt-clod shaped fungus that grows underground at the roots of certain oak trees, considered by everyone to be a delicacy. These gems are rooted out by female pigs that think they smell male pigs, and specially trained dogs. The white truffle is a specialty of Northern Italy, while the black truffle can be found in France and Spain.

variety meats   See *offal*.

zest   The flavorful outermost layer of a citrus fruit.

Index

A

à la carte service, 77
accreditation, culinary schools, 39-40
ACF (American Culinary Federation), 56-57
Advanced Professional Pastry Chef, 83
AIWF (American Institute of Wine and Food), 59
alcohol, avoiding, 172-174
Alphabet of Gourmets, An, 85
ambiance, restaurants, 247-248
American Cookery, 79
American cooking cookbooks, 79-81
American Culinary Federation (ACF), 56-57
American Institute of Wine and Food (AIWF), 59
American Society of Composers, Authors and Publishers (ASCAP), 248
apprenticeships, 87-89
    European, 89-90
armed forces cook, working as, 102-104
Art Institutes, 31
ASCAP (American Society of Composers, Authors and Publishers), 248
Associate's degrees, culinary schools, 42-43
attire, 135-136
attitude mentors, 160-161
auto liability, 255

B

Bachelor's degrees, culinary schools, 42-43
back of the house (BOH), 193
bain marie, 54
baker, job description, 193
bakeries, working for, 92-94
baking cookbooks, 83-84
banquet chef, job description, 194

bar blenders, for purées, 138
Basal Metabolic Rate (BMR), determining, 171-172
Batali, Mario, 13
BBGA (Bread Baker Guild of America), 189
Bear Pit, The, 243
Beard, James, 13, 36, 59, 79-80
béchamel sauce, 34
Beck, Simone, 70, 77
Becoming a Chef, 85
beggar's purse, 141
Bertholle, Louisette, 70, 77
Bertolli, Paul, 80
Bittman, Mark, 84
blacklists, creating, 156
BMI (Broadcast Music Inc.), 248
BMR (basal Metabolic Rate), determining, 171-172
Bocouse, Paul, 36, 82
BOH (back of the house), 193
Bone in the Throat, 86
books
    cookbooks
        American cooking, 79-81
        baking, 83-84
        classics, 76-78
        fish, 84
        healthy cooking, 84
        importance of, 75
        international cooking, 81-82
        pastry, 83-84
        references, 78-79
    wines, 85
Boston Cooking School Cookbook, 83
Boulud, Daniel, 13
Bourdain, Anthony, 86
Bread Baker Guild of America (BBGA), 59, 189

Breads of France, The, 80
breakfasts, 166
brigade system, 77, 97-100
Brillat-Savarin, Jean Anthelme, 85
Broadcast Music Inc. (BMI), 248
brunches, 166
burns, susceptibility to, 7
burr mixers, 61
business interruption insurance, 255
business life insurance, 255
business mentors, 161
business plans, restaurants, 234-236
butcher, job description, 194
Butter Table, measurements, 137

C

*Cakes, Great Cookies, Chocolate Desserts, Pies
  and Tarts*, 83
California Cuisine, 80
California Culinary Academy (CCA), 4, 32
calories, 170-172
Caprese salads, 144
capsaicin, 134-135
Caréme, Anton, 36
carnitas, 66
Casa Bonita, 243
cash flow, restaurants, 236
catering chefs, job description, 194
catering companies, 180-181
    laws regarding, 92
    working for, 91-92
CCA (California Culinary Academy), 32
Celebrating Italy, 81
celebrity chefs, influence of, 16
certification
    culinary schools, 42
    sanitation, 224-225
chain restaurants, working in, 107-108
charcuterie, 70
charitable organizations, volunteering for,
  182-183
chaudière, 80
checks, 51

chef
    average salaries, 7
    choosing a career in, 4-8
    good attitude, importance of, 26-27
    job description, 192
    patience, importance of, 24-25
    speed, importance of, 23-24
    stamina, importance of, 22-23
    stardom, chances of, 8
    teamwork, importance of, 25-26
    uniforms, 7
chef de cuisine, job description, 192
chef de partie, job description, 192
Chefs for Humanity, 58
Chez Panisse Cooking, 80
Chez Panisse Desserts, 80
Child, Julia, 4, 59, 70, 77
Chinese gooseberries, 84
Chocolatier magazine, 188
CIA (Culinary Institute of America), 31, 79
cigarettes, avoiding, 174
class sizes, culinary schools, 37
classified advertisements, finding jobs in, 120
Clayton, Bernard, 80
cleaning, time-savers, 143-144
cleanliness
    certification, 224-225
    food-borne illnesses, 225-226
    HACCP (Hazard Analysis Critical Control
      Point), 227
    importance of, 73-74, 224
    safety, 227-228
    viral contamination, 226-227
clothing, 135-136
club sirloin, 84
clubs, joining, 56-60
co-workers, maintaining relationships,
  155-156
coffee grinders, grinding spices with, 138
comfort, 133
    clothing, 135-136
    first-aid kits, 136
    hands, protecting, 134-135
    proper hydration, 133-134
    shoes, 136

communication skills, importance of, 150

competitions, entering, 188-189

Complete Book of Pastry, The, 80

Complete Book of Soups and Stews, The, 80

complete proteins, 169

concassé, 142

concepts, restaurants, 241-243

Consider the Oyster, 85

cook 1, job description, 192

cookbooks

    American cooking, 79-81

    baking, 83-84

    classics, 76-78

    fish, 84

    healthy cookbooks, 84

    importance of, 75

    international cooking, 81-82

    pastry, 83-84

    reading, 70-72

    references, 78-79

Cooking Across America, 80

Cooking of South-West France, 81

Cook's Tour, A, 86

cookware, purchasing, 67- 68

Cookwise, 78

cooling, time-savers, 139-140

corporate executive chef, job description, 192

corporations, restaurant ownership, 238

Corriher, Shirley, 78

Coupe du Monde de la Boulangerie, 189

courtesy, importance of, 153-154

Couscous and Other Good Food from Morocco, 81

cover letters, resumés, 118-119

covers, 26

Craft Services, 91

credentials, culinary schools, 41-43

cruise ship chef, working as, 105-107

cuisine du terrior, 71

Cuisine Minceur, 84

Culinary Artistry, 78, 85

Culinary Institute of America (CIA), 31, 79

culinary instructor, job description, 195-196

culinary schools, 31

    accreditation, 39-40

    alumni, speaking with, 33

    Art Institutes, 31

    attending

        advantages, 14-15

        disadvantages, 15-17

    attending and working, 18

    bad influences, avoiding, 60-61

    choosing, 32-40

    CIA (Culinary Institute of America), 31

    class sizes, asking about, 37

    clubs, joining, 56-60

    credentials, 41-42

        Associate's degrees, 42-43

        Bachelor's degrees, 42-43

        certificates, 42

    curriculum, studying, 34-36

    externships, 88-89

    finding, 32

    formats, asking about, 37

    instructors, interviewing, 37-39

    job placement data, obtaining, 40

    Johnson and Wales, 31

    kissing up, importance of, 49-50

    LCB (Le Cordon Bleu), 31

    mentors, 51

    networking, 51

    notebooks, importance of, 48

    paying for, 43

    professional organizations, joining, 56-60

    recommendations, attaining, 50

    reputations, researching, 32

    rules, following, 46-47

    studying, importance of, 47-49

    succeeding in, 40-41, 45-46

    working while attending, 54-56

culinary supervisor, job description, 192

Cunningham, Marion, 83

curriculum, culinary schools, 34-36

cuts, susceptibility to, 7

D

DD Factor—Professional Culinary Recruiters, 122
de Gaulle, Charles, 76
Dean & Deluca, 82
defrosting, time-savers, 139
delicatessens, working for, 94
demographic studies, restaurants, 243-244
Des Jardins, Traci, 13
dessert chef, job description, 193
dicing onions, 142
Dining Clubs, 59
dining room manager, job description, 193
Dinner Against the Clock, 77
disabilities benefit insurance, 255
disasters, restaurants, avoiding, 252-254
dishes, trying, 68-70
dogfish, 84
Dornenburg, Andrew, 78, 85
double boilers, 54
drugs, avoiding, 172-174
Drummond, Karen, 84

E

eaters, finding, 72
eating healthy, 165-167
    nutrition, 167-168
        calories, 170-172
        food groups, 168-170
        pyramid, 167-168
education, resumés, 114
emergency procedures, preparing for, 230
employees
    hiring, 214-219
    terminating, 221-222
    training, 219-221
employment, 192
    baker, 193
    banquet chef, 194
    butcher, 194
    catering chef, 194
    chain restaurants, working in, 107-108
    chef, 192
    chef de cuisine, 192
    chef de partie, 192
    cook 1, 192
    corporate executive chef, 192
    cruise ship chef, 105-107
    culinary instructor, 195-196
    culinary supervisor, 192
    dessert chef, 193
    dining room manager, 193
    entry-level jobs, obtaining, 101
    executive chef, 192
    executive pastry chef, 193
    executive sous chef, 192
    finding, 119-123
    food and beverage manager, 193
    food purveyor, 197
    food stylist, 197
    garde manger, 194
    general manager, 193
    hospitality supervisor, 193
    hotels, working in, 104-105
    independent restaurants, working in, 108-109
    interviews
        dressing for, 126-127
        equipment, 127
        initial contact, 128
        preparing for, 125-126
        succeeding in, 128-129
        tryouts, 127-130
    kitchen manager, 192
    line cook, 192
    line manager, 192
    maitre d'hotel, 193
    management, 214
        hiring employees, 214-219
        terminating employees, 221-222
        training employees, 219-221
    manufacturing, 196
    military cook, working as, 102-104
    nutritionalist, 198
    pastry chef, 193
    pâtissier, 193
    personal chef, working as, 101-102

probationary period, 131
regional executive chef, 192
research and development, 196
restaurant manager, 193
resumés, 114
    additional information, 116-117
    cover letters, 118-119
    education, 114
    fabricating information, 119
    headings, 114
    objectives, 114
    references, 116-118
    relevant information, 115
    work experience, 115
senior sous chef, 192
server, working as, 109-110
shift manager, 192
sous chef, 192
specialty merchandiser, 198
sushi chef, 195
enology, 36
entertaining at home, 180
entry level jobs, attaining, 101
equipment
    time-savers, 138
    training, 228-229
Escoffier, Auguste, 77, 97-100, 173
Escoffier Brigade System, 97-100
executive chef, job description, 192
executive pastry chef, job description, 193
executive sous chef, job description, 192
exercise, importance of, 174-175
expanding restaurants, 249-250
externships, 87-89

F

faculty, culinary schools, interviewing, 37-39
Fannie Farmer Baking Book, The, 83
Fast Food Nation, 86
Fearing, Dean, 151
federal crime insurance, 256
feng shui, 245

Ferran, Adria, 13
Field, Carol, 81
filberts, 84
filo dough, 139
financial assistance, culinary schools, 43
finger cots, 136
fire and extended coverage, 255
fires, avoiding, 252-254
first aid, learning, 228
first-aid kits, importance of, 136
fish, cookbooks, 84
Fish: The Complete Guide to Buying and Cooking 70 Kinds of Seafood, 84
Fisher, M.F.K., 85
flavors, matching, 160
floor plans, restaurants, 246-247
flounder, 84
FOH (front of the house), 193
food and beverage manager, job description, 193
food banks, volunteering for, 182-183
Food Chronology, The, 78
food groups, 168-170
food handling, 140-141
    time-savers, 138
        cooling, 139-140
        defrosting, 139
Food Lover's Companion, The, 78
food manufacturer, job description, 196
Food Network, influence of, 16
food preparation, time-savers, 141-143
food processors, 138
food purveyor, job description, 197
food stylist, job description, 197
food-borne illnesses, avoiding, 225-226
Foods of the World series, 81
footwear, 136
formats, culinary schools, 37
franchising restaurants, 250
French Chef, The, 77
French cuisine, importance of, 71
Friberg, Bo, 83, 105
From Julia Child's Kitchen, 77
front of the house (FOH), 193

fruits
    defrosting, 139
    purchasing, 144
funding sources for restaurants, identifying, 237
Fussell, Betty, 80

G

garde manger, job description, 194
garlic, mincing, 141
Gastronomical Me, The, 85
Gastronomique, 78
Gateaux Saint Honoré, 131
general liability insurance, 255
general manager, job description, 193
giradon, 15
Gisslen, Wayne, 79, 83
gloves, importance of, 134
Good Cook, The series, 76
Gourmet Magazine, 85
Great Desserts, 83
Guérard, Michel, 36, 82, 84
Guide Culinaire, La, 77

H

HACCP (Hazard Analysis Critical Control
    Point), 227
halibut, 84
Haller, Henry, 119
handling food, 140-141
    time-savers, 138
        cooling, 139-140
        defrosting, 139
hands, protecting, 134-135
Hard Rock Cafe, 242
haute cuisine, 71
    founding of, 36
Hazard Analysis Critical Control Point
    (HACCP), 227
hazelnuts, 84
headhunters, finding jobs through, 121-122
headings, resumés, 114
health insurance, 256

healthy cooking cookbooks, 84
Heatter, Maida, 83
Hefter, Lee, 13
Henri II, king of France, 72
Herbst, Ron, 85
Herbst, Sharon Tyler, 78
hollandaise sauce, 54
homeless shelters, volunteering at, 182-183
Hors d'Oeuvre and Canapés, 79
hospitality supervisor, job description, 193
hot line, 26
hot pan signal, 140
hotels, working in, 104-105
How to Eat a Wolf, 85
Howard Johnson's, 108
hydration, importance of, 23, 133-134

I

I Hear America Cooking, 80
IACP (International Association of Culinary
    Professionals), 57-58
ice baths, 140
ice wands, 140
immersion blenders, 61
In Madeleine's Kitchen, 70, 77
independent restaurants, working in, 108-109
ingredients
    experimenting with, 67
    purchasing, 144
    shopping for, 67
injuries, avoiding, 175
instructors, culinary schools
    as mentors, 51
    interviewing, 37-39
    job description, 195-196
    networking, 51
    recommendations, 50
insurance, restaurants, 254-256
International Association of Culinary
    Professionals (IACP), 57-58
international cooking cookbooks, 81-82
International Council of Cruise Lines, 59
Internet, finding employment on, 121

internships, 87-88
interviews (job)
  dressing for, 126-127
  equipment, 127
  initial contact, 128
  preparing for, 125-126
  succeeding in, 128-129
  tryouts, 127-130
Italian Baker, The, 81

J

James Beard Foundation, The, 59
job placement data, culinary schools, 40
jobs, 192
  baker, 193
  banquet chef, 194
  butcher, 194
  catering chef, 194
  chain restaurants, working in, 107-108
  chef, 192
  chef de cuisine, 192
  chef de partie, 192
  choosing, 110
  cook 1, 192
  corporate executive chef, 192
  cruise ship chef, 105-107
  culinary instructor, 195-196
  culinary supervisor, 192
  dessert chef, 193
  dining room manager, 193
  entry-level jobs, attaining, 101
  executive chef, 192
  executive pastry chef, 193
  executive sous chef, 192
  finding, 119-123
  food and beverage manager, 193
  food purveyor, 197
  food stylist, 197
  garde manger, 194
  general manager, 193
  hospitality supervisor, 193
  hotels, working in, 104-105

independent restaurants, working in, 108-109
interviews
  dressing for, 126-127
  equipment, 127
  initial contact, 128
  preparing for, 125-126
  succeeding in, 128-129
  tryout, 127-130
kitchen manager, 192
line cook, 192
line manager, 192
maitre d'hotel, 193
management, 214
  choosing, 203-204
  hiring employees, 214-219
  job description, 205-207
  motivational supervision, 210-212
  styles, 207-210
  terminating employees, 221-222
  training employees, 219-221
manufacturing, 196
military cook, working as, 102-104
nutritionalist, 198
pastry chef, 193
pastry cook, 193
pâtissier, 193
personal chef, working as, 101-102
probationary period, 131
regional executive chef, 192
research and development, 196
restaurant manager, 193
resumés, 114
  additional information, 116-117
  cover letters, 118-119
  education, 114
  fabricating information, 119
  headings, 114
  objectives, 114
  references, 116-118
  relevant information, 115
  work experience, 115
senior sous chef, 192
server, working as, 109-110
shift manager, 192

sous chef, 192
specialty merchandiser, 198
sushi chef, 195
Johnson, Howard Dearing, 108
Johnson and Wales, 31
Joy of Cooking, The, 76
Julia Child and Company, 77
Julia Child and More Company, 77
Julie and Julia: 365 Days, 524 Recipes, 1 Tiny Apartment Kitchen, 71
Julie/Julia Project, The, 71
julienne, 143
Jungle, The, 86

K

Kamman, Madeleine, 70, 77
Kansas City steak, 84
Keller, Thomas, 13
Kitchen Confidential, 86
kitchen managers, job description, 192
kitchens
as working environment, 6-7
dangers of, 7
reach-ins, 50
walk-ins, 50
kiwi fruit, 84
peeling, 141

L

laminate, 36
laying out restaurants, 246-247
LCB (Le Cordon Bleu), 31
L'Ecole des Trois Gourmandes, 77
Les Dames d'Escoffier International, 59
letters of recommendation, 118
lifestyle mentors, 161-162
limited partnerships, restaurant ownership, 238
line cook, job description, 192
line manager, job description, 192
lines, 26

liquor liability insurance, 255
loans, small business, 237
locations, restaurants, 245
lotte, 84
Louisiana Kitchen, 81
low-calorie options on menus, making available, 170
lunches, 166

M

Madeleine Cooks, 77
magazines, cooking, 187-188
maitre d'hotel, job description, 193
management, 214
choosing, 203-204
employees
hiring, 214-219
terminating, 221-222
training, 219-221
job description, 205-207
motivational supervision, 210-212
styles, 207-210
mangoes, removing flesh, 141
market studies, restaurants, 243-244
masa harina, 66
Mastering the Art of French Cooking, 70, 77
matching flavors, 160
McGee, Harold, 79
measurements, time-savers, 137-138
meat
defrosting, 139
rancid meat, 145
Medici, Catherine de, 72
Medieval Times, 242
Mediterranean Cooking, 81
mentors, 157-158
acting as, 163
attitude mentors, 160-161
being disappointed by, 163
business mentors, 161
finding, 56, 162
lifestyle mentors, 161-162

skills mentors, 158-159
taste mentors, 159-160
utilizing, 162
menus
collecting, 60
creating, 246
low-calorie options, making available, 170
military chef, working as, 103-104
military cook, working as, 102-104
mincing garlic, 141
mirepoix, 13-14
mise en place, 45
missions, volunteering at, 182-183
Modern Art of Chinese Cooking, The, 81
Mondavi, Robert, 59
monkfish, 84
Montagne, Prosper, 78
mortgage insurance, 255
mother sauces, 34
motor lodges, creation of, 108
music licensing, 248

N

Nasty Bits, 86
National Ice Carving Association, 59
National Restaurant Association (NRA), 58
National Restaurant Association Education
Foundation, 225
negativity, avoiding, 151
networking, importance of, 51
networks, expanding, 55
New Making of a Cook: The Art, Techniques, and Science of Good Cooking, The, 77
New Wine Lover's Companion, The, 85
New York strip steak, 84
notebooks, importance of in culinary schools, 48
nouvelle cuisine, 71
NRA (National Restaurant Association), 58
nutrition
calories, 170-172
food groups, 168-170

importance of, 167-168
pyramid, 167-168
Nutrition for Food Service and Culinary Professionals, 84
nutritionalist, job description, 198

O

Oaks, Nancy, 13
objectives, listing in resumés, 114
Occupational Safety and Health
Administration (OSHA), 228
On Food and Cooking: The Science and Lore of the Kitchen, 79
onions
dicing, 142
slicing, 142
open sores, health risks, 136
opening restaurants, risks, 234
orange roughy, 84
organization, importance of, 143
OSHA (Occupational Safety and Health
Administration), 228
ownership, restaurants, 237-239
Oxford Companion to Wine, The, 85

P-Q

Page, Karen, 78, 85
pantry cook, 92
partnerships, restaurant ownership, 238
pastry, defrosting, 139
Pastry Art and Design magazine, 92, 188
pastry chef, job description, 193
pastry cook, job description, 193
pastry cookbooks, 83-84
patience, importance of, 24-25
pâtissier, job description, 193
peeling
kiwi fruit, 141
tomatoes, 142-143
Penzeys Spices, 82
Pépin, Jacques, 76
perch, 84

periodicals, cooking, 187-188
personal chef, working as, 101-102
phyllo dough, 139
Physiology of Taste, The, 85
placement services, finding jobs through, 121-122
plastic gloves, importance of, 134-135
plating, 194
Powell, Julie, 71
prep cook, 92
probationary period, jobs, 131
product liability insurance, 255
Professional Baking, 83
Professional Chef, The, 79
Professional Cooking, 79
professional organizations
    ACF (American Culinary Federation), 56-57
    AIWF (American Institute of Wine and Food), 59
    IACP (International Association of Culinary Professionals), 57-58
    James Beard Foundation, The, 59
    joining, 56-60, 188
    NRA (National Restaurant Association), 58
    RBA (Retail Bakers of America), 58
    women's organizations, 59
Professional Pastry Chef, The, 83
Prudhomme, Paul, 81, 186
Puck, Wolfgang, 13
pyramid, nutrition, 167-168

quality management, 204
Quark's Bar, 243
Quintana, Patricia, 82, 141

R

Rancho Gordo, 82
rancid meat, 145
RBA (Retail Bakers of America), 58
reach-ins, 50
recommendation letters, 118

recommendations, obtaining for culinary schools, 50
red fish, 84
reduction, 186
reference books, 78-79
references, resumés, 116-118
regional executive chef, job description, 192
Reichl, Ruth, 85
relationships, co-workers, 155-156
research and development, job description, 196
Research Chef Association, 59
restaurant manager, job description, 193
restaurants
    ambiance, 247-248
    business plans, creating, 234-236
    cash flow, 236
    concepts, 241-243
    covers, 26
    disasters, avoiding, 252-254
    expanding, 249-250
    franchising, 250
    funding sources, identifying, 237
    insurance, 254-256
    laying out, 246-247
    locations, 245
    market studies, 243-244
    menus, creating, 246
    opening, risks, 234
    ownership types, 237-239
    owning, 233
    scouting, 187
    seatings, 235
    staffing, 248-249
    turning tables, 41
resumés, 114
    additional information, listing, 116-117
    cover letters, 118-119
    education, listing, 114
    fabricating information on, 119
    headings, 114
    objectives, listing, 114
    references, 116-118
    relevant information, limiting to, 115
    work experience, listing, 115
Retail Bakers of America (RBA), 58

RICE (Rest, Ice, Compression, and Elevation), 228
Riley Guide On-line Job Placement, 122
risks, opening restaurants, 234
Ritz, Cesar, 77
Robinson, Jancis, 85
Robo-Coup food processors, 138
rock cod, 84
rolling racks, 140
roux, 66
rubber gloves, importance of, 134-135
rules, following in culinary schools, 46-47

S

safety, practicing, 227-228
salaries, chefs, 7
sanitation
    certification, 224-225
    food-borne illnesses, 225-226
    HACCP (Hazard Analysis Critical Control Point), 227
    importance of, 224
    safety, 227-228
    viral contamination, 226-227
sauteuse, 68
saving food, 140-141
SBA (Small Business Association), 237
Schlosser, Eric, 86
scouting restaurants, 187
Scoville, Wilbur, 135
Scoville Heat Units (SHU), 135
seafood, cookbooks, 84
seatings, restaurants, 235
second jobs, taking, 178-179
Secrets of Baking, The, 83
senior sous chef, job description, 192
Serve It Forth, 85
server, working as, 109-110
ServSafe training, 225
sheet pans, 68
Sheila Shine polish, 47
shelters, volunteering at, 182-183
Shere, Lindsey, 80

shift manager, job description, 192
shoes, 136
SHU (Scoville Heat Units), 135
side-towels, 7
    auto parts stores, purchasing from, 73
    importance of, 144
Sinclair, Upton, 86
skills, honing, 177-178
    catering, 180-181
    entertaining, 180
    second jobs, 178-179
    volunteering, 182-183
skills mentors, 158-159
slicing onions, 142
Small Business Association (SBA), 237
small business loans, attaining, 237
smoking, avoiding, 174
Sofronski, Michael, 85
sous chef, job description, 192
spa cuisine, 84
specialty merchandiser, job description, 198
speed, importance of, 23-24
staffing restaurants, 248-249
stamina, importance of, 22-23
stealing, preventing, 256-257
storage, optimizing, 145
studying, culinary schools, importance of, 47-49
stylist (food), job description, 197
sugar, sifting, 141
Super Size Me, 86
sushi chef, job description, 195

T

tables, turning, 41
taste mentors, 159-160
Taste of Mexico, A, 82
teachers, culinary schools
    as mentors, 51
    interviewing, 37-39
    networking, 51
    recommendations, 50

teamwork, importance of, 25-26
Technique, La, 76
Tender at the Bone, 85
theft, preventing, 256-257
themes, restaurants, 241-243
time-savers, 137-141
   cleaning, 143-144
   equipment, 138
   food handling, 138
      cooling, 139-140
      defrosting, 139
   food preparation, 141-143
   measurements, 137-138
   organization, importance of, 143
tomatoes, peeling, 142-143
top loin, 84
trade shows, attending, 190
Trager, James, 78
training, equipment, 228-229
trends, keeping up with, 186-190
Tropp, Barbara, 81
tryouts, job interviews, 127-130
turning tables, 41

U–V

unemployment insurance, 255
uniforms, chefs', 7
   checks, 51

vegetables
   defrosting, 139
   purchasing, 144
viral contamination, avoiding, 226-227
volunteer work, 89-90, 182-183

W–X–Y–Z

Waitrose Food magazine, 188
walk-ins, 50
Waters, Alice, 13, 36, 80
WCR (Women Chefs and Restaurateurs),
 163

What to Drink with What You Eat: The Definitive Guide to Pairing Food with Wine, Beer, Spirits, Coffee, Tea—Even Water—Based on Expert Advice from America's Best Sommeliers, 85
When French Women Cook, 77
window, 226
wines, reference books, 85
Wolfert, Paula, 81
Women Chefs and Restaurateurs (WCR),
 163
women's organizations, 59, 163
work experience, resumés, listing, 115
working while attending culinary school,
 54-56
workman's compensation insurance, 255

Yard, Sherry, 83

zesters, 68

Check Out These
Best-Sellers

Grammar and Style SECOND EDITION

Rights and wrongs of sentence structure, word usage, spelling, and much, much more

Laurie E. Rozakis, Ph.D.

978-1-59257-115-4
$16.95

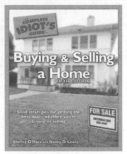

Buying & Selling a Home FIFTH EDITION

Solid strategies for getting the best deal—whether you're buying or selling

FOR SALE

Shelley O'Hara and Nancy D. Lewis

978-1-59257-458-2
$19.95

Being a Groom THIRD EDITION

Jennifer Lata Rung and Mark Rung

978-1-59257-451-3
$9.95

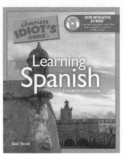

Learning Spanish FOURTH EDITION

Gail Stein

978-1-59257-485-8
$24.95

Investing THIRD EDITION

Expert advice on building a solid and diversified portfolio

978-1-59257-480-3
$19.95

Baby Sign Language

Over 400 signs you and your baby can use to communicate

Diane Ryan

978-1-59257-469-8
$14.95

Total Nutrition FOURTH EDITION

Food group fundamentals from the dairy, fruit, vegetable, and grain worlds

Joy Bauer, M.S., R.D., C.D.N.

978-1-59257-439-1
$18.95

Positive Dog Training SECOND EDITION

The most effective method for teaching your dog to be a good citizen

Pamela Dennison

978-1-59257-483-4
$14.95

The Bible THIRD EDITION

Timeless Stories from Genesis to Revelation and all the wondrous tales in between

James Stuart Bell and Stan Campbell

978-1-59257-389-9
$18.95

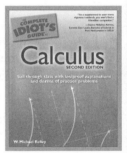

Calculus SECOND EDITION

Sail through class with foolproof explanations and dozens of practice problems

W. Michael Kelley

978-1-59257-471-1
$18.95

Music Theory SECOND EDITION

Michael Miller

978-1-59257-437-7
$19.95

The Perfect Resume FOURTH EDITION

Professional help in making your resume stand out from the pack

Susan Ireland

978-1-59257-463-6
$14.95

Playing the Guitar SECOND EDITION

Frederick Noad

978-0-02864244-4
$21.95

MANGA ILLUSTRATED

John Layman and David Hutchison

978-1-59257-335-6
$19.95

Knitting & Crocheting THIRD EDITION

Keep your stitches straight with hundreds of step-by-step photos and illustrations

Barbara Breiter and Gail Diven

978-1-59257-491-9
$19.95

More than *450 titles* available at
booksellers and online retailers everywhere